"A phantasticly phunny and excellently exciting read! ... a no holds barred tale of phlying, traveling, and partying on the road with professional commercial hot air balloon pilots."

—Denny Floden, aka Capt. Phogg,
1st World Hot Air Balloon Champion

"... a great trip down memory lane, and a reminder that we are privileged to fly and to share this sport with each other."

—Andy Baird, owner of Cameron Balloons

"What a ride! ... an excellent memoir and a tribute to the sky-bound dreamers."

—Scott Lorenz, president, Westwind Communications

"An entertaining and fascinating journey into the heyday of ballooning from the perspective of one person who lived and breathed it. ... a brilliant and engaging read."

—Larry Knight, lowly retired Balloonatic extraordinaire

"... a ripping adventure like no other. ... This book had me clutching my armchair as if it was a gondola caught in a thunderstorm!"

—Joshua Veith, author of the Sudden Quiet series

"An engaging and entertaining memoir. You'll gain insight into the art and science of hot air ballooning while enjoying 'laugh out loud' stories of Craig's and his fellow balloonatics' antics along the way."

—Linda Livezey, editor

"My mom always told me not to chase boys, but I always had to chase Craig in the chase vehicle so he'd come home from balloon flights. Our heads have been up in the clouds ever since."

—Michelle Elliott, Craig's wife

DIAGRAM OF THE TYPICAL CAMERON BALLOON SYSTEM

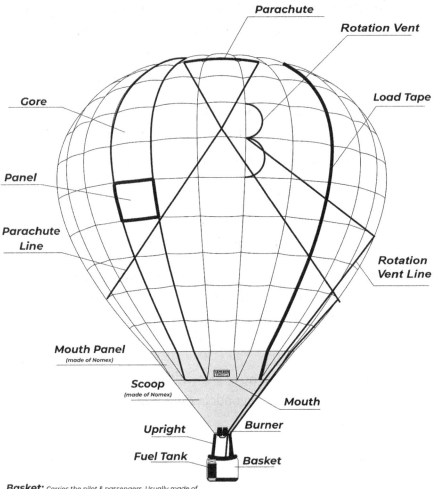

Basket: Carries the pilot & passengers. Usually made of rattan

Burner: Runs the fuel through coils & creates the flame needed to fly

Fuel Tank: Holds propane to be used by the burner

Gore: A full vertical row of panels

Load Tape: Webbing sewn onto the fabric to take the "load" of the balloon and give it strength

Mouth: The opening at the bottom of the envelope

Panel: One individually cut piece of fabric

Parachute: A valve at the top of the balloon that can be used to cool the balloon by venting hot air

Parachute Line: A line run from the parachute to the basket in order to operate it

Scoop: A large piece of the balloon made from fire-resistant Nomex that helps keep the balloon pressurized

Rotation Vents: Vent in the side of the balloon that spins it left or right

Rotation Vent Lines: Lines run from the turning vents to the basket in order to operate them

Upright: Poles that help support the burner assembly above the basket

THE BALLOONATICS

A Memoir of a Hot Air Balloon Pilot

Craig Elliott

M·P·P
www.MissionPointPress.com

Copyright © 2025 Craig Elliott
All world rights reserved.

This is a work of creative nonfiction. The events are portrayed to the best of Craig Elliott's memory. While all the stories in this book are true, some names and identifying details have been changed to protect the privacy of the people involved.

No part of this book may be reproduced, stored in a retrieval system, or transmitted in any form or by any means electronic, mechanical, photocopy, recording, or otherwise, without the prior consent of the publisher.

Mission Point Press

Published by Mission Point Press
www.MissionPointPress.com

Cover illustration: Basket art designed by Terry O'Connor; balloon envelope art by Andrew McComas; original design by Dan Stephens
Book and cover design: Deirdre Wait

Hardcover ISBN 13: 978-1-965278-73-4
Paperback ISBN 13: 978-1-965278-74-1

LCCN: 2025910045

Printed in the United States of America

Photo: Dave Hodgkin, BH Photographic

About the Author

Craig Elliott is a rare bird, a professional Hot Air Balloon Pilot for 40 years. Somewhere along the road he took on the pilot nickname of "Capt. Sunshine." While this may seem a bit whimsical, one only needed to watch him in action as his enthusiasm for hot air ballooning radiated.

He began as a ground crew member for Dr. John Hall, a local balloonist, in 1976, after graduating from Okemos High School in Okemos, Michigan, and soon began taking flight lessons in Hot Air Balloons. He obtained associate degrees in Architecture and Solar Technology from Lansing Community College and started his own company, "Elliott and Sun Builders." Craig then began employment with Balloon Corporation of America (BCA) in Fenton, Michigan, in 1983.

Following extensive travel throughout the USA with the Buick Olympic Balloon, Capt. Sunshine returned to BCA to begin and manage a hot air balloon passenger ride program that grew to be one of the largest and most prestigious in the Midwest. Competing in many balloon events over the years sharpened Capt. Sunshine's skills. In 1984, flying the Buick Olympic Balloon in the Great Preakness Balloon Race in Baltimore, Maryland, he placed third. Flying the Tony the Tiger shaped Balloon for Kellogg's at the National Balloon Rally in Statesville, North Carolina, he won the top prize in 1985 and returned to take first place again out of one hundred and forty other balloons in 1986. Several other smaller events were also won. He competed in the Battle Creek International Balloon Championships flying the Buick Olympic Balloon in 1986. He also competed at the Albuquerque International Balloon Fiesta in 1986 while flying passenger rides and took first place in the McDonald's Race, and in 1989 flying the Virgin Jumbo III Special Shape Balloon for Virgin Atlantic Airways he won second place in the Special Shape Rodeo event at Fiesta.

Capt. Sunshine excelled in other aspects during his ballooning career as well. He and his wife, Michelle, planned, and Craig acted as Balloon Meister, for the TV 9&10 Balloon Classic in Traverse City, Michigan. They did the same with the Seven Lakes State Park Balloon Race for ten years running, and five years with the Trans-Michigan Balloon Race.

Capt. Sunshine retired from ballooning in 2019 after 43 incredible years of wonderful adventures and excitement. This book will bring you along for the ride. He currently lives in Michigan on a small farm with his wife, Michelle, where they raise chickens and tend several large vegetable gardens.

Dedication

First, I dedicate this book to all the unsung heroes, the ground crew. Without them, we would never get off the ground or back again after the flight. I have been blessed with many wonderful ground crew heroes, and many of them have become great friends over the years. A sincere, heartfelt thank-you to all of the ground crew heroes everywhere!

I want to thank Dr. John Hall for teaching me and my best friend, Larry Knight, how to fly hot air balloons, and for the great art that he supplied for my book cover from an old poster he kept. And thank you, Larry, for bringing me along as well!

In addition, a huge thank-you to my good friend Denny Floden, aka Capt. Phogg, for hiring me way back in the day, thus leading to this book.

And of course, many thanks to my wife, Michelle, for sticking with me through all the ups and downs.

Special Dedication

On the left is my dad, Don Elliott, and on the right is Dr. John Hall, my ballooning mentor and flight instructor. This photo was taken by me in 1977 or 1978 while we waited for the wind to die down so we could fly both balloons over a Michigan State University football game in East Lansing, Michigan. As I recall, the winds never allowed us to fly that day.

My dad died while I was writing this book, and Dr. Hall passed a few months before publication. This page is a special dedication to these two great men who are sorely missed by all who had the pleasure of knowing them.

Excerpt: 1998

I felt my heart racing as the balloon ascended. Years of work planning, negotiating, and overcoming setbacks had led to this moment, and I was realizing my dream. I floated up gently in our new 100-foot-tall, tethered, helium-filled balloon—one of only a few like it in the entire world! It was an extremely proud moment.

As I rose into the night looking down at the twinkling lights below, I envisioned selling night flights to groups, party flights with food and drinks, wedding flights, and more. I radioed down to Hugh telling him how fantastic it was. I ascended to 100 feet, still moving straight up. At 150 feet, a remarkable scene unfolded—the dazzling lights of Frankenmuth in the distance. This was awesome!

I continued a gradual ascent to 200 feet, then 250 feet, mesmerized by the view, until—WHAM!—the balloon entered a fast-moving wind shear. The gondola, suspended some 50 feet below the bottom of the balloon, was instantly pulled sideways at an incredible angle. I was thrown against the side as the floor tilted at a 30-degree angle. Struggling to reach the controls on the other side of the gondola, I radioed Hugh that I was coming down. Before I was able to reverse course, the gondola entered the wind shear. The strong wind that had so violently interrupted my peaceful and triumphant first night ride buffeted me! Swinging back and forth like a pendulum, the entire system was tilted at an angle of 30 to 40 degrees. I hung on for dear life, praying the system would hold together in this craziness.

*"Aging is an extraordinary process whereby
you become the person you always should have been."*

—David Bowie, as quoted in
Happiness Is a Choice You Make

Contents

Foreword 1

A Brief History of Hot Air Ballooning 3

   • Sixties and Seventies 7

   • Eighties 43

   • Nineties 208

   • The Beginning of the End 277

   • A New Century 305

Afterword 313

Scan this QR code to visit www.theballoonatics.com and see the photos that are featured in this book in full color—plus many more full-color photos and videos that go with these stories!

Foreword

For most every story in this book, there are many beautiful, full-color photos and videos showing the glory and craziness of the heyday of Hot Air Ballooning in the '80s and '90s. I have organized them on my website, www.theballoonatics.com, so that you can easily see how they correspond to the book. Included with these stories in the book there are a few related images along the way, but in black and white, they aren't as grand. Please take some time while you're reading, or when you've finished, to peruse the photos and videos on the website that I'm so excited to share.

I am not proud of many things I talk about in this book. Despite alcohol's influence on idiocy, I must truthfully recount the tale to be just to my readers. Sure, I could make myself look great and only talk about the good stuff, but that would be a cover-up. Also, many of the embarrassing stories are quite funny. The story needs humor because that is life.

Thank you for joining me on this adventure!

A Brief History of Hot Air Ballooning

by the Anderson Abruzzo International Balloon Museum

Hot air ballooning has only been around for a little over two centuries, but it has a rich history filled with many important events. The history of ballooning is the history of flight because humans first achieved flight with balloons. For almost 150 years prior to the airplane, ballooning permeated many areas of human life and human achievement. From travel and mapping to research, military, photography, and entertainment, this article will cover some of the main highlights from the history of hot air ballooning.

There are two types of balloons that are flown today, hot air balloons and gas balloons. The envelope is the part of the balloon that holds the hot air or gas. Hot air balloons fly as a result of a hotter air temperature inside the envelope than outside. Gas balloons fly using a lifting gas inside their envelopes. The gas pilots use will either be helium or hydrogen, with hydrogen being more common due to it being cheaper and more available than helium.

A Brief History of Ballooning

September 19th, 1783—The first hot air balloon was launched by a French scientist named Pilatre De Rozier and was called *Aerostat Reveillon*. The balloon carried three passengers—a rooster, a duck, and a sheep—and was only in the air for 15 minutes before crashing back to the ground.

November 21st, 1783—Just two months later, two French brothers, Joseph and Etienne Montgolfier, attempted the first manned flight. They launched their balloon in Paris, and the flight lasted 20 minutes, birthing hot air ballooning.

1785—Jean Pierre Blanchard, a French balloonist, and John Jefferies, his American co-pilot, became the first people ever to fly a gas balloon across the English Channel. This marked one of the longest distances a balloon had ever flown and was a major step toward long-distance balloon travel.

1785—That same year, Pilatre De Rozier (the world's first balloonist) died while also trying to cross the English Channel. His balloon exploded shortly after takeoff on account of his experimental design of using a hot air balloon and a hydrogen balloon tied together.

January 7th, 1793—Jean Pierre Blanchard became the first person to fly a hot air balloon in North America, with President George Washington watching the launch.

1800s–c. 1950—For the next 150 years, hot air ballooning was overtaken by gas ballooning, and the practice of flying via hot air balloon was all but abandoned.

1950s—A man named Ed Yost worked to revive hot air ballooning by engineering a redesigned fueling system that would allow balloons to fly for longer distances and become more maneuverable.

October 22nd, 1960—Ed Yost launched the first modern hot air balloon flight in Bruning, Nebraska, which lasted for 1 hour and 35 minutes.

1972—Sid Cutter organized a gathering of 13 balloons in Albuquerque, New Mexico. This event would go on to become the Albuquerque International Balloon Fiesta, the largest balloon event in the world.

1987—Richard Branson and Per Lindstrand became the first people in history to cross the Atlantic in a hot air balloon, flying 2,900 miles in 33 hours.

1991—Branson and Lindstrand re-teamed to cross the Pacific in a hot air balloon. Their flight launched from Japan and traveled to Canada, flying 6,700 miles in 47 hours.

2011—The Anderson Abruzzo International Balloon Museum in Albuquerque, New Mexico, became the home of the International Ballooning Hall of Fame to commemorate the history of hot air ballooning and all those who have played an important role.

One of the best ways to learn even more about the history of hot air ballooning is to visit the Anderson Abruzzo International Balloon Museum (www.balloonmuseum.com). The museum has a variety of exhibitions detailing the history of lighter-than-air flight, aircraft, and artifacts from important events.

Sixties and Seventies

1960-1970

I've always been adventurous. When I was a kid growing up in Michigan in the sixties, my favorite toys were little green army men and G.I. Joes. My friends and I would spend hours setting up elaborate battle scenes and then dramatically blowing them to pieces. When I was around eight years old, I told my mom that when I grew up, I would join the Green Berets and die for my country. She was not very happy with this idea, and, fortunately, it never worked out.

When I joined the Boy Scouts, I wasn't interested in advancing through the ranks, earning badges, or any of that stuff. All I wanted to do was go on camping trips. I never did progress beyond the rank of Tenderfoot, but I did have a few adventures! One of my most memorable camping trips involved a pack of stray dogs wandering in and joining our troop, and me meeting a pretty girl at the camp store, sneaking out of camp to meet her that night, getting my first kiss, and then being chased off by her dad who threatened to shoot me with his rifle. To top it off, the dogs announced my return to camp late at night, and I barely made it into my tent before the scout masters rushed out to see what was going on.

A few years later, the day after I graduated from high school at the age of 17, two friends and I drove straight through from Michigan to Lake Tahoe, California, in 40 hours. We spent a month touring California on an epic adventure that I will tell in my next book, *California Trippin'*.

But I digress. This book is not about those adventures, so let us begin.

1976

My ballooning adventures began in the summer of 1976 after I'd graduated from Okemos High School in Okemos, Michigan. I had become good friends with a new guy who had moved to town in my junior year. He was in the same grade, and we hung out a lot together. His name is Larry Knight, and he became the boyfriend of one of my best high school friends, Gretchen Fritz.

The summer after our senior year, we were hanging out at Larry's mom's house when he got a phone call. After he hung up, Larry asked me if I wanted to go with him to crew for a hot air balloon flight. I said, "What the heck is that?"

Hot air balloons were completely unknown to me. Larry told me that a family friend, Dr. John Hall, was a hot air balloon pilot, and Larry had been crewing for him and following him in the pickup truck to pick him up after the flight. I said, "Sure, that sounds interesting."

A few hours later, we drove to Williamston, where Dr. Hall lived, about 10 miles east of Okemos. Larry introduced me to Dr. Hall, his wife, Bonnie, and several others who were there to help crew the flight.

Dr. Hall was quite the character! Six foot two and about 280 pounds, with curly red hair balding at the top, big red curly sideburns, and a gregarious, happy-go-lucky personality. I liked him right from the start. He informed us that the winds and weather were favorable for flying. We loaded up his green-and-white four-door Ford pickup with the balloon and some other equipment. It was all so new and cool. I was extremely excited!

We drove just a few blocks down the street to a cul-de-sac in his neighborhood where we unloaded the balloon. The gondola (the compartment that pilot and passengers rode in later called a basket when made of wicker) consisted of square aluminum tubing with fiberglass sides. Two big stainless-steel propane tanks sat on the floor with some crazy-looking propane burners at the top. We laid the gondola down on its side and attached the balloon, which Dr. Hall said was called the "envelope," to the gondola. The envelope, which weighed over 200 pounds and was almost waist high, was stuffed in an enormous canvas bag.

We dragged the canvas bag away from the gondola, revealing the envelope bit by bit. It was green and white, just like the pickup truck, and it seemed like it would never end. It was huge! Dr. Hall then positioned two small gas-motor-driven fans on either side of the gondola and started assigning everyone their crew jobs to help get the balloon ready for flight, an operation he called "the inflation."

I was assigned the task of holding the mouth of the envelope open so the fans could blow air into the balloon. The mouth is at the bottom of the envelope, which is open. Before we started the fans, we sealed up the big opening at the top of the balloon using Velcro to ensure that the envelope would hold the air. Dr. Hall told me that the opening at the top was called the "deflation port" and was used to deflate the envelope at the end of the flight. To deflate the envelope, you pulled on a red strap that was attached to the top cap and ran down the inside of the envelope to the gondola.

Dr. Hall explained how he would inflate the envelope using fans and heat the air with the burners to make the balloon stand upright. He told me and a crew member on the other side of the mouth to hold the fabric of the balloon up so the mouth was open and the fans could blow the air in. Then, when he started using the burners, we were to keep holding the fabric up and out of the flame so it did not get burnt.

It was windy during the inflation and we struggled to hold the mouth open for a while, but it got easier as the envelope inflated. When the envelope was almost full of air, Dr. Hall used the burners, and holy cow, were they hot! I had leather gloves on that Dr. Hall had given me but was wearing a short-sleeved T-shirt and felt the heat on my arms and face.

The wind started gusting up a bit as Dr. Hall carefully blasted the burners to heat the envelope. The fabric of the balloon was being blown down into the flame. I had to use all my strength to hold it up out of the flame, and I really felt the heat on my right forearm. Ouch, it hurt!

A minute later, the balloon stood up, and I then used the rope that was attached to the mouth of the balloon to hold the fabric out of the flame as it stood up. About then I realized that my right arm was really hurting. Dr. Hall had two passengers get in the balloon with him as we put all our weight on the outside of the gondola. Dr. Hall instructed us to hold it down, and he kept heating the envelope with the burners. After a few more minutes, Dr. Hall told us all to let go, and he sailed up, up, and away.

Larry asked me to help him load the fans into the truck and said that we were going to be the chase crew now. As Larry drove off with me in the passenger seat, I realized that the underside of my right arm from the wrist to the elbow was very red and hurt badly. A short time later, the skin started to bubble up, and I said, "Wow this is not good." Larry said there was a cooler in the back of the truck with lots of ice, pop, and beer. We pulled over, and I grabbed a few cans of Pabst Blue Ribbon beer and some ice and used the cold cans and the ice to stop the burn from hurting so much. Then I drank the beer, which also helped.

After about an hour of following the balloon, Dr. Hall found a landing spot, and we arrived to help pack up the balloon. Larry told

The green-and-white balloon.

Dr. Hall about my burn, and when he looked at it, he said, "What the hell happened?"

I told him, and he said, "Why didn't you let go and get out of the way?"

I said, "You told me to not let the fabric get burned." He said if that ever happens again, he would rather the fabric get burned instead of my arm, and then he got a first aid kit and treated my arm.

When we got back to his house, he told me I had second-degree burns—thank God, not third. He treated my arm again and gave me more dressings to keep changing for a few days. After that, we always wore long-sleeved shirts, and we got bigger gloves that covered more of the forearms for the two crew members who were tasked with holding the mouth open.

So that was my first hot air ballooning experience. I found out why they are called hot air balloons—but I was hooked!

~ ~ ~

It was so cool and exciting to help set up and inflate that enormous balloon and then watch it slowly lift off the ground and gently drift off with the wind.

Then the "chase" is on. At least that is what we called it. We were known as the chase crew even though it was more of a slow following rather than an actual chase most of the time. The balloon goes with the wind, not the roads. It was always a logistical challenge to follow the balloon using local maps and talking to the pilot on two-way radios.

Our job was to be at the landing spot before the balloon landed, or at least shortly thereafter. It did not always happen, so we had a backup plan in place for the few occasions that we "lost" the balloon. Remember, this was back in the seventies. There were no cell phones, GPS, or computers. We had a designated "lost balloon" phone number to a landline. That was all there was back then, landlines: a big phone on the wall or tabletop connected to telephone lines that ran along with the power lines. The phone line was monitored by either Dr. Hall's wife, Bonnie, Larry's mom, or my mom, who stood by until they got a call from us later that all was well.

If we lost the balloon, the pilot would have to walk to the nearest house and ask to use their phone or find a pay phone, then call the "lost balloon" number to give the monitor the address and directions to where they had landed. And we, the crew, would have to do the same to get that address and directions, then go find the balloon using our local road maps.

Larry and I loved being the chase crew. It was a ton of fun and sometimes very challenging. We also loved the cooler with a bottle of champagne that we usually gave to the landowner where the balloon landed as a traditional gift, and the Pabst Blue Ribbon beer that was for the pilot and crew afterward. Dr. Hall was not very strict about drinking age limits back then, but he was strict about the rule to never drink before flying. We always adhered to the old saying of "eight hours from the bottle to the throttle." We told Dr. Hall that we wanted to be his chase crew every time he flew, and that is what we started doing.

That first summer, Larry and I crewed every flight. Gretchen often came with us, and we invited some of our friends as well.

~ ~ ~

Dr. Hall was larger than life and the life of every party! He was a lung specialist at a local hospital, and his wife, Bonnie, was an anesthesiologist, so they were financially well off. They did not come off that way, though, and were very likeable, down-to-earth people. They actually divorced twice and got married to each other three times! The third time was the charm, as they are still married as of this writing and have a son and a daughter who were very young when we started flying balloons together.

Dr. Hall loved fast cars, airplanes, and boats, and he had them all. He enjoyed working on them and had a very fast Corvette that he had souped up himself. He made our chase truck super cool as well. It was a brand-new green-and-white Ford F-250 with four doors (which was rare back then) and a long bed with a lift gate. He had tweaked the motor to make it faster, put on a throaty-sounding dual exhaust system, and converted it to a dual fuel vehicle that ran on gasoline or propane. He mounted a 100-gallon propane tank in the bed and that gave it a range of over 1,200 miles! And if needed, we could refuel the balloon propane tanks right from the truck. It was one of the coolest balloon chase vehicles at all the ballooning events we soon began attending.

He named his balloon company Ballooney Tunes, a takeoff from the Warner Bros. "Looney Tunes" cartoons. He had a logo made with his likeness in place of Porky Pig, and when he would take off in the balloon, he would yell out, "Pigs in Space!"

Dr. Hall lived about 15 miles from East Lansing, Michigan, home of the Michigan State University Spartans, whose colors are green and white. He had a contract with a local radio station to fly his balloon over the MSU football games carrying two large WVIC banners attached to the envelope. In keeping with Spartan spirit, both his chase vehicle and balloon were green and white.

That fall I turned 18 (and my mom 39, as we share the same birthday). The legal drinking age in Michigan at the time was 18, so now both Larry and I were of legal age to access that cooler in the chase vehicle.

Dr. Hall also gave Larry his first hot air balloon pilot lesson that fall. The weather cooperated, and Larry logged 15 hours of pilot training over four months with me, Gretchen, Larry's younger brother Danny, and an assortment of friends following along as the chase crew. Several of these training flights were over the MSU football games, which were always exciting, especially since they took place in the middle of the afternoon (more on that later).

1977

The summer of 1977 was big for us. Larry and I attended our first ballooning events, and I started taking pilot lessons. Dr. Hall decided it was a good idea for all of us to be able to fly the balloon, and I certainly agreed!

My first lesson took place during the Capt. Phogg Balloon Classic held that year at the Bishop Airport in Flint, Michigan. Capt. Phogg was the first World Hot Air Balloon Champion, a title he won in 1973 at the first championship event in Albuquerque, New Mexico. His real name is Denny Floden, and he had taught Dr. Hall how to fly and sold him the green-and-white balloon.

How did Denny become Capt. Phogg? The credit goes to another pilot, Bruce Comstock, whom Denny had also taught to fly balloons. Here is the story direct from Bruce himself:

> During the summer I was being trained by Denny, I thought having a flight suit might be useful, as it would give me pockets in which to store strikers and other small items while flying. I grew up around a mother who was constantly sewing clothing, mostly for herself and my two sisters, so I was generally familiar with the process of using patterns and body measurements to sew clothing. After I started my balloon pilot training, I bought a generic flight suit pattern and a bunch of bright yellow fabric of the right type and sewed a flight suit for myself. When I showed up for one of my lessons wearing this, Denny exclaimed something like, "Oh my gosh, it's a big yellow canary!" Since his proclivity was to name everyone around him "Captain something-or-other," I immediately became "Captain Canary," a title I never really embraced. That is the real story of where the appellation started.

According to Denny:

> Bruce Comstock showed up one morning in a bright yellow flight suit. I told him he looked like a giant herniated canary, so I would call him Captain Canary. He responded that I was no prize early in the morning, so I should be Captain Fog, which became Phogg.

Denny, a skilled promoter and salesman, embraced this and rebranded himself as Capt. Phogg—inspired by Phileas Fogg, protagonist of Jules Verne's novel and the movie adaptation *Around the World in 80 Days*. The rest, as they say, is ballooning history!

~ ~ ~

I will never forget how excited, nervous, and a bit scared I was before that first lesson. I had crewed about 25 times over the past year and had taken one short introductory flight a week prior. This would be my first time actually piloting a balloon.

About 20 balloons attended the event. We took off from the main runway at the Flint Bishop Airport. Dr. Hall walked me through the inflation process, and I passed the first test without melting the fabric. He guided me in heating the envelope until it became buoyant, instructing the ground crew to release their hold on the gondola and regain it as needed. I then gave it a bit more heat, said "weight off," and up we gently sailed.

I was sweating bullets by the time we lifted off. I felt a little faint, but that quickly subsided, and I almost instantly felt exhilarated and enthralled. This was awesome! So crazy cool, I was not afraid at all. Instead, I was completely amazed at how gentle and peaceful it was. I literally felt like we were suspended, and the earth was rotating below us. There was no sense of movement at all!

Slowly, everything below became smaller and smaller till it looked like one of those model cities with the miniature train set running through it. I had no fear of the height, as it just seemed unreal and totally peaceful. Even when we got to 1,000 feet above the ground, I really did not notice a sense of height at all. You could hear the road noise and dogs barking below. "This is incredible," I told Dr. Hall; he just smiled and said, "I know." Now I was really in love and hooked on this crazy "sport."

I can relate my experience to a wonderful description of balloon flight by Anthony Smith from his brilliant book *Throw Out Two Hands*. The book describes in detail his adventures flying a balloon from the island of Zanzibar to the African mainland and his many flights across the African continent filming great herds of wildlife in 1963.

> Instantly, the miracle of a flight started once again. Without a bounce, without any apparent movement, we were flying into the air. We said nothing to harm those first few moments when the incredible repeats itself and a balloon takes leave of the earth with a grace that is unforgettable. Up we went, and smaller grew the people. The crowd broke through the police and darted onto the field. How minute they were! How remote already! And how inaccessible! Our point of no return had already been reached. As if by a signal we three turned round in the basket and looked ahead to see what chance and fate had in store for us.
>
> A balloon, unlike any other craft, enables you to feel part of the elements. A ship is an intrusion, bouncing about on top of the waves. An aircraft, and even a glider, crashes through everything; but a balloon is a cloud, a shape on its own, and going with the wind as part of it.
>
> I repeat that flying with the wind means that you feel no wind. It is not like sailing. It is not like gliding. It is an experience entirely of its own. The wind takes you as fast as it pleases,

and yet causes not a single hair to ruffle in the process. This complete lack of draught of any sort is extremely hard to comprehend for the novice balloonist. He looks down, as we did, upon a buffeted world, and yet he coasts along above it all, unblown, untouched by the wind, and yet in the very midst of it.

Dr. Hall instructed me throughout the flight. To regulate the balloon's heat, he advised doing short, frequent burns instead of long, infrequent blasts on the burner. He instructed me to ascend to 1,000 feet and then maintain that altitude. Then we went down to 500 feet, and I tried to hold that altitude. Despite the overwhelming amount I had to learn, he kept encouraging me, saying I was doing great for my first time. That gave me confidence, and I truly enjoyed the entire experience despite some butterflies and apprehension.

These ballooning events almost always involved some kind of competition and were often called "balloon races." However, there was no real "racing" involved. Balloons travel at the same speed when at the same altitude because they simply drift with the wind. Winds are usually different at different altitudes, and that is how you can "steer" a balloon. By ascending or descending into different altitudes that have different wind speeds and directions, you can often direct the balloon accurately.

Sometimes the winds at different altitudes are all going pretty much the same way, so every flight is unique. That's the true beauty of ballooning. You have no actual destination in mind but are just out to be free, literally floating along, drifting with the wind wherever it takes you.

The competition during my first flight lesson was a "Hare and Hound" race, where one balloon was chosen as the Hare and the rest were Hounds. The Hare balloon takes off first, and the Hounds must wait 15 minutes before they can launch and follow the Hare. The aim was to land closest to the Hare's landing spot to win.

I soon learned that this was not in the best interest of the Hare balloon. Dr. Hall and I were somewhere in the middle of the pack flying toward the Hare balloon. After the Hare balloon landed, we watched three consecutive balloons in front of us literally crash into the Hare balloon!

Now, when I say "crash" here, I must emphasize that there were no injuries except perhaps to the pilots' egos and the Hare balloon's envelope. The initial balloon collided with the Hare balloon, knocking it down. The Hare balloon then stood back up, and the second balloon flew into it, knocking it over again! At this point, the Hare balloon pilot decided he'd had enough and pulled out the top on his balloon to deflate it. Then the third balloon came down fast and landed right on top of the deflating Hare balloon envelope. There were some heated discussions at the next morning's pilot briefing.

The next year, the rules were changed, yielding a historical demarcation in the annals of ballooning history. The Hare balloon would carry a big X target made of bright orange fabric. A passenger would place the target at the landing spot, and then they would move the Hare balloon out of the way.

The organizers gave all the Hound balloon pilots a bean bag with their name on it. A fabric streamer about three feet long was attached to the bean bag. The pilots would throw the bean bag at the orange X target as they flew by, thus avoiding future collisions and damage to the Hare balloon.

Dr. Hall and I did not get near the Hare balloon on that first flight. We flew past and landed gently in a field a mile or so beyond the Hare balloon. Then we celebrated my first successful flight lesson with the crew, champagne, and lots of Pabst Blue Ribbon beer!

~   ~   ~

The rest of the weekend was a real blur. We flew several more flights with Larry as the pilot in training and me as part of the chase crew. We had a great time at the post-flight dinners and parties that followed. Our host, Capt. Phogg, and his ex-wife, Laraine, did a fantastic job of making this event special.

We stayed at a pleasant hotel in Flint, just a mile away from the airport. The hotel had a cool restaurant and aviation-themed bar called Mr. Gibby's. Alas, both are now long gone, but they were real hot spots back then. Pilots and up to four crew members enjoyed royal treatment at the event. Free hotel rooms and food were provided for the entire weekend, along with a lavish awards ceremony where pilots received many gifts and awards.

There was one very low point that happened Saturday evening at the airport during the refueling of the balloons after the flight. Many balloons were transported in enclosed trailers, and the refueling would take place inside the trailer. Refueling in an enclosed trailer was a perilous situation, as we discovered that day.

Some propane gas vapors escape during the refueling process, and that vapor, being heavier than air, will sink and dissipate if you are out in the open. In an enclosed trailer, it can collect on the floor. That happened to one of the balloon crews, and that very explosive vapor somehow ignited, perhaps by a spark or most likely simply static electricity from someone's nylon jacket rubbing on something.

An explosion and fire ensued inside the trailer while several people, including the pilot's young sons, were in it refueling their balloon. Several people ended up in the hospital, with one of the young boys sustaining severe burns on his face, neck, and hands. Luckily, there were no fatalities. From then on, the event prohibited refueling inside enclosed trailers.

~ ~ ~

The rest of the summer and that fall, we crewed and received more pilot lessons from Dr. Hall. I remember two flights over the football games that fall. The first was Dr. Hall and I flying the WVIC green-and-white balloon over MSU Stadium at halftime.

After launching close by, we encountered turbulence at 500 feet and began a rapid ascent. Being a new pilot trainee, I did not notice our ascent right away. It soon became evident. Not only were we going up fast, but the gondola began to rock in a circular motion. As soon as we encountered the turbulence, Dr. Hall instructed me to look up and make sure the mouth of the balloon was open and, if so, put heat in it. (On rare occasions, severe turbulence can close the mouth of the balloon temporarily, and if you use the burners to add heat at that moment, you can severely damage the envelope.) Although I noticed some distortion, the mouth was open, so I added a long blast of heat.

We had been flying level when we encountered the turbulence, and we were now going up at about 700 feet per minute, according to the instruments. Also, the gondola started swaying around in a circular motion—a uniquely terrifying experience even for the most fearless aeronaut! Dr. Hall, the fearless aeronaut, sat on a propane tank and instructed me to add heat, but to always check if the mouth was open. I asked, "Why should I heat it when we are going up so fast already?" He explained that we were currently in a thermal—a rising mass of hot air—and would soon exit into a downdraft outside of it. Unless the envelope stayed at the same temperature as it was when we were flying level before the thermal, we would plummet and struggle to recover from the rapid descent.

I watched the temperature gauge carefully and kept adding heat to keep the envelope temperature steady. Our ascent increased to about 1,000 feet per minute, and the gondola and envelope were now rotating and swinging noticeably in a circular motion. Dr. Hall was not enjoying it as he stayed seated and kept telling me to keep the heat up to temperature.

Being 18 and adventurous, I thought it was a fun and cool ride! We continued up to about 10,000 feet in less than 10 minutes. Then, as

Dr. Hall had mentioned, we were spit out of it and encountered some turbulence again. The circular motion gradually stopped, and we were now in a very fast descent of about 1,000 feet per minute. I kept on adding heat, using the burners a lot, to slow our descent, and at about 1,000 feet above the ground we regained control and quickly descended to find a landing spot. We had a normal, but bumpy, landing of 8–10 miles per hour not more than a couple of miles from where we first encountered the turbulence and went for our thermal ride!

Here's Wikipedia's definition of a thermal: "A thermal column is a rising mass of buoyant air, a convective current in the atmosphere, that transfers heat energy vertically. Thermals are created by the uneven heating of Earth's surface from solar radiation, and are an example of convection, specifically atmospheric convection."

When a balloon encounters a thermal, the thermal usually takes control of the balloon from the balloon pilot. Thermals generally only happen in the middle of the day when the sun is high in the sky and directly striking the earth's surface. Balloon flights are much safer early in the morning right after sunrise before the thermals start forming, or late in the day before sunset when they have dissipated.

Larry and I were crewing for the second football flight. We attached a brand-new WVIC banner on the balloon using Velcro, and Dr. Hall flew off.

Dr. Hall had stressed the importance of attaching and securing the banner correctly; however, after the balloon launched, we realized the banner wasn't secure. A corner had begun to peel off and flap as the balloon went up or down.

We had launched the balloon two miles away from the MSU stadium because the campus police were not balloon friendly, not even to a green-and-white balloon! They had kicked us off MSU property twice before. One time when they did this, we had the balloon all inflated and ready to take off. We had to deflate it, pack it all back up, then drive a mile or so off MSU property to find another launch site. By then, we had missed our halftime window and missed flying directly over the stadium by about half a mile!

Anyway, we radioed Dr. Hall that the banner was peeling off on one corner, and he advised us to keep a close eye on it as it had cost $1,200! As he approached the stadium, we radioed to him it was coming off, and we saw it fall off and drift slowly down toward the student section on the south side of the stadium. Dr. Hall told us to drive there and retrieve it if it did not go into the stadium.

Luckily, it just missed drifting into the stadium and fell harmlessly only 100 feet short of the stadium in the south parking lot area, where we were waiting to catch it. Good thing, as I can only imagine what would have happened if it had fallen into the student section! It turned out the banner was too small. Dr. Hall sent it back to the manufacturer, and they added an extra six inches of fabric to the top and sides. It then fit perfectly and never came off again.

~ ~ ~

Larry's younger brother Danny helped us crew a flight late that summer. After the flight, we ended up back at Dr. Hall's house and finished the cooler. Around 10 p.m., Danny said he wanted to drive into Williamston to look for someone who owed him money. I had driven my car that day, so off we went in my 1967 Oldsmobile Delta 88 that I had bought a few months before for $100.

Back then, you could buy a 10- to 15-year-old car for $100 that still ran well. They were beat up and burned oil. Every time you filled up with gas, you also had to add a quart of oil.

Anyway, it was a big old car, and off we went cruising through town. Soon, Danny yelled, "There he is, driving his truck!" We pulled up alongside him, and Danny started yelling, "Where is my money?" The truck took off, and Danny yelled, "Go after him!" With liquid courage and a touch of stupidity, I pursued the truck.

Turning right, he drove out of town on a two-lane highway, with us in pursuit. The truck had a huge, strong rear bumper that I only noticed when he slammed on his brakes and, despite slamming on my own brakes, I ran into it at about 15 miles per hour. BAM! He took off again. Furious, I chased after him.

Unbeknownst to me, my car had sustained some damage to the hood-latching mechanism. When we got up to about 50 miles per hour, the car hood flipped open and slammed into the windshield (but did not break it, thank goodness). I slammed on the brakes, came to a stop, jumped out, and slammed the hood back down in a rage, then took off after him again.

Once again, when we got up to about 50 miles per hour, the hood slammed up against the windshield, this time breaking the driver's side hinge and leaving it attached only by the passenger-side hinge. Slamming on the brakes and skidding to a stop, I jumped out again. In a senseless drunken rage, I grabbed the huge car hood and started shaking it back and forth until I ripped it off completely and threw it in the ditch.

I got back into the car, which had a smashed front, steam coming from the radiator, and no hood. As we resumed the chase, Danny said, "Craig, you are bleeding really bad."

I said, "No, I'm not!"

To which Danny responded, "Yes, you are. We better go back to Dr. Hall's house and have him check it out."

This time I looked and saw that my thumb was badly cut and bleeding profusely. I drove back to Dr. Hall's house. Upon seeing it, he immediately advised, "You must go to the hospital NOW." Dr. Hall wrapped it up quickly, and I drove with Larry and Danny in the steaming, smashed-up car with no hood the 15 miles to Sparrow Hospital in Lansing.

They did surgery to repair my left thumb, which I had almost severed. It was cut to the bone 80 percent of the way around, just below the joint, right through all the tendons. Sporting a new cast and nursing a hangover, I was unceremoniously sent on my way a few hours later.

It was getting to be sunrise the next morning as we three tired amigos drove home in the car with no hood, a smashed-up front end, and steam rolling out of the radiator, but still driving! We were hungry and tired and stopped at Dunkin' Donuts on the way. I parked in front, turned off the car, and we saw them.

Three police officers sat at the counter looking out at us. Nothing to do at that point but casually walk in. The police officers stared at the smashed and smoking car without a hood as we three sad sacks emerged, me with a new cast on my hand. Upon entering, they glanced at us, shook their heads, chuckled, then resumed sipping their coffee. Guess they figured we'd had enough for one night and decided to leave us alone!

~ ~ ~

Thanks to Dr. Hall, I accumulated 10 hours and Larry logged 4.9 hours of flight instruction in 1977.

1978

Dr. Hall landed another commercial contract, this time with the American Cancer Society. They bought him a white balloon with a multicolored top and 20-foot-tall red letters on both sides that read "No Smoking." This was back in the early days of the government's anti-smoking campaigns. Part of the contract was to fly this new balloon along with the green-and-white WVIC balloon over the MSU football games. So now Dr. Hall needed at least one more pilot.

We brought the No Smoking balloon to an event that spring in Decatur, Alabama—the Decatur Alabama Jubilee. Larry and I had never been to Alabama, and to get to travel on such a long trip with Dr. Hall was a real honor. I remember arriving and learning on the first night that it was being held in a dry county. We had not stocked up the cooler on the way, so the next day we had to drive quite a way to the next county to do so.

The weather did not turn out great that weekend as there were thunderstorms all around on Saturday. One balloon flew, however, to the disbelief of everyone else. A pilot nicknamed Weird Harold took off and headed straight for the big thundercloud anvil that was about 15 miles away.

We all watched in amazement and trepidation as he just kept flying low, going toward it for what seemed like a very long time. We watched as he ascended quickly and did a 180-degree turn at about 1,500 feet to fly right back at us and land near the event launch field! He came back a bit later, all excited and happy about what a great flight it was, while we all just shook our heads in disbelief. Weird Harold's crazy storm trooper flight was the highlight of the event, and I will never forget watching that one!

Sunday morning, the weather was much better. Dr. Hall and Larry flew the No Smoking balloon. Thanks to favorable winds, they were able to "box" the field, meaning they used different winds at different altitudes to fly away then fly back so they landed right back at the event site field where they had launched. This thrilled Dr. Hall. He was concerned about landing out in the countryside where they grew tobacco in a "No Smoking" balloon! Sunday evening's flight, I got to fly with Dr. Hall.

~ ~ ~

Dr. Hall bought a trailer to hook up to the chase truck so we could haul and fly two balloons with one chase vehicle. We did not always

The "No Smoking" balloon.

fly both balloons since Dr. Hall only got paid to fly them over the football games and at a few other contracted events. For fun and training flights, we usually flew just the green-and-white balloon.

The No Smoking balloon included a brand-new wicker "basket." The basket featured a padded suede bolster on top and padded suede uprights supporting the updated burners. This was much nicer than the aluminum bucket gondola we flew under the green-and-white balloon.

That summer of 1978, Dr. Hall said I was ready for my first solo flight. He said that if I could complete a couple of touch-and-goes and landings safely, he would step out and let me go solo. I did well enough for him to hop out on the second landing. It was a beautiful calm morning with just a little breeze starting at about 300 feet.

I was flying the green-and-white balloon attached to the new wicker basket. We planned to continue doing this and use the aluminum bucket gondola only when we flew both balloons, as they were interchangeable. The wicker basket was nicer and much more flexible and forgiving on hard, bumpy landings than the old aluminum and fiberglass gondola on the green-and-white balloon. And those hard, bumpy landings happen much more often than they need to when training new pilots!

So off I went flying by myself, quite nervous but also quite proud and happy to be doing so. I did a few more touch-and-goes while flying low in the countryside. Then I came across a large cattle farm, where I ascended to about 1,000 feet to avoid scaring the livestock. It took around 15 minutes to clear the farm.

I began descending and noticed a road ahead. It was surrounded by open fields with no power lines nearby. I radioed down that I was going to land on that road. My thinking was that I would do a nice stand-up landing and let Larry jump in to get a short flight in with me from there. Unbeknownst to me, the winds on the ground had picked up while I was flying high over the farm. They were no longer as calm as they had been during my earlier landings and touch-and-goes.

The Balloonatics

I came in nicely, touched down on the road, and pulled the side vent line hard to stop. The balloon had a side vent to release hot air and cool down the air inside to make the balloon heavier. This would cause it to descend or allow for a smooth landing in calm winds. The side vent opening happened to be on the downwind side when I touched down, and the wind gusted up even higher as I hit the road. I quickly skidded across the road and into a small ditch on the other side of the road, all the while holding the side vent open, thinking I was going to stop soon.

As soon as I hit the ditch, the balloon and basket laid down on its side. I was pulling even harder on the vent line with one hand while trying to hang on to the basket with the other hand to stay in the basket. The wind blew the balloon, basket, and me across the corn stubble field at a fast clip as the basket dragged through the field with the envelope acting as a sail.

I continued to pull that vent line to no avail; the vent opening was now on the downside of the envelope, dragging along the ground, so not really letting any more air out. With the brand-new beautiful wicker basket in tow, I bounced over the corn stubble rows for about 100 yards. Eventually, a fence row that divided the fields finally brought me to a halt.

I was lucky that the heavily overgrown fence, with its soft bushes, prevented any damage to the envelope that had dragged over it into the next field. Dr. Hall's nice new basket got a little damaged. The leather that protected the wicker at the bottom of the basket was all scuffed up, as was some of the wicker on the side that dragged on the ground. The top suede bolster that covered the padding on the top rail of the basket was scuffed up as well. The brand-new expensive basket, with just a few hours of flight time, no longer looked brand new.

When Dr. Hall and Larry arrived in the field with the chase vehicle, they were upset. They asked why the hell I had not pulled the red rip line to pull out the top of the balloon, which is what you must do on a windy landing so you don't drag along forever! I sheepishly said that I didn't realize it had gotten so windy and just forgot in the heat of the moment and kept pulling the vent line. They drilled me on that and kept telling me over and over that if you must stop the balloon, RIP OUT the TOP using the red rip line! And after that, I was no longer allowed to fly the not-so-new-anymore wicker basket.

Gretchen reminded me of the time I was inflating the green-and-white balloon for a solo flight before taking my Federal Aviation Administration (FAA) check ride. She was one of the two crew members holding the mouth of the balloon open, and when I blasted the burners, the flame blew way too close to her and actually singed off her eyebrows and most of her beautiful eyelashes!

I believe it happened because it was an early morning flight, and I learned that when you first blast the burners in the cold, they can put out an initial large fireball because the preheat coils are not yet hot. The preheat coils, when hot, vaporize the liquid propane coming from the tank so you burn vapor, and the flame is narrow and straight. When those coils are cold, the liquid propane is not vaporized, and the subsequent flame comes out as a much larger and wider fireball at first.

I learned to be very careful about that from then on! I did not even realize what had happened until after the flight when she showed me. She was upset that she looked bad without eyebrows and eyelashes, but I told her she was still beautiful. She was a waitress at the time and was not happy to have to go to work looking like that!

~ ~ ~

It was never easy for Dr. Hall to find the time and have the weather cooperate for flying balloons, so our flights were spaced out to average about two to three per month. I was able to log a couple more training flights with Dr. Hall and one more solo flight, this time with a much better landing! I had accumulated 22 hours of flight instruction time, and Dr. Hall said I was finally ready to take my private FAA check flight to get my private license. We scheduled an FAA flight examiner from the Grand Rapids area, on the west side of Michigan. I remember little about the flight except for the landing.

Back then, there were just a few hot air balloon manufacturers around, and the two largest in the USA were Raven Industries and Barnes Balloons. Most pilots remained fiercely loyal to the brand they were trained in, creating a rivalry between the two camps. My FAA flight examiner was a Barnes Balloon pilot, and we were loyal Raven guys.

One difference between the two was in the design of the deflation port on the top of the balloon envelope. Tracy Barnes, who developed and built Barnes Balloons, had designed a unique and simple parachute top system that was used in all his balloons. It worked great, but back then it did not dump hot air out of the envelope as quickly as the Raven rip-top system did. On a windy landing, Barnes balloons were more prone to drag farther along the ground before deflating and coming to a complete stop. Raven balloons used a Velcro rip-out top that quickly deflated the balloon, preventing it from being dragged along. Both had their advantages and disadvantages. The other major difference was in the basket design. Anyway, I was all gung-ho Raven, and my examiner was not. I sensed he was not comfortable flying with me in our Raven system. Consequently, I set out to prove to him that I was an excellent pilot and that our Raven balloon was superior.

After completing the in-flight exam requirements, we set out to land. It was windy, and we were moving along at about 15 miles per hour. I saw a small field ahead that was bordered by six-foot-tall fences and said I was going to land there. The examiner said, "That looks too small to me." I leveled off at about 15–20 feet, cleared the first fence, and ripped out the top.

We hit the ground with a thud in the aluminum bucket and tipped over while the envelope deflated without dragging more than five feet. The examiner was impressed and said, "Wow, that was good." So, on July 15th, 1978, I passed the exam and became an FAA Certified Private Pilot with the following limitations: operating a lighter-than-air free balloon equipped with an airborne heater. Larry took his commercial pilot exam flight the next day and passed it as well, so we both now had our hot air balloon pilot's license.

~ ~ ~

The week after getting our licenses, Larry and I flew together in the green-and-white balloon with the aluminum bucket gondola. Dr. Hall and Gretchen were our chase crew. We had a great flight and were looking for a landing site when Dr. Hall urgently radioed that we must land in a big field ahead. On the other side of the road from the field there was a vast track of state land with no access.

We said, "Okay, looks good," and started our approach. We were moving along at around 10 miles per hour, so Larry reminded me we need to rip out the top on this landing. There were high-voltage power lines running through the middle of the field. It was an enormous field, with plenty of room to clear the power lines safely and then descend quickly and land before the road.

Larry was flying, and he leveled off about 100 feet above the approximately 75-foot-tall power lines. As we approached them, he told me to be ready to rip out the top after we cross the lines when he tells me to. I only heard "rip out the top after we cross the lines" (and I was remembering my solo flight when I forgot to rip out the top).

Larry had the balloon in a perfect trajectory to cross over and clear the lines by about 100 feet, then descend and level out over the field at about 10 feet when he would tell me to rip out the top. Instead, I ripped out the top at about 75 feet above the ground after we crossed the lines. We crashed so hard it almost knocked us out. Incredibly, we landed in a big deep mud puddle that made the impact less drastic and probably saved us from serious injury.

The Balloonatics

We were bruised and shook up but so relieved when we saw how lucky we had been to hit that mud puddle smack dead center! The puddle was only about 20 feet in diameter, and everything around it was dry. There were other areas of the field that were wet as it had been raining a lot that year, but the envelope had lain down on dry ground. The aluminum bucket was stuck about a foot deep in the mud and took a lot of work to extract, but it was worth it, considering what could have been. We had to take it home and hose all the mud off of it later while drinking a few beers and nursing our bruised tailbones! (Referring to tailbones and the rigid aluminum gondola, it is not recommended to impact the horizontal bar or the 20-gallon lay-down fuel tanks with one's tailbone. It may have been this flight that led to Larry's lower-back surgical fusion some 40 years later.)

We learned a valuable lesson about sharing control of the balloon between two pilots. I also learned the hard way to never completely rip out the top of the balloon from a height exceeding 25 feet. (Dr. Hall had told me that many times, unless absolutely necessary to avoid a worse outcome.)

~   ~   ~

Larry and I had another flight that year that involved our first encounter with an upset landowner. We took off one evening in midsummer with light winds traveling slowly at about four to five miles per hour. Late in the flight, the slight breeze we had been traveling on slowly came to a halt over a large farm.

Sunset was about half an hour away. Our plan was to land after passing over a huge soybean field. However, we were currently hovering over the field without any movement. We went way up but still made hardly any movement, so we came back down and got nowhere. After about 20 minutes of this, we realized we had no choice but to land in the middle of that soybean field.

After landing, Larry stayed in the inflated balloon while I got out and walked toward the farmhouse, which was about a half mile away. Our chase crew was on the road by the farmhouse, and we had radioed them to go there and see if anyone was home. As I was walking, I saw someone walking toward me from the farmhouse, and we met about halfway.

It was a large older farmer, and he was not happy! He asked me in a very loud and unfriendly tone, "What the hell are you doing in my bean field?" I apologized profusely and explained that we did not intend to land here, but the winds stopped, and we had no choice. I said we would pay for any damages to his crop if he would please let us drive our pickup out to recover the balloon.

As soon as I said we would pay for any damage, he seemed to relax and calm down. He said, "Okay then, I appreciate that, but I do not want you to drive out here. I will get my tractor and trailer to recover it with." I apologized again and thanked him for his understanding and said our crew was waiting to come help. He said they could walk out behind his tractor and trailer.

After we packed up and loaded the balloon on his trailer with him watching closely, he drove it out to the green-and-white chase truck. We again thanked him over and over and asked him how much damage he thought we did to his beans and what we owed him. He thought for a minute and said, "Aw, hell, most of those beans will pop back up and be harvested. You did minor damage. Just give me $20 for my time and use of my tractor." What a relief that was! I wish all landowners had his great attitude.

~ ~ ~

That fall, we had an awesome flight over the University of Michigan football stadium! Now, if you are from Michigan, you know there is a fierce rivalry between Michigan State University and the University of Michigan that dates back over 100 years. U of M had won six straight games against MSU and was favored in this matchup at their home stadium in Ann Arbor, only an hour's drive from MSU in East Lansing. We took the green-and-white balloon and chase vehicle into our rival's campus, and somehow, with no resistance, we found a launch location upwind from the stadium. We were literally right next to the stadium, only 200 yards away! No way could you get that close or get away with inflating and flying a hot air balloon anywhere near a major stadium like that today, but remember, this was 1978.

We tried to time our flights over the football games at halftime. However, this time we were running a bit late, or maybe early, I am not sure. Dr. Hall and I quickly ascended after taking off near the stadium. We had to climb fast and used the burners at full blast until we cleared the top rim by about 100 feet.

The side we launched from turned out to be the home team's side, and the MSU fans were on the opposite side. As we came up over the stadium, the MSU fans clearly saw the huge green-and-white balloon popping up over the stadium. Once we realized we had generated sufficient lift to cross the stadium, I ceased burning the balloon's burners. Back then, those burners were quite noisy, and being inside the gondola made it very difficult to hear anything else.

Suddenly, we were met with an overwhelming roar from the MSU fans! It was incredible! We were simply enthralled with ourselves, and our heads swelled up thinking they were all cheering for us. We started jumping up and down and waving to our adoring throng! And then we realized MSU had just scored a touchdown, and the crowd was roaring for that, not us.

The timing could not have been more perfect, and I am sure that our appearance at that moment made the touchdown even more special for any MSU fan who was there. Once we came down from our momentary high and imagined fame, we settled down and enjoyed a pleasant flight over the city of Ann Arbor. We congratulated each other on a job well done!

Competition is an interesting human characteristic, in football and ballooning. While the balloon was in flight, one of the local balloon pilots (who would eventually become well known in the industry) stopped our chase crew. Gretchen was driving and remembers the pilot scolding and yelling at her about us flying over the U of M stadium and then telling her to get out of Ann Arbor. Apparently, this pilot was not happy about the competition.

~   ~   ~

Thanks to Dr. Hall, I gained 12 hours of flight instruction in 1978 and passed my private license check flight. Additionally, I logged another nine hours of flight time as pilot in command, working toward my commercial license. Larry logged nine more hours of training and passed his commercial license check ride. Larry used his previously accumulated fixed-wing training hours toward his commercial balloon pilot license. As a result, his first FAA check ride was for the commercial license.

1979

My 1979 logbook shows a couple of local flights every month starting in April, including one at the Capt. Phogg Balloon Classic in Flint in August. Several of these were solo flights, and several included high-wind landings.

I recall two of these flights in particular. The first one was when I took my mom up for her first balloon ride. We had a wonderful time together, and she loved it, except for the landing. The wind was not strong, maybe six to seven miles per hour. I landed against the grain in an unplanted farm field with corn furrows and stubble. We dragged and bounced over the rows for 20 to 30 feet before stopping. I had instructed my mom on how to hold on tight and slightly bend her knees to absorb the shock of landing, but I didn't realize that she had positioned herself with her shins right next to one of the unpadded lay-down 20-gallon propane tanks on the floor.

She was facing the way we were landing, so her shins banged into the tank with every bump. Ouch! I felt so bad after we came to a stop and she told me what had happened. Despite her pain, she didn't complain about her two bruised shins, showing her toughness. I felt awful and made a point to warn passengers about the tanks on future landings.

The other flight I remember was my dad's first flight. We took off from Kinawa Middle School in Okemos. A tall communications tower was located about one-half mile from the school, and the wind was unusually calm that day. It was an evening flight, and we became becalmed over that tower. I spent half an hour going up and down trying to find any wind to take us away from it and finally landed on the other side of it—just a mile away from where we had started after an hour's flight!

~ ~ ~

Another adventure happened that spring that did not involve ballooning. Larry and I hitchhiked to Florida. We went to visit a friend who was living in Jacksonville. We often hitchhiked locally, so a long trip sounded like an adventurous idea. Because all the schools were on their spring break, we assumed it wouldn't be difficult to catch rides. Our mistake was going south from Lansing on highway 127. Had we gone east toward US-23, then south on I-75, we would have been going with the flow of most of the students heading to Florida. We thought we would just start south and make our way to I-75 later. Big mistake.

Our first ride gave us a clue how this trip was to go. A cemetery truck carrying a burial vault picked us up! We both piled into the cab with the driver, noting his striking resemblance to Lurch, the butler on TV's Addams Family, and the fact that he spoke very little. Fifteen miles down the highway, he exited and let us off in the countryside to hitch our next ride. Hitchhiking was only allowed from on-ramps, so we'd go to the very end for better visibility to passing cars. It took a long time to get another ride, which didn't take us very far. This continued over and over all day.

We had agreed that we would not hitchhike after dark, so we eventually stayed at a motel along the highway where one of our rides left us. The following day, we encountered similar circumstances and reached an exit with just 45 minutes until nightfall. We hitched at the on-ramp's end, with a motel nearby as a backup plan.

As darkness fell, I suggested ending the night when a young blonde woman sped by. We actually made eye contact with her as she passed. To our surprise and delight, she put on her brakes and, braking hard, pulled over about 100 yards down the highway. Larry started running toward her car and I thought, *She will not pick up two guys.*

I was certain she was messing with us and would speed away before Larry got there. Larry just yelled, "Come on, man!" I shook my head and started walking that way, and, lo and behold, she stayed. Larry opened the door, poked his head in, and yelled at me to hurry. I could not believe our luck! She was a beautiful gal and picked up two male hitchhikers just as it was getting dark. We were certainly no threat to anyone, but it didn't seem like a safe decision to me. Anyway, she was nice, and during our conversation, she revealed she was going back to her college, which was east of Atlanta. At least we had a ride to Atlanta now.

We got to Atlanta in the early evening the next day. She drove the entire way, making several stops, which resulted in a lengthy trip. When we arrived in Atlanta, she dropped us off at a highway hotel,

The Balloonatics

and we bid farewell. Once she left, we exchanged glances and realized we hadn't even asked her to join us for dinner and drinks. Anyway, she probably would have said no.

We stayed at that hotel and got up early the next morning. We got a ride in the first five minutes! The guy who stopped was in a pickup truck, so we piled in, with me taking the middle seat. The driver was an older guy in his sixties, I guessed, and he had an open bottle of Jack Daniels in one hand! He was in wonderful spirits as he asked us where we were going. He took off and was driving fine as he passed the bottle around and we had a toast!

An hour later, he said he should let one of us drive, and Larry took over. The man told us he was heading back home to Miami and had been working in New York. He took out a huge wad of bills from his front shirt pocket and gave me about $60 for gas and said he was going to take a nap.

Larry drove, and somehow, through the Jack Daniels haze, we ended up taking a wrong exit, taking us 100 miles west of Atlanta before we noticed it! We continued on after finally turning east while the owner of the vehicle continued to sleep off his Jack Daniels–induced slumber. He was still sleeping when we got to where we needed to go east toward Jacksonville. We pulled over and tried to wake him up, but he was out cold and snoring with a huge wad of bills sticking out of his front pocket.

We locked him in his truck and headed east before it got dark, hitchhiking the rest of the way to our friend's house. In hindsight, we should have driven all the way to Jacksonville and tried to revive him there. Hopefully, he was okay and got to his destination safely.

Because of our travel delays and work obligations, we could only stay in Jacksonville for three days. Our friend drove us to I-75, and we promptly got a ride from college guys in an old van heading to Michigan. They were lucky to have picked us up because their old van broke down twice on the way, and Larry, being an auto mechanic, fixed it both times and got us home. We finally made it across the Michigan border with no further problems, and they dropped us off at Larry's front door!

~   ~   ~

That summer the Capt. Phogg Balloon Classic moved from the Flint airport to Crossroads Village, a county park that featured a re-creation of an 1850s-era village. Most of the buildings had been moved from their original locations and rebuilt there. It is well done and very large, including a working farm and a full-scale steam railroad that takes passengers on a circle tour of the village. It is still a major local attraction to this day.

This time, we had two balloons to fly. Dr. Hall flew the No Smoking balloon, and Larry and I flew the green-and-white balloon. As usual, the event provided a first-class experience, and everyone, including me, had a ton of fun with beautiful flights over the surrounding Genesee County countryside.

A unique part of the Crossroads Village Capt. Phogg Balloon Classic was the antique cars. Each balloon was assigned an antique car as its "special pilot chase vehicle." The aim of each race was for the balloons to all fly out from Crossroads Village and remain airborne for 45 minutes or five miles, whichever came first. Then the balloon would land, and the pilot would jump in the antique car (after making sure the balloon was safely down and secure on terra firma first, of course). The antique car would race the pilot back to Crossroads Village, and the first pilot back won the race.

Some cars were fast and some were not, but it really didn't matter as it was all just for fun and show. It was a real crowd pleaser since all the balloons took off from the event site. The crowds saw all the balloons launch and float away, and then the announcer would keep them excited waiting for the pilots to race back one by one in the antique cars. The event organizers ensured that the car drivers were treated as well as the balloon pilots, which resulted in many longtime friendships between the pilots and car owners.

Larry and I always wanted to have one particular car and driver. We wanted Bob Conlee because he was a great guy with a magnificent car, a 1913 Rolls Royce. He also always had the best cooler, filled with ice-cold Moosehead beer and Crown Royal whiskey. And Bob would let us drive the Rolls Royce back after the flight!

Another really cool thing that Capt. Phogg did was award everyone a first-place trophy since the event and the competitions were just for fun.

~ ~ ~

Soon it was fall, and the exciting new college football season of 1979 was here. I remember the one and only football flight the weather allowed that year. Larry and I were flying low late in the flight looking for a place to land.

We were crossing a corn stubble field, and I was planning a descent to skim over it when we got hit by a big downdraft, most likely caused by a nearby thermal. It slammed us down into the ground with a good thump, although not nearly as hard as our crash into the mud puddle the year before! Then we rebounded and crashed down again.

This time as we dragged along, bouncing over the corn stubble, we noticed that one of the two 20-gallon propane tanks was bouncing around with us in the gondola and was attached to the burners by just the fuel lines! Larry grabbed the red line and ripped out the top, bringing us to a stop in the middle of the field.

The bolt securing that tank strap to the floor broke on impact, causing the tank to come loose. Our previous crash into the mud puddle may have damaged it. We replaced both tank strap bolts and never had the issue again.

Craig Elliott

~ ~ ~

In 1979, I logged 11.25 hours of flight time as pilot in command and now had 42.25 total hours, 7.25 more than the minimum needed for a commercial LTA pilot's license.

Eighties

1980

In January 1980, Dr. Hall signed me off for my FAA commercial pilot check flight. On January 20th I went with two of my friends, Rick Scott and Rick White, as my crew to fly with a different FAA examiner. We arrived an hour before sunrise.

That winter had been quite mild with little snow. No snow covered the ground, and the temperature was in the low 40s. We set the balloon up on the examiner's front lawn and I inflated it. He jumped in before the sun had risen, and off we went. Rick White, a photography enthusiast, took some nice black-and-white photos of the flight.

The examiner told me to ascend to a certain altitude and level off, then descend to another and level off. About 15 minutes into the flight, he told me to land in the field ahead. I questioned him about which field he was referring to, and he said the one before the power lines. I told him I wasn't comfortable landing there and preferred flying over the power lines to land in the enormous field beyond. I felt it wasn't safe to land before the power lines, so despite his unhappiness, I landed immediately after crossing the lines. The entire flight lasted just 20 minutes.

The examiner hastily signed off my logbook and left us to pack up the balloon. He had someone tailing us in his car. He hurriedly returned to join another pilot and balloon that had arrived as we were taking off. I was just thrilled to have my commercial pilot's license, so I thought little about it. My crew and I celebrated with some champagne. I was now a commercial hot air balloon pilot and could get paid to fly balloons!

Dr. Hall told me that the examiner called him later that week and said he was not happy with me and my performance. He told Dr. Hall to better prepare the next pilot he sent to get his commercial check ride. I don't understand his reason for saying that. I did everything he asked me to do on that very short check ride except land in front of power lines.

~ ~ ~

We again went to the Capt. Phogg Balloon Classic and had a blast. I logged one flight over an MSU football game that fall and noted in my logbook that we had a high-wind landing.

Soon, our balloon flying settled into a lull as we scattered and pursued different paths. For a few years, Larry worked as a mechanic and managed a Shell service station. He decided he wanted to be a fighter pilot in the Air Force, so he joined the Air Force ROTC.

I had been working nights as a custodian at the AFSCME (Michigan's public service workers' union) headquarters building in Lansing while working on an associate degree in architecture from Lansing Community College. The No Smoking and WVIC balloon contracts ran out and were not renewed. Ballooning became less important to Dr. Hall after he bought an airplane. He sold the No Smoking balloon and then sold the green-and-white balloon, along with his company Balloony Tunes, to Larry.

I logged only 2.25 total flight hours and five flights, including my commercial pilot check flight. Larry logged just five hours of flight time in 1980.

The Balloonatics

~ ~ ~

Late in the fall of 1980, disaster struck. Larry and I went out one weekend evening to a local club in East Lansing called Coral Gables, a great venue for bands. We stayed too long and then decided to drive the 15 miles to Dr. Hall's house and surprise him at 1 a.m. Alcohol makes you do stupid things, and this was one of our stupidest.

I had recently bought a brand-new Toyota pickup truck, which back then was a small truck with a four-cylinder engine and four-speed manual transmission. Neither of us was competent to drive, but I got behind the wheel while Larry piled into the passenger seat, and off we went. In our drunken stupor, we ended up taking a wrong turn and were going around Lake Lansing when I fell asleep at the wheel. Larry was also asleep. We left the road while going around a sharp curve, rolling the small truck through two old wood utility poles that we snapped in half with the little truck.

I walked away with a badly bruised head and body; I believe my injuries were relatively minor because I was wearing my seat belt. Larry, however, had not worn his seat belt and suffered severe injuries. Larry ended up in the hospital for three days in a coma. Those were the worst three days ever, praying he would wake up and be okay. He finally did and endured a long and painful recovery. The coma and head trauma meant he was no longer eligible for pilot training in the Air Force, and he had to quit the ROTC program.

1981

The next year, Larry, thank God, had recovered from our terrible accident, and we did a few flights and commercial jobs with the green-and-white balloon that he now owned. I logged three flights that year and two hours as pilot in command. Larry logged 14 total hours that year.

~ ~ ~

One of our trips was to Gary, Indiana, where we tethered the balloon at a truck stop, of all places! (This means we tied the balloon to the ground so it could only go up and down, not fly away.) Larry's younger brother Danny came with us on this trip. It was Larry's birthday that weekend as well. Once we finished tethering the balloon, we returned to our hotel and decided to celebrate Larry's birthday at a strip club we had noticed nearby. Turns out it was not a real classy place. The first dancer to emerge seemed to be around six or seven months pregnant. We did not stay long.

On our way back to the hotel, we stopped and bought some beer. As we drove through the hotel parking lot, I noticed a girl alone on her second-floor hotel balcony. I told Larry to stop the van and called up to her, asking how she was and if she wanted to join us for a beer. Initially, she declined, but after some conversation, she invited me up for a drink. I told the guys, "See ya later," and went on up to meet her. She was a pretty gal with long, straight black hair and sad green eyes. I introduced myself, and she did the same. I do not remember her name.

We went to the balcony, where she poured us drinks, and we began talking. Eventually, I noticed her deep sadness and inquired about the cause. She started crying and told me that her boyfriend had just broken up with her, and something else traumatic had just happened. She was truly depressed. Then she confessed that she had been on the balcony contemplating suicide.

Wow, that really hit me like a ton of bricks. I had never dealt with anything like that. Somehow, I was able to talk with her for about an hour and console her and help her realize that what had happened to her was not worth taking her life. I told her she had lots of good things to look forward to. She relaxed and stopped crying

The Balloonatics

and said yes, I was correct. She needed to take time for healing.

After having a few more drinks, I spent the night. The next morning, we all went out to breakfast. She was happy and talkative. We exchanged phone numbers, and then we left. It was Sunday, and we all had to get back to our respective homes and jobs. Later that week, I was out in the yard of my small house in Lansing, Michigan, tending my vegetable garden. She showed up out of the blue. We hadn't communicated, yet she appeared unexpectedly, frantically expressing her desire to be with me and causing me to panic. How had she found me? All I had given her was my phone number.

I wasn't interested in a serious relationship with her or anyone else. However, she surprised me by saying she wanted to move in together. She had all her stuff in her car ready to do just that! I had to tell her no. I was sorry, but that was not happening. Moreover, I had another girlfriend who, coincidentally, was visiting me that day and was in the house. The young woman got very upset and drove off. I never saw her or spoke to her again. I felt terrible after that and just hoped she would be okay.

~ ~ ~

That fall I did a flight that was supposed to be over an MSU football game. Larry's mother was the owner of a women's health clinic, and she had bought a banner for the balloon to advertise the clinic. Larry requested that I cover one of the football game flights due to a scheduling conflict. I invited a girl I liked for the balloon ride, and she joined me. Lisa and I had graduated from Okemos High School in the same class, in 1976. My friend Marty, who was renting a room in my house, came along as ground crew. I believe Lisa's younger brother Ron also came and crewed with Marty.

We searched for a launch site to fly our balloon over the MSU football stadium. I found a suitable spot, and we departed after obtaining permission from the landowners. Unfortunately, I miscalculated the winds or the launch spot or both, and we missed the stadium by a mile. We were now flying straight for the city of Lansing and would soon enter the airspace for the Capital City Airport.

I did not have an aircraft radio to call and get permission to fly into the airspace, so I had to land fast. We flew from the south side of East Lansing into Lansing and crossed over the intersection of Grand River and Highway 127. Because it was a highly populated area, finding a suitable landing spot was challenging. However, luck was on my side as I spotted a schoolyard ahead and swiftly descended. We came down perfectly over the schoolyard and had to clear some playground equipment before dropping into an open area to land at about 8 to 10 miles per hour. An exciting tip-over landing ended the flight! Lisa, her brother Ron, and I have stayed in touch and are still good friends today.

1982

In 1982, I logged 4.5 hours as pilot in command during four flights. Three flights were local, around East Lansing. One, of course, was again at the Capt. Phogg Balloon Classic, which we never missed. Larry flew 15 flights that year, logging 19.6 hours. I recall little from that year except too much partying with my friends at my little house in Lansing. All I seemed to care about back then was sex, drugs, and rock 'n' roll, sad to say.

1983

In 1983, I did not fly all spring, summer, or fall. In the meantime, Larry was flying like crazy. He logged 25 hours of flight time through

The Balloonatics

August and then, unbeknownst to me, started a commercial job for Buick Motor Division out east, where he logged another 30-plus hours from September through November.

~ ~ ~

In July, I went with Larry to the first annual Jackson Jubilee event in Jackson, Michigan, as his crew. He flew several flights there. At one, the organizers put $100 bills in envelopes attached to the top of eight-foot-tall poles set out in a field for the pilots to fly by and grab.

It was a breezy day, and they set the poles too close to a road that had huge, gnarly oak trees lining the opposite side of the road. I was parked on that road in Larry's chase van, watching as the balloons came in with the pilots trying to grab the envelopes. Several of them did not clear the oak trees as they went over the road. One balloon was badly damaged when it hit an oak tree about halfway up. As it dragged through the tree, I watched it rip the envelope apart from the equator on down. The basket came over the top of the tree at a 90-degree angle!

I was amazed and greatly relieved that no one fell out of that basket, and they kept on flying! Another balloon tried to grab an envelope but missed and then dragged along the ground, crashing into a parked car behind me. Larry was in the back of the pack, and I radioed to tell him what was going on. He forwent a try at the money poles.

~ ~ ~

The year 1983 had not been a very good one for me. After earning my associate degree in architecture in 1980, I continued studying at Lansing Community College (nicknamed "Last Chance College" by my friends who went to MSU) when I discovered they had just started a new solar energy program and now offered an associate degree in solar technology. I was thrilled by the novelty of it, thinking I could contribute to a better world by designing solar-heated homes.

I pursued that degree for two years while continuing to work nights at my custodian job for AFSCME. I was about four or five credits short of receiving that solar degree when I decided I didn't really need that piece of paper but just needed to start doing the work. So I started studying for my builder's license instead. Despite my limited knowledge of residential building, in January of 1983 I passed the test and became a builder. I started my own company and named it Elliott & Sun Builders. Then I quit my good custodian job and soon thereafter regretted doing so.

With the country facing a tough recession and residential building at a standstill, starting a building company was a bad decision. I struggled to make ends meet by helping other builders as a laborer whenever I could find work, and I landed a few minor jobs myself here and there, including one roofing job. I was struggling financially but fortunately had two renters in my house renting rooms. My renters had also become good friends. I was just able to get by.

That summer, one renter left, followed by the other a month later. My girlfriend moved in. She had graduated a year before from General Motors Institute (now Kettering University) with honors from the automotive engineering program. I believed she'd find a great job, contribute financially, and maybe we'd have a future together. However, she promptly informed me of her decision to forgo work and take a break for a couple of years. Unsure how I would manage financially, I faced the looming arrival of winter.

As I rapidly progressed into the financial abyss, one day in mid-December of 1983, Larry knocked on my door, and my world changed instantly for the better. The first thing I remember him saying when I opened the door was, "Pack your bags, dude, we are going on the road!" I said, "Where to?" He came in and told me he had been on the road the past few months flying a hot air balloon

The Balloonatics

for Buick Motor Division's nationwide tour.

Capt. Phogg had landed the contract and hired Larry as one of the pilots. The tour promoted Buick's involvement as a major sponsor and the official car of the 1984 Summer Olympic Games in Los Angeles, California. They needed two more pilots for the tour, and at Larry's request, Capt. Phogg had agreed to hire me as one of them!

Larry then told me we had to meet at Capt. Phogg's home office the next morning. I could not believe it! *What a blast,* I thought, and accepted immediately. Larry said he would pick me up early the next morning, and that was that.

Holy cow, I was on cloud nine! I called my mom to tell her, and she had lots of questions that I had no answers for. I just told her I could not pass up this opportunity. My live-in girlfriend said she was happy for me. I packed my bags, and Larry picked me up in the morning. We drove to Grand Blanc, Michigan, to Capt. Phogg's residence and met in the basement, where he had a pleasant office set up.

I have already mentioned how interesting a character Dr. Hall was. Capt. Phogg was just as much a character and maybe a bit more! He was the ultimate salesman, a member of the MassMutual Leaders Club and the Life Insurance Industries Million Dollar Round Table. He could have been a stand-up comedian with all the one-liners and jokes he told.

Capt. Phogg was also very serious in business and a stickler for details. He named his balloon company Balloon Corporation of America and referred to it as BCA (in stark contrast to the whimsical and humorous name of Dr. Hall's company, Ballooney Tunes). He made sure that everything on this Buick Tour was first class.

That day was a whirlwind of information and meeting the other pilots on the tour. Lots of paperwork to read and fill out. Uniforms to fit, equipment to buy and load into chase vehicles. The tour was comprised of two balloons and two crews consisting of two pilots traveling with each unit. One team would work east and one west of the Mississippi River. Larry and I were to start immediately with our first job in 10 days in Phoenix, Arizona, on December 27th.

The pilots' salary was $500 per month, with an additional $25 per diem when traveling and an hourly rate of $125 when the balloon was inflated in tether or free-flight mode. I thought that sounded good. If we could operate the balloon an average of 10 hours a week, we would do very well financially and have a blast doing it.

We scrambled to get everything in order. Another chase vehicle was being completed, and the second balloon had just arrived. Our chase vehicle was a GMC four-door pickup truck that had just served as a fire truck emergency vehicle at that year's Indy 500 auto race. It had to be tuned down (as it was too fast and not street legal) and modified to accommodate carrying the balloon and support equipment.

Capt. Phogg had secured what was called a Balloon Kakoon trailer that was modified and mounted in place of the truck bed. It was awesome, painted red, white, and blue to match the balloons with the Buick Hawk and Buick Olympic logos emblazoned on the sides, back, and even the top. It was just the coolest chase vehicle, period.

The truck-mounted Balloon Kakoon was amazing! The hydraulics opened the top, while the back opened onto the ground. The balloon basket was now standing upright on the open back hatch. It was an incredible display in and of itself. All we had to do was tip the basket over on its side and then pull the attached envelope out of the basket, and we were ready to inflate!

When we did a job for a dealership, they gave us a car to drive, and we parked the chase vehicle in front of the dealership (with the Balloon Kakoon opened to display the balloon) when we were not tethering or flying it. Some dealers gave us a nice car; the best one was the new Buick Grand National. We worked harder for the dealers who gave us a Grand National to drive, and maybe not as hard when they gave us a Skylark!

Larry and I left Michigan a few days later for Phoenix, Arizona, and our Buick Olympic Balloon Tour's first job. I recall Larry driving

The Balloonatics

the chase vehicle through a mountainous area in Arizona, navigating a sharp left curve. I was in the passenger seat looking down the mountain with only a short guardrail between us and a sheer 500-foot drop. I started yelling, "Slow down, she is leaning!" That scared the heck out of me, while Larry was just laughing away at me!

Turns out the truck needed some shoring up and stabilization of the suspension because of the weight of the Balloon Kakoon and all the equipment mounted on the bed. We drove it slower around sharp curves from then on until we had that issue fixed.

~ ~ ~

Our first job took place on December 27th as part of the College Football Fiesta Bowl festivities, which Buick sponsored. However, we

Larry and me before leaving Michigan with the new Buick Olympic Balloon chase vehicle.

almost did not make it to that job and came very close to ending our Buick Olympic Balloon Tour before it ever got started. Here is Larry's account of that story.

> We met with dealership the day before for the usual introduction and site survey. They invited us to join them at an all-you-can-drink-for-$ night. We did. We didn't have a dealer car yet, so we drove the balloon truck there, emblazoned with Buick Olympic identification. Of course, being the good stewards of the Buick name with a need to impress the dealership personnel with our capabilities, Craig and I proceeded to drink all we could for our hard-earned spend.
>
> Leaving the pub, we had to take the expressway to get to the other side of the city to check into the hotel. I was driving. En route, we came upon a construction zone with a merge to one lane. There was a car in front going slow, and I did not want to be stuck behind it in one lane. So, being at that level of extreme intelligence which imbues the intrepid drinker, I passed the vehicle to get in front. As I was sliding by, I noticed it was a cop. That revelation caused me to swerve into their lane, almost cutting off the car.
>
> Well, that made things interesting, as the cop had no sense of humor. There we were, a fully emblazoned Buick Olympic Balloon chase vehicle and in full uniform on the side of the road with a cop car flashing its lights. Well, as fate would have it, an attractive female police officer (even more attractive in her cop uniform) came to greet me and, I thought, regale me for my astute driving technique. I was in fine spirits as she handcuffed me and escorted me to the back seat of the awaiting squad car. Lo and behold, her mother was with her, doing a ride-along. The officer then went to the other side of the vehicle to ask Craig if he could drive.

The Balloonatics

In the meantime, well, the mom and I hit it off during the ensuing 15 minutes alone while the officer dealt with an irate and drunk passenger who, I assume, the officer concluded was in no shape to drive. Indeed, apparently that didn't go well at all, for the officer finally came back to the car and told me that my buddy was going to get us both arrested. Imagine my surprise to find I was not yet under arrest! You had to love the early '80s—the cops would still give drunk drivers some slack!

About this time, a second squad car had pulled up behind us, into which Craig was escorted. Now, I can't speak for Craig's experience with his chauffeurs, but now I had both the officer and her mother in the car. Having had a good 20 minutes in the car with the mother, I was certain she was close to giving me the green light to marry the daughter (or maybe hit on me herself). Thinking that might provide at least a short-term solution to my problem, I began working toward that goal on the 20-minute ride back to the station after the tow truck arrived and left with the chase vehicle and the balloon—which were needed for the job in the morning at the dealership.

This was Craig's first Buick job, so he was impressed, for sure, that this might be his only one. Fortunately, he had had some time for self-reflection and a little sobering up by the time we got to the cop shop. I am certain that this, plus my flirting with the officer and her mother, helped to calm the potentially dire prospect of spending the night in jail, as not only did she not jail us, but she gave us a ride to our hotel. While I didn't have to marry her, it did cost me a dinner date (and a $400 ticket).

It was a restless and short time at the hotel, for our troubles weren't over yet. We still had to get a job done at the dealership in a few hours, with no vehicle or balloon, and no clue where or how to get them. I don't recall how we got the information, but somehow, we found the impound lot, paid the piper to get the vehicle out, and got the job done with a huge hangover, still semi-intoxicated, and no one the wiser. And we still had a job!

~ ~ ~

That first job in Phoenix (the morning after retrieving the chase vehicle from the impound lot) was for Addams Buick. Our logbooks show that on December 27th we did a "high winds" tether using the Raven super pressure system for one and a half hours.

The super pressure system used an electric fan to pressurize the envelope, which helped it withstand a lot of wind and allowed you to tether the balloon in much higher winds than you could without it. It was a significant inconvenience to use and required extra effort to set up and inflate the balloon, so we only used it when absolutely necessary.

That night we tethered again using the super pressure system for an hour and a half, according to my logbook. On the 29th, the logbooks say we did a tether in the morning for one hour and in the evening for one and a half hours, again using the super pressure system. On the 30th, logbooks say "normal" tether for just under two hours, which means the winds must have calmed down so we didn't have to use super pressure. It was the same the next day, the 31st; we tethered for two hours on the parade route during the Fiesta Bowl Parade. Aside from the near-arrest and the leaning truck on the mountain, I remember little about this trip.

1984

My January 1, 1984, log shows we free-flew the balloon in Mesa, Arizona. This tour had no rhyme or reason as far as the logistics were concerned. Buick mailed out a press release kit to every Buick dealer in

The Balloonatics

the country to inform them about the balloon tour and offer the balloon to them for $500 per day. Dealerships across the country began booking the balloons for sales events or large community events they sponsored.

We went to wherever the next job was booked, which was a mystery until we received a hotel fax that provided instructions. No cell phones or GPS in the eighties meant relying on the Rand McNally Road Atlas and local maps from gas stations to find our way. We did a lot of driving back and forth across this big, beautiful country! After Arizona, we worked in California, Texas, California again, Nevada, Colorado, Washington, Idaho, and so on.

I remember driving on Highway 101 from Los Angeles to Seattle, then looping back to LA, into Texas, and beyond. Loving it, we played Willie Nelson's song "On the Road Again" repeatedly on the cassette tape player. We listened to several tapes while on the road, including some motivational and self-help tapes by Brian Tracy that Capt. Phogg had given us. Our contract limited us to driving only 500 miles a day, a simple task with two drivers.

We often drove a lot farther and reached our destination a day or two early, allowing us to take a couple of days to relax and enjoy the sights. It was a tough job, but somebody had to do it! We did not fully appreciate how lucky we were but took full advantage of the opportunity to have as much fun as we could doing what we considered fun back then. Which, unfortunately, was mostly drinking and chasing women.

~ ~ ~

Larry's dad lived in Las Vegas and was a poker dealer at the Palace Station Casino. It was great to visit him and Larry's grandmother while driving back and forth. Several times on the tour, we took advantage of this and flew the balloon directly over the Strip, giving rides to his dad and others. Vegas was small back then. The area around the Strip was wide open in every direction. It was easy flying.

We thought about going back there after the tour was over to start a balloon ride operation. Looking back, I imagine where we might be if we had done so back then and bought some property! Oh well, lost opportunities lead to other opportunities, and you can only do so much. I like a quote from a famous insurance salesman, Art Williams: "All you can do is all you can do, but all you can do is enough."

Larry and I weren't into gambling or skilled at poker, so we didn't play much. Larry's grandmother loved to play bingo, and she often won money doing so. She convinced us the first time we visited to join her, and we did so kind of reluctantly to please her and so Larry could spend time with her. Turns out we loved it too! Heck, where else could you spend $20 on a few bingo cards, get free drinks for two to three hours, and have a chance of winning $10,000?

One time I was only one number away from winning $10,000, and it was incredibly exciting as they called out number after number for about five calls till someone else very close to me yelled BINGO! Larry's Grandma won money one of the times we went with her. I was amazed by how she could keep track of all the numbers on the many cards she bought! Larry and I could only keep up with half as many. I am sure it is good brain exercise for anyone to play like she did. And, unlike Larry and me, she was only drinking Coca-Cola, so I'm sure that helped her keep up as well.

~ ~ ~

Another time when we were in Vegas, Larry had gone somewhere with his dad and grandmother. We were staying at a casino, and I decided to drive the Buick Olympic chase vehicle to a nearby bar.

It was a hopping place with a big dance floor and lots of pretty ladies dancing and drinking. I danced with a few gals and ended up sitting in a booth with one and buying her a drink. She was from Vietnam, beautiful, and kind of shy. We had been sitting and talking for just a few minutes when I heard some guy yell, "You bitch!" I turned to look, and he threw a drink at the lady I was sitting with. It flew right past my nose and hit her in the chest. He ran for the door, and I jumped up and ran after him.

I caught up with him just before he reached the exit, which had two sets of double doors and a small lobby in between, where the bouncers checked IDs. I shoved him through the first set of doors, and he fell into the small lobby. Jumping on top of him, I started pounding on him. The bouncers pulled me off. He got up and ran out the second set of doors into the parking lot.

Quickly, I told the bouncers what had happened, and they let me go. I ran out in the parking lot to look for him. When I caught up with him, he turned and yelled something at me. I decked him with a straight right punch that caught him on his left cheek, just below the eye. He did not get up. Blood was dripping from his cheek.

I returned to the bar and found the girl still at the booth, crying and drenched from his drink. She said she was okay and that he was an ex-boyfriend. I suggested leaving and changing into dry clothes. We left in the Buick chase vehicle. She lived alone not far away in a trailer park. I told her I was staying at the casino and that she could stay with me if she did not feel safe at home. She agreed she should not stay there alone that night. She changed and gathered items while I stayed in the vehicle, on the lookout for the creep.

We went to my room at the casino and had a fantastic time! Turns out she was older than she looked and had a big scar on her lower belly from two C-section deliveries. She told me her kids were living with her mother in Vietnam. The next morning, we went out to breakfast, and I drove her home. She said she had to go to work waiting tables later that morning. I never saw her again.

~ ~ ~

Our first job in 1984—after the almost-final first one of the tour in Arizona at the end of December—was in Pasadena, California, for Thorson Buick, and our logbooks show we tethered the balloon on January 7th for five hours! I remember that one. The dealership parking lot was right on the 210 Freeway, and we tethered the balloon only 200 feet from the freeway.

Arriving, I questioned whether it was a good idea to tether the balloon in that cramped lot with numerous light poles and a freeway almost on top of us. However, Larry was always the optimist and would find a way. We lucked out with perfect weather and almost no wind. The sight of our balloon snarled rush hour traffic on the freeway even more than it usually was. It surprised me that the police never showed up and told us to take it down!

The next day we tethered for three hours and then had a few days off due to windy weather. On the 13th, we did two one-hour tethers, one in the morning and one after dark, which was cool. Our last day in Pasadena was the 14th, when we tethered for two hours.

~ ~ ~

I remember two things about that Pasadena job:

1) The smog! We stayed at a hotel overlooking the freeway and hills outside the city. When the wind was calm, we couldn't see the hills through the smog that hung in the air, obscuring visibility. When the wind was blowing, we could see the hills, and it was a delightful view.

2) Annette. I met Annette in the hotel bar one of the first evenings, and we hit it off right from the start. She was a few years older than me. We got along very well and had tons of fun together. One day we went to Disneyland with Larry and his girlfriend, Gretchen, who had flown from Michigan to be with us. We all had a memorable time there. Annette and I spent a lot of time together during that week in

The Balloonatics

Larry, Gretchen, me, and Annette at the top of the Palm Springs, CA, Tramway.

Pasadena, and she came to visit for a few days while on our next job in Rancho Mirage.

~ ~ ~

Larry and I began our next job on January 16th in Rancho Mirage, California, just outside of Palm Springs. Buick was a sponsor of a PGA Golf Tournament, which was being held at the Westin Rancho Mirage Golf Resort. Gretchen was staying on for a few weeks and was also with us.

Usually, we were responsible for finding our own lodging. Sometimes the office would book us ahead of time at a hotel near a job, but we really preferred to pick for ourselves. We had a company credit card for gasoline, propane, lodging, and other expenses, and a lodging budget that exceeded our needs.

We quickly learned that the two best places to stay were Holidome and La Quinta Inn. Holidome, back in the day, was a Holiday Inn with a large indoor pool under a dome-shaped roof. It also had a large bar with a stage and a dance floor and booked good bands on the weekends with plenty of ladies to hustle and dance with. The new La Quinta Inns chain had a fantastic free happy hour and free food buffet every night. Staying at a Holidome meant no need to leave for fun, while at La Quinta Inn the free drinks and dinner let us save our per diem for the bar later.

After the Pasadena job ended, we drove to the Westin Resort in Rancho Mirage, California, that was hosting the golf event. All the rooms were booked and exceeded our budget. We then drove back toward Palm Springs on Highway 111 looking for a hotel. Larry saw what he thought was a nice-looking hotel a few miles down the road. I remember it was a large hotel that was located a bit off the road and was painted pink.

Larry drove up, entered, and suggested we wait in the truck. Gretchen said she would stay in the truck, so I went with Larry. We walked in and went to the front desk, where Larry asked about availability and price. The front desk guy struck me as odd, but I ignored it.

I noticed a massive wall of windows overlooking a courtyard and pool. While Larry continued to talk with the front desk guy, I walked over to check out the pool area. It was beautiful, but something was missing, and I felt out of place. Suddenly it hit me: there were no women! The clientele consisted of guys in speedos, many of whom were hugging and hanging onto each other. I exclaimed, "This place isn't for us!" and hurried back to the front desk, where Larry was just about to book two rooms.

I told him, "Stop! We're not staying here." Puzzled, Larry looked at me and asked why not. I grabbed his arm, led him over to the windows, and told him to look. He said it looked very nice. I said, "Look harder. Do you see anything missing or strange?"

He looked for a minute and said, "Oh yeah, I see. Let's go!" And out we went. Gretchen and I had a field day ribbing him about that for the next week! I do not remember where we ended up staying, but I do know there were women there.

~ ~ ~

On January 16th we did a free flight from the Rancho Mirage Westin Resort in California. On the 17th, we flew two free flights and tethered the balloon at the resort. On the 18th, Larry and I free-flew together from the resort in the morning and evening. The next morning on the 19th, I flew solo from the resort. You gotta love that California desert winter weather! Coming from Michigan, I found this amazing. We were flying every day!

Now, this place was incredible. Palm Springs and the entire Coachella Valley had huge, beautiful golf resorts sprinkled throughout the valley, like green palm oases interrupting the drab brown desert floor. Surrounded by snowcapped mountains, it was simply paradise on earth.

I had been to California and spent a month traveling from Lake Tahoe to San Francisco and down the coast to San Diego after I graduated from high school. Yet we never reached this place, and nothing else came close to comparing. Flying above it in a hot air balloon, traveling so slowly while ascending to several thousand feet, and seeing the entire valley, from the San Gorgonio pass to the northeast to the Salton Sea to the southwest, was incredible. Descending and gently skimming over the palm trees was an extraordinary experience. We got paid for this! We felt like the luckiest guys in the whole wide world.

I recall we created quite a stir and had lots of complaints from the locals who were not used to balloons flying around low over their million-dollar resort homes. We found out later that there was an ordinance prohibiting balloons from flying and landing in Rancho Mirage. Some local balloon ride operators cautioned us about creating a disturbance that could impact their future landings. We were never notified by any authorities.

There were several balloon ride companies operating in the valley. It was a rapidly growing minor industry, along with the rapid growth of the tourist business and golf development that was happening there back then. We met with several balloon operators and became friends with some, whom I would later come back and fly for after the Buick Tour was over.

~ ~ ~

Our next job was in Thousand Oaks, California, on January 21st and 22nd. We both got to fly, taking up Buick executives and their spouses in Simi Valley, with Larry logging two flights and me one, and we did a one-and-a-half-hour tether at the local dealership in Thousand Oaks.

We met several nice local balloonists who flew in the area and were told that the Simi Valley was where they filmed the TV show *Bonanza*. The place was beautiful, with wide-open spaces for miles and light winds during our visit. The three flights we took there were lots of fun, with several other balloons flying alongside us.

A very wealthy man, whom we heard about from other pilots but never actually met, flew a standout balloon. The artwork was beautiful and must have been quite costly. The balloon resembled the night sky, complete with stars and constellations. It was very elaborate. His chase vehicle was a matching motorcoach. His crew would set the balloon up and inflate it, and then he would walk out of the motorcoach with a different beautiful woman on his arm every flight. He and the lady would step into the basket, and off they would go a mile high ... to enjoy the scenery, I am sure!

~ ~ ~

Next, we went to Perris, California, and on January 26th I did a flight from the balloon field there. This was a cool place with another bunch of local pilots who had their own designated launch field, complete with a 1,000-gallon propane tank on site for refueling. We again met many nice pilots, and the one who stands out is Fred Kreig. I do not remember a lot about him except that he was a super nice guy who heartily welcomed us and showed us around. He must have impressed me because I noted that I met him in my logbook. He lived in a beautiful, large stone house up on a big hill nearby.

After Perris, we were off to Wilmington, California, and on the 28th and 29th we did two four-hour tethers at the Good Buick Dealership in Wilmington. Our next job was in Albuquerque, New Mexico, aptly named "The Hot Air Balloon Capital of the World," where Larry flew one free flight on February 1st and we met a ton of great folks at World Balloon Corporation, including Sid and Jewel Cutter. Then we were off to Dallas, Texas, for a one-day job at Ewing Buick on February 6th. Luckily, the weather just barely cooperated, and we were able to pull off a three-hour tether in the morning and another two-hour tether that evening using the super pressure system.

~ ~ ~

During our time in Albuquerque, we decided to go skiing and were told that Taos was the best place to go. The drive from the New Mexico desert to the Taos mountains was a beautiful one. As we drove into the parking lot at the ski resort, we almost turned around and left. Our eyes were immediately drawn to an unbelievably steep, colossal run that appeared to ascend the mountain indefinitely. It was covered with the biggest, wildest moguls we had ever seen. It scared us, to be honest! Fortunately, the resort staff were aware of the problem and strategically positioned a noticeable billboard that said, "Don't panic! We have many easy runs too!" So we stayed.

It was early in the morning when we arrived at the lodge. We booked two rooms, had breakfast, and rented our equipment. Both of us had skied in Michigan, but this was on another level. We had an absolute blast skiing all day while taking frequent breaks in the lodge for drinks and food.

At the end of the day, they announced that the mountain was closing in 30 minutes, and everyone had to return to the lodge. To reach the lodge from the runs we were at, a good speed was required to cross a long, flat area. Otherwise, walking would be necessary for a while. At the top of the run, I challenged Larry: "Last one to the lodge buys drinks!" Off we went, racing down the hill. Just before the long flat stretch, a sharp turn leads to a bridge over a stream. In the lead, I raced over the bridge and coasted to victory at the lodge. When I stopped and turned around, Larry was nowhere to be seen. I thought, *Wow, I really beat him bad!*

As I waited and waited, I wondered what could have happened to him. Finally, I started walking back toward the bridge, and that is when I saw him. He was limping along slowly, carrying his skis and poles. His clothes and hat were all disheveled and wet, and he looked like a truck had run him over! He had missed the turn on the bridge and gone headfirst into the small ravine and stream, which was full of rocks and boulders.

I helped him carry his equipment back to the lodge, where we turned everything back in. Then we went straight to the bar for that drink he owed me and stayed for many more. The next day, Larry had difficulty walking, and bruises covered his entire right side. Luckily, he did not break any bones or his skull, at least that we knew of. He

The Balloonatics

was in awful shape for several days after that.

~ ~ ~

Do you recall the house I owned in Lansing, Michigan, that I left with an unemployed girlfriend living in it? After some consideration, my mom and I decided I should rent it. I had decided to break up with the girlfriend the day that I left, and I finally called her and did so. I also told her she had to vacate the house soon because we were going to rent it. So now I was totally committed to this Balloonatic life!

~ ~ ~

Next it was back to California. (Remember I said there was no real rhyme or reason to this tour?) In Long Beach, we did a three-hour super pressure tether along the route of the Long Beach Marathon Race on February 12th. February 18th and 19th we had a job at Clark Buick in Compton, California, and we tethered at the dealership both days in the morning and evening for a total of seven and a half hours.

Driving from Compton one evening, somehow we ended up lost in Watts, which was a dangerous area back then. It was getting dark, and here we were in a beautiful, shiny, red-white-and-blue pickup truck with Buick Olympic Balloon logos all over it. We decided we would not stop for anything. Larry carefully ran all the red lights and stop signs while I was reading the map, trying to figure out how to get back to the freeway!

~ ~ ~

The day after finishing the Compton job, we headed off to Elko, Nevada, where we were scheduled for a weekend job from February 22nd through the 24th. We drove straight through from Compton and arrived the day before to scope out the area. It was beautiful, with snow-covered mountains on both sides of the valley and the Humboldt River running through the middle.

Elko was a tiny town in 1984, sitting along I-80 midway between Reno and Salt Lake City. Nothing else existed within a hundred miles. It really reminded me of the Old West, and the tiny downtown area had many old buildings still being used, including the largest and most prominent one, the historic Stockman's Casino Hotel.

The fax we received with our job info said to report to Cooper Motors and see the owner, Clark Cooper. On the 21st, we met him there. Clark, a friendly and fairly young dealership owner, was a great guy. He wanted us to tether the balloon in his parking lot by the road like all the car dealers did. We were all about flying if the area permitted, and this was an incredibly beautiful area to fly in.

We convinced him to bring his wife with him in the morning for a flight. He had not realized we could fly the balloon and thought that was an awesome idea. We also asked him to call the local newspaper to get some free press.

He knew the newspaper editor, so he called him while we were there. The editor assured us he would attend. We asked him to bring additional people for balloon setup and packing after landing. The next morning, we all met at the airport, and the weather was perfect, if cold. I have a copy of the newspaper article that appeared on the front page of the paper the next day.

The winds took me and Mr. and Mrs. Cooper gently down the valley. After a half-hour flight, I landed literally in the open field across the street from their dealership, Cooper Motors. Larry arrived in the chase vehicle, and we quickly prepared the tether ropes. We spent an hour taking dealership employees and anyone else who wanted to go on a tethered ride up and down.

Now, of course, after that opening performance, we were heroes! Later that day, Clark invited us out for dinner. We went to the historic

The Balloonatics

Stockman's Casino Hotel downtown and had a fantastic steak dinner with Mr. and Mrs. Cooper and a bunch of his employees and friends.

The one I remember most was his service manager. I will call him Gene. He was an older guy, maybe 70, and had lived out there all his life. Gene had a deep, raspy voice and wrinkled, leather-like skin, and he was all of about five feet tall. He sat next to us at dinner and was a real hoot, telling jokes and stories that kept the entire table laughing throughout dinner and lots of drinks. Clark invited us to join him at the craps table after dinner. We declined, as we were unfamiliar with the game and simply planned to observe.

We all kept on drinking and watched as Clark went on a roll, so to speak, and just kept on winning! As we drank and cheered Clark on for about an hour, I spotted him motioning for Gene. He whispered into Gene's ear and gave him a stack of bills. Gene walked back to Larry and me and said, "Come on, boys, we're going out on the town!"

Following him out to his pickup, we all jumped in the front seat, and Gene started driving. We asked where we were going, and he just said, "You'll see." We went a short distance down the main road and then turned onto a residential street. Gene stopped in front of a house, and we followed him up to the front door. When Gene knocked on the door, someone slid open a small viewing window at about eye height and said, "Who is it?" Realizing who it was, they then said, "Oh, hi Gene. Come on in," and opened the door.

I recall entering a sparse, gray room, roughly 20 feet wide and 30 feet long, with a makeshift bar on the left. The lady who opened the door identified herself as the barmaid and inquired about our drink choice. We all ordered whiskey. Bad move.

After finishing our first drink, we ordered more and more. At one point, I remember the barmaid's husband coming over and talking with Gene. Not long after, I heard a commotion behind us. We turned around to see a dozen stunning young ladies lined up before us. Gene just smiled and said, "Well, boys, take your pick." Larry and I, being quite drunk, just said, "Oh boy!" We had quite a night and quite a hangover when we woke up the next morning and had to get up and tether the balloon in the dealership parking lot. We tethered for more than two hours and then took a long nap in our hotel rooms.

That evening we free-flew again and did two more free flights the next day. One flight was southeast of Elko in the valley closer to the Ruby Mountains. Larry took nine passengers up by doing several short flights, landing to change the passengers, and flying off again. I have some incredible photos of that flight. Some look like the balloon was flying over the snowcapped Ruby Mountain!

We met some local folks who took us out to the river, where we partied like there was no tomorrow. I met a gal named Kendra at the hotel bar the second night we were there. She was beautiful, with long black hair and a dark complexion, and was half Native American. She and I spent a lot of time together while we were there.

One day, Kendra and her friends took us to many beautiful places near the river and mountains. We had a blast and never wanted it to end. Larry and I decided we wanted to come back after the Buick Tour ended and discussed a business idea with them. I said we could start a flying bordello using one of the big new balloons with a partitioned basket we had just read about in one of the ballooning magazines.

They believed in the idea, but sadly, it never happened. We never returned to initiate that one, and I am unsure why. It would have been another great story, for sure, had we tried it! Reluctantly, we had to leave February 25th for our next assignment in Colorado Springs, Colorado.

~ ~ ~

We always looked in the Balloon Federation of America (BFA) membership book to find balloon pilots living near where our jobs were and called them for advice about flying in the area. Capt. Phogg suggested we call Dewey Reinhardt before we got to Colorado Springs, and he turned out to be a great help and all-around wonderful guy. We spent some time together and had dinner with him and his lovely wife. He gave us advice on flying in the area and avoiding the air force base and airfield.

I was flying along highway I-25 just north of downtown Colorado Springs in the morning on March 2, 1984. The wind was very light, and I ended up being becalmed over the city dump! Luckily for me, there was a very wide road going through the middle of the dump, and I was able to land on the road. The folks working at the dump found it amusing and treated us well, so it was all good. My passengers, who were from the Buick district sales office, also came away with a great story to share!

~ ~ ~

The next day, on March 3rd, Larry and I each logged a one-hour tether, one in the morning and one in the early evening at Deane Buick in Denver. We then went to Littleton, Colorado, and tethered at Dale Buick on the 8th. On the 10th, we tethered at Dreiling Buick in Lakewood, Colorado.

~ ~ ~

I remember our first tether in Denver. The night prior, I encountered a charming lady at the bar, and we had a night-long celebration in my hotel room. I literally got no sleep. During the tether I had a terrible hangover, and when I returned to the hotel after the tether I was bummed out to discover that she was gone and had just left a note with her phone number. I never saw her again.

~ ~ ~

One day at Breckenridge, Larry and I went skiing and had a great time with no mishaps. This time we didn't race back to the lodge. After that, we returned to Michigan. As we drove back home, the transmission in the Buick chase vehicle burned out in the middle of nowhere in Nebraska. We had it towed to the closest Buick dealership.

It took nearly a week for the replacement transmission to be delivered and installed. I remember being stuck in a small town and bored due to the lack of activities. Larry confessed it was his fault for coasting down the mountains in neutral to see how fast we could go. I remember we got going very fast indeed!

~ ~ ~

When we arrived back in Michigan, I immediately embarked on the road out east with pilot Bob Grimes. Larry headed back out west with another pilot. My next logged entry was on March 31st in Charleston, South Carolina, and involved a one-hour tether at a local Buick dealership.

Regrettably, I rarely noted in my logbook the names of the dealerships like Larry did. So mostly only when I was with him do I have those names. On April 6th, when I made my next logbook entry, I was in Springfield, Missouri!

Crazy, right? We drove halfway across the country for one job that was scheduled for two days and tethered once, for one and a half hours, at the local dealership there. Then we headed back east again. My logbook says on April 12th I free-flew over Middletown, New York, and we were "mobbed by kids" at the landing site.

The next job involved working at the Philadelphia Buick District for five days. Bob had to leave, so Chris Mooney, who lived in Philadelphia, was hired by Capt. Phogg as my crew chief. After meeting up with Chris, I free-flew in New Hope, Pennsylvania, on April 22nd. My logbook says "tree bounce."

The Balloonatics

Chris Mooney was a tall, jolly, redheaded guy of Irish descent, and we had a great time together. His familiarity with the area proved beneficial in various ways. We tried all the great places to eat, and I genuinely loved the vintage diners. They were a deal—delicious and inexpensive!

After the initial flight, the weather deteriorated, with constant wind and rain for three consecutive days. I visited the hotel bar one evening for a drink and a burger. Feeling bored and having finished my meal and drinks, I asked the bartender if there was a nearby night spot for meeting women. He responded, "Yeah, right here." That surprised me because it was a small place, and I was the only one there. He said there was a hospital across the street, and the nurses' shift change was at 10 p.m. "Nurses will pack this place," he assured me. I thanked him and returned to my room to freshen up.

I came back down too soon, had too many drinks, and then it happened. The place filled up as he had promised. Seated at the bar, I noticed a table with six nurses sitting right behind me. I started a conversation with one of them and they invited me to join them. After a bit, I was making eye contact with a cute blonde across the table. I ended up sliding one of my room keys across the table to her and she winked.

Shortly thereafter, I went back to my room and fell asleep. I was awoken by a large woman in a silky nightgown who was sitting on my bed. It was her, the blonde. I recognized her cute face. Apparently, the table had not allowed me to see how large she was! I didn't care. Who was I to disappoint her when she was cute, present, and eager for a good time? And we did have a great time! I remember rolling off her a few times and just had to get back up there. Eventually I was exhausted and passed out.

Because Chris and I had an early morning appointment at a Buick dealership, I had arranged a wake-up call with the hotel. When they called to wake me up, she was gone. After unlocking the door for Chris in case he arrived early, I showered.

Minutes later, I heard him come in and say hi. Then he broke out in hysterical laughter. I yelled, "What is so funny?" Throwing open the shower curtain, Chris came busting into the bathroom, holding up a huge silky nightgown, and laughingly asked, "Who the hell's tent is this?" She had left her nightgown hanging in the open closet. It was extremely large, and I was busted. Chris and I still laugh about that!

~ ~ ~

Our last scheduled day for the Philadelphia job was on April 26th. We had scheduled a morning free flight from the King of Prussia Mall for the district manager and his wife. The day prior to the flight the weather didn't look good, and another "weather out" seemed likely.

I was staying at a hotel near the mall. The evening before the scheduled flight, I ended up at the hotel bar and, later, in my room with another attractive blonde. I got little sleep before the 4 a.m. wake-up call. When I received it, I immediately contacted flight service and was dismayed to hear that the weather was suitable for flying. I called Chris, and he concurred that the weather looked good.

The forecasted wind direction was favorable for a flight from the mall, taking us away from Philadelphia toward suitable landing spots. I called the Buick district manager and told him to meet us at the hotel by the mall at 6 a.m. We drove to an open field near the hotel, inflated, and took off.

Unfortunately, the wind direction was about 90 degrees different from what was forecasted. We immediately headed for downtown Philadelphia at a good clip. I tried to find a landing spot ASAP, but there were none, and the land was getting more and more built up and congested every minute. Continuing at a good 15 to 20 miles per hour, we flew on toward the city and the Philadelphia International Airport.

I soon realized that I had to call the airport control tower and ask for permission to fly through. Luckily it was a Friday morning, there

The Balloonatics

was not a lot of traffic, and it was 1984. Today we would be in big trouble for doing that without prior permission. Using my aircraft radio, I called the airport tower. Thank God that radio was working; this was the first time I had to use it!

After explaining my predicament, the tower replied, "Hot air balloon—what?" To which I replied, "I am very sorry, the wind direction was forecasted to take me away from you, and it did just the opposite. So here I am, requesting permission to fly through." After a long pause they came back with, "Hot Air Balloon 230LY maintain your altitude." Then a minute later they gave me permission to fly through at my current altitude, which was approximately 1,000 feet above ground level.

Moving along at about 20 miles per hour, we were rapidly approaching the airport's north end. I could see nowhere to land for as far as I could see, so I asked permission to land on the extreme north side of the airport in a large, open grassy area. Believe it or not, they then granted me permission to land! Although I could not believe it, I was glad to oblige.

I started a fast descent, and we came down literally 10 feet above the 10-foot-tall chain-link fence on the north side of the field. We flew directly along the fence line, so I could not land. "Damn," I exclaimed. "Missed it by that much." I called the tower again and told them about the fence and that I was going to have to fly on into New Jersey. They came back with something like, "Okay, have a pleasant flight."

Man, those were the days, for sure! Imagine the trouble I'd be in if I did that today. Considering that I am writing this around the same time a Chinese surveillance balloon was shot down off the coast of South Carolina, my flight would probably have had a much different outcome today.

So, on we went over the Delaware River into New Jersey at 15 miles per hour, about 100 feet above the river, with lots of boats and cars honking at us. It was really pretty cool! During this flight, I had only communicated with my chase crew, Chris, once on our two-way radios. Now that I was flying low, I couldn't reach him and figured he was stuck back somewhere in the morning rush-hour traffic.

I flew on and ascended to get a better view of what lay ahead. The wind was 15 miles per hour and gusting at the surface, so I briefed my passengers on the rough landing we may be in for. I finally got a brief and hard-to-understand reply from Chris but was not really concerned about where he was. My only desire was to find a landing spot and safely land as soon as possible.

Flying along at about 500 feet, I soon saw a large gravel pit ahead. I again briefed my passengers about a possible rough landing. As I descended into the gravel pit about 100 feet below ground level, the air was calm. We ended with a soft stand-up landing on a road that ran through the gravel pit.

Since I had briefed my passengers about a rough landing, they were prepared to go bouncing and dragging along. A few seconds after landing, they asked if they could relax and stop holding on and bending their knees! I laughed and said, "Yes, you can relax now, but please stay in the basket."

They said, "Wow, if that was a rough landing, you sure have a cushy job!"

Right then I looked up the gravel road we had just landed on and saw the chase vehicle coming down the road into the gravel pit, with Chris waving out the driver's window! I could not believe he even found us, let alone managed to be there right after we landed. He had to drive over 30 miles right through rush-hour traffic in Philadelphia, over the Delaware River, and into New Jersey with no help from me to find us.

A bunch of the gravel truck drivers stopped and gawked, and some even came out to help us pack up. After flying for one and a half hours, we had covered approximately 30 miles. To this day, it was one of my most exciting flights ever!

The Balloonatics

~ ~ ~

After tethering at a dealership in Erie, Pennsylvania, on April 28th and 29th, I proceeded to Baltimore, Maryland. Sadly, Chris could not go with me. I went to Baltimore on my own to fly in the Great Preakness Balloon Race that Bob Waligunda had organized.

Boyle Buick, my host in Baltimore for the event, left a great impression on me. My logbook says, "Boyle Buick my sponsor for Preakness Race and they were great people!" I remember having a fantastic time with all the people at that dealership. They were also excellent ground crew for me the entire time.

Their staff also crewed for a tether on May 5th at the dealership. The contract specified that the dealership would provide two to three helpers, but usually there were two pilots also. We had such a wonderful time together. For the next few days, the weather did not allow for any ballooning.

On May 9th, I took the Boyle Buick folks up for a free flight from Bel Air, Maryland. My logbook says we landed in Forest Hill, Maryland, after a one-hour flight. We did several short flights, landing and switching passengers. It was a blast. They were some of the best people I met on this entire tour.

~ ~ ~

Weather conditions were unsuitable for flying for several days prior to the Great Preakness Race. On May 12th, the morning of the event, we managed to pull it off despite a fog delay. We started from a park near downtown Baltimore with a Hare and Hound event. I remember taking off and heading east toward the Chesapeake Bay and lots of water!

The Hare balloon did not fly long and soon landed in a schoolyard, thank goodness. I also landed in the schoolyard, relieved to be on the ground. There were few open areas in the city and a lot of open water beyond that! My trusty crew from Boyle Buick was right there to retrieve the balloon, which took a while as we had to track down someone to open the locked gate into the schoolyard. It was early on a Saturday morning, so that took some doing.

Once all the balloon teams returned to the park, we had brunch and an awards ceremony. I won $300 by coming in third place and was ecstatic! We celebrated, drank champagne, and told stories. Then my friends recommended we have dinner at a seafood restaurant.

We all drove to the restaurant and ate, drank, and told more stories. Hours later, when we had had enough, one of the other, slightly older and wiser pilots (I think it was Roy Caton) offered to drive me and the Buick chase vehicle back to my hotel. I happily accepted, and his crew followed us there, where we said our goodbyes and I thanked him for driving me!

Upon waking up the next morning, I felt terrible. Damn, why had I drunk all those Long Island iced teas? I had a flight to do in Ellicott City that evening, so I checked out of the hotel and checked into one in Ellicott City. I flew a one-hour free flight from Ellicott City back into Baltimore that evening, May 13th.

~ ~ ~

My next job was a two-hour tether at a dealership in Southfield, Michigan, on May 17th, and then a three-hour tether in Boonville, Indiana, on May 19th. I then went to New Castle, Pennsylvania, and Bob Grimes joined me again. I did a one-hour free flight on May 24th, and my logbook just says "foggy."

~ ~ ~

Bob and I then traveled to Pittsburgh, Pennsylvania. At one of our jobs, the wind was too strong to tether in the dealership's parking lot.

The Balloonatics

The manager was not happy about that and told Bob he didn't care if it was windy and that he would bring out chains to hold the stupid thing down. He ended with, "Just put the fu–ing balloon up, damn it!"

Bob told him, "Okay, but I need you to hold the crown line while I inflate it." I thought Bob was crazy inflating in this wind. Turned out he knew what he was doing. The balloon was tethered to two cars. As the balloon inflated, it started to drag the cars through the parking lot. At the same time, the manager was frantically trying to hold on to the crown line and being thrown around in the process. Realizing that attempting to get the balloon up was futile, he gave up before causing damage to the cars and possibly injuring himself. That manager learned the hard way why we don't tether or fly in strong winds.

~   ~   ~

On the 26th of May, I flew out of a dealership parking lot in downtown Pittsburgh. I remember that flight very well! It was windy, but not dangerously so. After inflating the balloon, I had people hold it down, heated it up, and loaded my two passengers into the basket. I miscalculated and poured a bit too much heat into it, and we took off like a rocket! Bob said it "pancaked a bit," so it was an exciting takeoff, and quickly we were about 1,000 feet in the air.

I leveled out, and from then on, we had a beautiful flight. We did a "splash and dash" in the Monongahela River right next to a big factory, touching the water with the basket in flight. My passengers warned me against it, stating that the river was polluted and might rot my basket. But we were traveling along with the current at about the same speed, and I just could not resist.

We flew on after our successful "splash and dash" and, after a beautiful one-hour flight, had a breezy landing in a small farm field that was anything but flat. Bob surprised me by driving in to pick us up, even though we had no radio contact. He was right there when we landed.

~ ~ ~

The next morning, I flew from Monroeville, Pennsylvania, for a half hour, and the logbook says we had a "dry swamp landing." I don't remember that one. That evening, I tethered the balloon at a local dealership for one and a half hours. On May 31st, I tethered in Monroeville, Pennsylvania, for one hour.

Then we went back to Michigan on June 2nd for a one-hour tether in Midland. On June 9th, I went back to Pennsylvania and spent a total of three hours tethering in the morning and evening. On June 14th and 15th, I tethered once each day for one and a half hours in Washington, New Jersey. On June 16th I tethered in Catskill, New York, for two hours.

While Bob was with me, we switched off flying and crewing. He flew and tethered just as much as I did. I do not have his logbooks so can't list his flights and tethers. We were very busy, and the weather cooperated more often than not.

~ ~ ~

Next stop was back to Michigan, where I teamed up with Larry and we headed out west again. Our first stop was in Burley, Idaho, where we both recorded a two-hour tether at Bonanza Buick, one in the morning and one in the afternoon, on June 29th. I also recall that Larry and I were told about a great local hangout bar where we met two nice gals and had a great time with them.

We were very excited to go back to one of our favorite places for our second stop—Elko, Nevada, and Cooper Motors! On July 2nd, Larry took our buddy Gene up for a one-hour flight over Elko, and his logbook says, "went nowhere." The next morning, I flew two folks

The Balloonatics

from Cooper Motors, and my logbook says, "no wind." That evening we went out into the valley to a place called Spring Creek, and I flew some more folks for a short half-hour flight. My logbook says, "windy 10-15 miles per hour landing." We again had a blast with all our friends in Elko.

I fondly remember meeting up with Kendra again. Larry and I joined a bunch of her friends the following day and returned to the river, where we spent the entire day partying and splashing about in the cold water. Then we went to a western bar. It was closed, but we took advantage of the outdoor patio and continued to party and have a picnic. Larry got crazy, dancing on the tables and doing a strip show for everyone while the girls threw dollar bills at him!

~ ~ ~

Our next assignment was in St. George, Utah, on July 6th and 7th, and the weather turned out fantastic! Flying in this area was incredibly beautiful. Larry took advantage of it the first day with an awesome morning one-hour free flight where he noted in his logbook, "great flight over mountain and down the valley." He took two passengers from Peterson Motors Buick along. We went back to the dealership and tethered for two hours that same morning and that evening we tethered at the dealership for another two hours. We did the same the next day, both morning and evening.

~ ~ ~

Then we were off to Seattle, Washington, where we had a job scheduled July 14th and 15th with Hurling Buick in Auburn, Washington, a suburb of Seattle. We arrived three or four days early and checked into a Holidome near Auburn. I remember this adventure with great clarity.

The weather gods once again smiled upon us, and the bar at the

Holidome was hopping every night. For a couple of days, we had fun in the bar and the indoor pool, simply enjoying a relaxing time. As always, we contacted the local balloonists through the BFA membership guide. They invited us to come fly with them from a small private airfield in Snohomish, which is just about 25 miles northeast of Auburn.

Two days prior to the job, we met with the Hurling Buick team and persuaded them to join us in Snohomish. We all met at the Snohomish airport on the 13th with the local pilots. I don't remember names, but they were great.

They instructed us to fly low in the winds flowing down the valley toward the river, over a prison, and then land at a big farm on the other side of the prison before the river. We were warned not to cross the river due to unfriendly landowners and their dislike of balloons. The area is incredibly beautiful, with snowcapped, massive Mount Rainier looming in the not-too-far distance.

I flew the first flight, and it was fantastic. I followed the local pilots down the valley and up over the prison, which was on a tall hill, and then quickly descended on the other side of the prison to land on the huge farm on the "friendly" side of the river. No question about it; this flight ranks among my coolest and most scenic ones.

Larry and I each flew two more flights down the valley for the next two days. Having had so much fun, the folks from Hurling Buick decided that there was no need to tether at the dealership. This was another one of our best Buick Tour adventures, for sure!

I remember the last flight on the evening of the 14th. The balloon envelope we had been flying (4101L) needed to be replaced. The Velcro that held the top cap in place during flight was getting weak, and we had been using safety pins to help hold it in place for the past few flights. The top cap's fabric was also weak, and we had ordered a new Buick Olympic Balloon envelope that was due to be delivered to the Sacramento Airport. After we landed, the crew, local balloonists, and

The Balloonatics

passengers helped me tear the top of the balloon up, and they all took home pieces of it for souvenirs.

~ ~ ~

As previously mentioned, the bar at the Holidome was lively every night. I had a very interesting time there one evening. I met an exquisite lady, and we danced and drank and danced and drank. At last call, I invited her to go out and see our awesome Buick Balloon Chase Vehicle and join me for a bottle of champagne, which we always had in the cooler.

We sat in the back seat, which doubled as a custom-made bed, and got cozy drinking out of the bottle. Soon I suggested relocating to my room for a more comfortable experience. She agreed.

Upon arrival, I opened the door, and she immediately panicked, refusing to enter. I asked what was wrong. She revealed that someone had raped her in a hotel room years ago. I was shocked and just said I was sorry. I did not mean any harm. It was past 2 a.m., and the bar was now closed. She was in the hallway, and I was on the room's threshold. We were just hugging, and I kept saying I was sorry and asked, "What do you want to do?"

Without saying a word, she got on her knees, undid my belt, unzipped my pants, and dropped them to my ankles. I could not believe what was happening! There I was, just inside the door, and she was in the hallway on her knees. I looked up and down the hallway, hoping no one would appear.

I remember looking at the door to the room across the hall, hoping they did not hear all the commotion going on and were not looking out the peephole. Then I said to myself, "What the hell; they will get some cheap entertainment if they are," and I decided to just enjoy the new experience. After we were done, she simply stood up as I thanked her. She said goodbye while I tried to keep my composure and not fall over as I clumsily pulled up my trousers!

She departed, never to be seen again! I had asked for her phone number earlier in the evening and tried calling several times over the next few days. I never got an answer and never saw her again. And I really wanted to! She was drop-dead gorgeous.

~ ~ ~

On July 21st, our logbooks show that Larry flew with the new envelope (4393D) in Sacramento, California, for 1.3 hours, on assignment to the Graham Buick dealership. We had picked up the new envelope from the Sacramento airport the day prior. On July 23rd, I logged a one-and-a-half hour flight, and the logbook notes, "school yard landing." The next day Larry again free-flew for one hour, and his logbook notes, "landed one mile from McClellan Air Force Base." I doubt we would get away with that today!

On July 27th, I flew from Tracy, California, which is about 60 miles east of San Francisco. My logbook says it was a one-and-a-half hour flight taking "Olympic Soccer People" as passengers.

~ ~ ~

On August 4th I flew in Perris, California, and the log says, "mini rally in the fog." According to Wikipedia's entry about the city, "Perris is an old railway city in Riverside County, California, United States, located 71 miles (114 km) east-southeast of Los Angeles and 81 miles (130 km) north of San Diego. It is known for Lake Perris, an artificial lake, skydiving, and its sunny dry climate. Perris is within the Inland Empire metropolitan area of Southern California. Perris had a population of 78,700 as of the 2020 census."

I am surprised Wikipedia does not mention hot air balloons in its description of Perris! Both times I was there, I flew with 10–15 other balloons from their designated balloon launch field. Many of those balloons were taking up the skydivers that are mentioned. Of course, many more skydivers were jumping out of "perfectly good aeroplanes," as the saying goes, taking off from the local airport. Anyway, it was a great group of diverse balloon pilots who flew there often, and they were very accommodating to us.

Capt. Phogg, Bob Grimes, and the other Buick balloon joined Larry and me in Perris. They had come the week before for the Summer Olympic Games taking place in Los Angeles. This time in Perris we met someone who would be very instrumental in my future ballooning career, Kinnie Gibson.

Kinnie and his wife, Sheri, invited us all over to their house on Lake Elsinore for dinner after a flight. We had a wonderful time together. Their house was beautiful. We went swimming, and suddenly some of us started yelling, "Ouch, what the hell was that?" Kinnie laughed and said, "Oh, it's just the fish. They are hungry!"

Never had I encountered anything like this in my life, despite growing up in Michigan and swimming in countless lakes. Lake Elsinore's small blue gills and sunfish swarmed like piranhas around you. If you stayed still for a few seconds, one would come up and bite your nipples. And it hurt! That was nuts.

We seemed to make a special bond with Kinnie and Sheri. Kinnie was a successful Hollywood stunt man (he spent many years as the stunt double for Chuck Norris) and an accomplished balloon pilot. He was also known as the "Rocket Man" because he flew a jet pack and was the first to do so in movies and in demonstrations at major events all over the world. A remarkable person and an invaluable contact to have, no doubt!

~ ~ ~

The 1984 Summer Olympics took place in Los Angeles from late

July through mid-August. The East Coast balloon and chase vehicle, along with pilots Bob Grimes and Sheryl Conlee, joined us along with Sheryl's husband, Bob Conlee, Capt. Phogg, and Gretchen. We stayed at an amazing resort just outside of LA and had the opportunity to go to many Olympic events.

A few individuals from the group did attend the events. However, it was such a logistical hassle and took so much time to get there and back that most did not. Larry, Gretchen, Bob Grimes, Bob Conlee, and I preferred to hang out at the huge, impressive outdoor pool and drink when we were not flying.

We did a lot of flying over two weeks, taking Buick VIPs for fantastic flights in the Simi Valley and Moor Park. We completed nine flights with both balloons flying together for a total logged time of almost 30 hours. Many flights were over two hours in duration. The rich guy with the constellations balloon flew alongside us for several flights, each time with a different beautiful lady, going up a mile high!

And then it ended. It all went by so fast, and now it was over! An incredible life-changing adventure ended, but little did we know it was really just the beginning. We packed up and drove back to Michigan.

~ ~ ~

We got back to Michigan with no time to rest. The Capt. Phogg Balloon Classic took place on the 18th and 19th. The weather was perfect, and we flew both days.

I remember one flight in particular from that weekend. I was flying the Buick balloon with a Buick executive and his wife. We went over a small lake, and a balloon flying ahead of us had just done a nice "splash and dash." I decided to do the same, but I screwed up and came in too fast. We went into the lake almost up to our waists! Not a nice "splash and dash" but a "dunk and dash"! How embarrassing.

The Balloonatics

Luckily, my passengers were not very upset, although it was obvious they did not appreciate it.

~ ~ ~

After the Capt. Phogg Classic, we did some paid rides and commercial jobs. Capt. Phogg had sold a balloon to the local Anheuser-Busch distributor. It was an all-black 105,000-cubic-foot Michelob balloon with the "Michelob" logo spelled out in yellow on opposite sides in 20-foot-tall letters.

We were training the owner, Mike Ryan, and some of his employees to fly the balloon. Larry took the balloon along with Mike Ryan and his crew to the Forrest Park Balloon Race in St. Louis, Missouri. At the same time, I took one of the Buick balloons to Mount Kisco, New York, for a weekend job at the local dealership. Larry then took one of the Buick balloons to Glens Falls, New York, for the Adirondack Balloon Race.

At the end of September, I flew two paid ride flights for Bobby Grimes in one of his balloons on the west side of Michigan, and then the first week of October I flew for him again at a small race event he put on in Niles, Michigan, where he lived. Larry did another Buick balloon job at the Buick Headquarters in Flint, Michigan, in mid-October, and on October 13th, I flew two flights in the good old green-and-white balloon around East Lansing. One of these flights was my last over an MSU football game! Larry flew a few more paid rides and training flights in Michigan through the end of October.

~ ~ ~

On October 15th I left on my motorcycle for Palm Springs, California. Meeting Kinnie Gibson in Perris, California, that summer on the Buick Tour proved to be very advantageous for me. He told me he was starting a new balloon ride company in Palm Springs in the fall and may need a pilot. I told him I might be interested. Over the summer we agreed that I would come out to fly for his new company.

Larry and I had been riding motorcycles since the year we graduated from Okemos High School. I had a very nice Honda 650. It was a new model with shaft drive and a water-cooled V-twin, a very smooth ride and perfect for one person. Not having much money, I decided that riding the motorcycle out would be inexpensive and another great adventure! Also, I would need transportation while I was living and working there, and in California all you really need is a motorcycle.

I will never forget how upset my dad was about this. He begged me not to do it and actually cried when I rode out of the driveway with his army duffel bag strapped on the seat behind me along with two side-saddle bags and one tank bag full of my gear. Later, he told me he did not think I would come back. He thought I would find some beautiful California girl, fall in love with her and California, and stay there. He was almost correct. I told him I'd be back in the spring to fly again for Capt. Phogg.

I took the fastest route, Highway 80, and had an epic solo ride with no issues except the cold through the mountains in Colorado. It was freezing! I did not enjoy that part of the ride at all. (Do you remember the scene in the movie *Dumb and Dumber*?) The rest of the ride was beautiful, and I made my way to California in five days. I stayed at cheap motels along the way and stopped little for any sightseeing.

~ ~ ~

My first stop in California was at Annette's house in Duarte, near Pasadena. I stayed with her for a few weeks because Kinnie did not have everything together with his new company yet and I had nowhere else to stay. Luckily, Annette was fine with that arrangement for now. I enjoyed my time there, helping her around the house and

The Balloonatics

watching her children a couple of times while she worked. However, it was almost a two-hour motorcycle ride through Los Angeles to Palm Springs where I worked, so I had to get a place much closer soon.

With the new company not yet operational, I desperately needed money and searched for work. I called all the local balloonists and started crewing for some of them for pay. One of them was Bill Henry. He gave me a few paid rides to fly in addition to crewing for him.

The dynamics of the ballooning business in the Coachella Valley in 1984–85 were quite interesting. There was a bunch of small balloon companies competing for the passenger ride business. The desert's rapid growth and new golf resorts created abundant business opportunities.

In late fall, winter, and early spring, the weather was fantastic, allowing for morning and evening flights almost every day. The tourist and large convention business was booming, and all the companies were vying for that business. A guy named Dan Glick owned one of the first companies that started it all, called Sunrise Balloons.

Dan was an interesting guy. The other balloonists did not seem to like him much, but, then again, none of them seemed to like each other. It was a very tense and competitive working environment. They had to work together because one of the largest blocks of business was the convention group business.

They all worked hard to "lobby" and garner favor with all the group tour operators. However, none of them had enough balloons or pilots to fly a large group. When any of them had a large group to fly, they had to subcontract most of the passengers out to the other companies.

Many times, if the group was large enough, they would call in balloon companies from Perris, San Diego, and all over Southern California. I am amazed when I think back about how they would coordinate with so many companies and balloons, sometimes 20 to 25 balloons to fly a large group! Back then, most of them flew Barnes balloons that only carried 4 to 6 passengers each.

Flying in the desert was unique. The Coachella Valley, where Palm Springs is located, was wide open at that time. It was full of farm fields, date palm groves, and golf resorts spread out all over the valley. But mostly it was wide-open desert. Combined with the amazing weather, balloon flying was easy 99 percent of the time.

As always, Mother Nature and the nature of balloon flying sometimes turned even the most serene flight into an exciting, or even slightly scary, event. Compared with flying back home in Michigan, where landing sites are often small and few and far between, the desert back then was a breeze. One big difference was landing in the desert. The spaces were wide open, but there were lots of minor obstacles like scrub bushes (tumbleweeds), cactus, and the like that you had to avoid.

Packing the balloon in the desert was a dusty job and required a four-wheel-drive vehicle to reach the landing spot and return. It was like the Wild West, sometimes with balloons landing all over the big open desert and four-wheel-drive vehicles driving all over the place to pick them up. Unlike in Michigan, where we almost always had to ask permission from a landowner or farmer, out in the desert back then it was a free-for-all! The desert was our playground, and no one ever bothered us.

Dan Glick's company, Sunrise Balloons, was the only company that actually owned property to fly from in the valley. He had a ten-acre balloon field between the small cities of Indio and Thermal. He purchased the land after flying in the area for several years and deciding that it was a perfect location for flying both morning and evening flights. In the morning, the calm, cool air would drain slowly down the valley toward the Salton Sea. Then in the late afternoon and early evening, that flow reversed, with the warmer air now going up the valley toward Indio and Palm Desert.

Dan's balloon field was irrigated and covered with lush grass, something only seen elsewhere in the desert on the many golf courses and resorts. Some of the other balloon companies would pay Dan to fly from his field, especially if they had a large group. Otherwise, they would just find any open desert field to fly from.

Dan also flew helicopters and had two of them. I befriended him, and he once took me up in his small two-man copter from his field up into the mountains. It was awesome! I loved that one and only helicopter flight of my life. Except for all the noise and vibration, flying low and slow in a helicopter was the closest thing to ballooning.

~ ~ ~

The second week of November, I went with Bill Henry and his wife, Nina (one of the few female hot air balloon pilots around back then), to the Thunderbird Balloon Event in Glendale, Arizona. They took two Barnes balloons. I crewed and flew three flights in one of their balloons, which was a first for me, having flown only in Raven balloons up to then. The Barnes Balloon system had a triangular basket instead of a rectangular one, among other distinctions. But I soon realized they flew and operated similarly, and I was simply content to fly.

I recall many details from that Thunderbird event and have numerous photos of it. I carried a camera and took many photos my first few years of flying. Later, I realized it was a bad idea. It was easy to get distracted taking photos when I really should have been focusing all my attention on flying. Back then, a camera was a big, clumsy thing that you had to focus, not a little smartphone that you could just point and click.

The weather was fantastic, and the balloons flew daily. On one morning flight, however, the weather turned in a bad way. I was not flying, thank God, or crewing either, as I had met a nice gal there and had spent the night and most of the day with her. I recall dining with pilots that evening when Bill and Nina told me what had happened. A freak downpour had forced a bunch of the balloons down in the desert, completely drenching them.

Another flight I will never forget was one I crewed for Bill and Nina. They used an old Chevy Blazer and a large flatbed trailer for both of their balloons. They had finished flying passenger rides, and we had a big crew. After packing up the balloons and loading them onto the trailer, we filled the Blazer with as many people as possible. About six more of us had to ride in balloon baskets strapped on the flatbed trailer.

Bill made an interesting choice as he drove back to the launch site when another chase vehicle (one that was not grossly overloaded or pulling a trailer with passengers in the baskets) passed us going very fast. Bill decided it was time to race and took off after him. Soon we were speeding like a bat out of hell, with those of us in the baskets getting bounced around and fearing for our lives!

We all started screaming for him to "Slow the f— down!" He finally did, after way too long. We all gave him a HUGE earful when we got back to the launch field!

~ ~ ~

After we returned from the Thunderbird event in mid-November, I continued to crew and fly a few flights for Bill and Nina in the Palm Springs area. I took another trip with them to Las Vegas; Bill had just landed a contract to fly a balloon for the Landmark Hotel & Casino. The artwork on the balloon depicted a desert landscape, with the hotel tower on both sides.

The Landmark Hotel & Casino resembled Seattle's Space Needle and was located on the Strip. The Vegas Strip was small back then. We flew the balloon from the hotel parking lot down the Vegas Strip with no issues. Oh, the things you could do back in the day!

The Balloonatics

That whole valley was wide open, and you could land just about anywhere.

When we returned from the Vegas trip, I found a tiny apartment closer to Palm Springs in Desert Hot Springs. It was only $175 a month! I learned why the price was so low the first night when I could not sleep due to the thousands of crickets chirping both in the apartment and outside.

Also, it was still about a 45-minute ride through the high desert down into the valley where we flew. It was quite cold in the early mornings before sunrise when I had to ride my motorcycle in to crew or fly. Fortunately, I only stayed there for a month before Kinnie Gibson and his brother-in-law Ron Frusher launched their new company, American Balloon Society, in mid-December. They rented a beautiful three-bedroom house in a country club right on a golf course in a gated community. What a relief, and what a stark difference from my tiny apartment!

Ron was my age, very laid back and easygoing. We got along well and became good friends. His sister, Sheri, was Kinnie's wife. Ron had been working with Kinnie to get the company going and oversaw its Palm Springs operation. He was a student pilot, and I was going to help train him.

We started out with an older Barnes AX-7 balloon that could fly a maximum of four passengers plus the pilot, but that was really pushing it. It would have been more appropriate to fly the balloon with only two passengers. Because flying in the desert south of Palm Springs was easy back then due to the wide-open spaces, we generally flew with four passengers plus me.

The year ended well, with the new company American Balloon Society off to a good start and my new friend Ron and I living in luxury in our huge country club house on the golf course!

1985

I continued to crew and fly for Bill and Nina in January because American Balloon Society was not very busy yet. My logbook shows I flew only six paid passenger flights the entire month of January for American Balloon Society.

I remember two flights that I did for Bill in January during the Indio Balloon Race. One was a passenger ride with four passengers in one of his old Barnes AX-7 balloons. The flight was great. We landed going about 6–7 miles per hour in a small open spot in the desert in between scrub bushes. It was hard packed, as I recall, almost like concrete.

I disliked the triangle basket and the hard wooden uprights of the Barnes balloons. The uprights come up at an angle to a point at the top where the burner attaches and intrude into the space where everyone is standing. It is easy to bump into them with your face on a bumpy landing. I told everyone to hold on tight, bend your knees, and keep your face away from the uprights on every landing, including this one.

We landed and bumped along a few times before coming to a stop. Everyone was fine and laughing except one lady who had bumped her lip on an upright and it was bleeding a bit. Nothing bad, and she said she was fine. We packed up the balloon and returned to the launch field to meet Bill and his passengers, where we had our traditional post-flight champagne celebration.

I recounted the story of the lady with the split lip to Bill, and we both kept checking on her well-being. She kept insisting she was fine while continuing to drink champagne. She stayed with us for quite some time, partying and dancing at the post-flight event dinner.

The next day, she showed up in a neck brace. I think someone told her she could get some money that way. Regardless, I completed extensive legal paperwork and shared my side of the story, as I am doing now. I heard nothing more about it.

The Balloonatics

The second flight at that event was competing for the key grab. They had a new vehicle up for grabs if you could fly into the event field and grab the keys off a 15-foot-tall golf flagpole. You were required to launch at least two miles away from the pole.

Annette visited me at my new country club house for the weekend, and I took her up with me on this flight. The winds were light and variable, and balloons took off from all over the place, trying to get to the pole and keys. I recall we flew for almost two hours. We ascended to 6,000 feet two times after I realized my track would not take me toward the pole. I found winds up high going back the other way, allowing me to position myself again and then descend fast to try to get the keys.

The second time was the charm. I lined up perfectly and flew right to the pole. I was the only balloon left flying, and someone yelled to me that the keys had already been taken when I got within 20 feet of the pole. Well, that was a bummer! I flew right into the pole, grabbed it as we flew by and pulled it out of the ground in frustration. Then we landed on the field and celebrated a fun flight with lots of champagne!

Because I was flying so little, I started looking for other work besides ballooning. Early in January I took a job with a solar energy company selling solar hot water heating systems for homes. Once a week, the company held a seminar at a hotel in Palm Springs.

I began as a salesperson, pitching solar hot water systems to attendees. I sold a couple, and things were going okay, then the seminar presenter left, and they offered me his job. That job promised to pay much more. I received commission on all system sales, not just my own. I received a small portion of the commissions on the systems I had sold to date. They promised to pay me the remaining amount once the systems were installed.

I started running and presenting the seminars in mid-January. We had a good team of four salespeople, and we were selling a decent number of systems. Everything was going well, and we all looked forward to getting paid soon.

We arrived one night to find the room locked. The front desk clerk said the company hadn't paid rent for two months and had come and taken all the supplies and equipment. We were all in shock.

The next day, we all piled into one of the salesperson's cars and drove to the company headquarters in Los Angeles. We found it abandoned and realized we had been taken! Unfortunately, so had all the folks we had sold systems to. They still owe me over $3,000 in promised commissions!

~ ~ ~

Ron and I were living in that amazing house in a gated community on the ninth tee of the golf course. The entire neighborhood had a wall surrounding it. Residents had to enter and exit through guarded gates and show a pass to prove they lived there.

We were totally out of place with our big four-wheel-drive, four-door pickup truck with a lift gate on the back, a hot air balloon in the truck bed, and my motorcycle! Neighbors complained right away, so we had to unload the balloon after every flight and put it and my motorcycle in the garage and close the garage door. *For Pete's sake, you cannot leave your garage door open, you hoodlums!* It was a hassle, but we loved it anyway as we were living in the lap of luxury. Ron's master bedroom had an immense fancy bathroom and hot tub spa, and my bedroom had its own large fancy bathroom and hot tub that Annette and I thoroughly enjoyed as well.

Kinnie and Ron had gotten an amazing rental deal on the house, and we found out why soon after we moved in. Ron and I were watching the Super Bowl one afternoon, sitting on the couch drinking beer, when suddenly, the locked front door swung open. In walked four guys in suits!

We all kind of jumped back, thinking, *What the hell!* The suits were from the bank, and they had come to repo the house! Turns out the owner who was renting it to Kinnie and Ron had neglected to pay the

The Balloonatics

mortgage for quite some time. After the initial shock of both parties seeing someone in the house they did not expect, Ron showed them the rental agreement from the former owner. The bank eventually decided to let us stay for the remaining six months of the agreement as long as the rent was paid to them.

~ ~ ~

By February, Ron and Kinnie had successfully launched the company. That month, I flew 28 paid flights, which helped ease my financial stress. We also got a newer, larger Raven AX-8 balloon that comfortably flew four passengers plus me.

In March I flew 22 paid rides, and in April only 11. Flying in the desert gets tricky as summer approaches and things start to heat up. The weather does not cooperate as often, and it just gets too darned hot! We flew into mid-May that season, flying nine paid rides, with the last one on May 19th.

~ ~ ~

Two months after the Indio Balloon Race when Annette visited and went on that awesome flight at the race with me, she broke off our relationship. She said she met someone else who was also divorced with two young children and thought that this new relationship could provide a better situation for her and her kids. I was sad and disappointed and continued calling her a few more times until she asked me to please not call anymore. I never saw her again.

~ ~ ~

On St. Patrick's Day, I went out by myself in search of love to a popular place in Palm Desert called the Red Onion. It was a Tex-Mex restaurant bar that had a happy hour where if you ordered a drink, you could partake in an all-you-can-eat Mexican buffet. Ron and I went there often, but that night I went by myself.

I drove a used Toyota four-wheel-drive pickup that Ron had just bought for the company. I had fun but had no luck finding love, and we had a flight scheduled in the morning, so I took the back way home. After stopping at a four-way stop in the desert about a mile from home, I saw flashing lights behind me, pulling me over.

I asked the officer why he pulled me over, and he said there was a taillight out on the truck. I explained that we had just bought it and were unaware of the light issue. He asked what I was doing out so late and if I had been drinking. He said he could smell alcohol. Well, I got busted, and the police took me to the Indio County Jail for a pleasant evening in the drunk tank. Ron had to cancel the morning flight after I called him from the jail and told him the sad story.

I called around and found an attorney who agreed to take my case in trade for a balloon ride for his family. I bartered whenever I could, and this was much needed as I had no extra cash on hand. Thank God it was 1985, and I only received six months' probation, a $500 fine, and two points for a DUI. Ron only charged me for the propane and a little gas for the chase truck, and I paid the ground crew for the attorney's family's flight the next season.

~ ~ ~

On one flight in March, we flew four ladies in the Barnes balloon. Two were older, and two were the same age as Ron and me. Our flight was incredibly enjoyable, and the champagne celebration evolved into a lively party.

I was very interested in one of the younger gals. She was beautiful, blonde, and loved champagne! What was not to love about that? We made plans to get together, and I went out with her a few days later.

The Balloonatics

Both gals came out and crewed for us a few times, and one time they invited Ron and me to their house for dinner.

They lived together and were both nurses. I do not remember their names, but the blonde that I was interested in had a nice sports car, and I remember driving with her in it a few times. Anyway, I was interested in turning our friendship into a more amorous affair. We ended up in their hot tub, but things didn't go as I had hoped. When I reflect on it, I'm relieved that things didn't work out between us that night. If we had hit it off, my dad's fears of me not returning home to Michigan might have been realized.

~   ~   ~

One of the great things about flying for American Balloon Society in the desert was the local crew. Ron was the crew chief on most flights, but he had also hired some locals to help. All were Hispanic, with Dave as the head guy.

Dave and his number-one guy, Frank, spoke English well. Most of the other Hispanic crew members who occasionally came out did not speak English. Dave was a big guy, about six feet, four inches and 250 to 260 pounds. Frank was not much smaller, both very strong and hardworking. Having them along was great because it allowed me to focus on flying and interacting with the passengers while they took care of preparing and packing up the balloon.

We became good friends after a while and began partying together. Smoking pot had been a big part of my life since I was around 15 (I will go into detail on this in an upcoming book, *Tokemos High*). When they found out about that, they started inviting me out with them to party. They also took me to the best places to eat after our flights.

After one morning flight they took me to a small store/restaurant in the desert surrounded by date palm trees. A Hispanic family who didn't speak English owned the establishment, and it was mainly frequented by Hispanic field workers. Dave and Frank asked what I'd like to eat. I had no idea, so I asked them to get me whatever they were having.

They went to order while I waited at a table outside under the palm trees and returned a short while later with a variety of food. One thing I remember was something they called shrimp cocktail. I'd said I liked shrimp cocktail, but what they set in front of me I had never seen before. It was in a big, clear plastic glass with a big straw and consisted of a reddish liquid filled with small whole shrimp and small pieces of other things I couldn't identify. I was not sure about it but found it was quite good. It tasted kind of like a shrimp Virgin Bloody Mary.

~ ~ ~

May 4th was the highlight of the season. We, along with a group of other hot air Balloonatics, received an invitation to fly from the Palm Springs Airport while the gas balloons were being inflated for the Gordon Bennett Gas Balloon Race!

I found this history of the event on the internet at https://www.fai.org/gordonbennett:

COUPE AÉRONAUTIQUE GORDON BENNETT

The Coupe Aéronautique Gordon Bennett, the FAI World Long Distance Gas Balloon Championship, is the oldest and most prestigious event in aviation and the ultimate challenge for the pilots. It is a story full of adventure, skill, courage, survival and luck. The goal is simple: to fly the furthest non-stop distance from the launch site.

The international competition was initiated by adventurer and newspaper tycoon James Gordon Bennett Jr. in 1906, when 16 balloons launched from the Tuileries Gardens in Paris, France. Little did the crowd of 200,000 spectators know that

The Balloonatics

this race was to continue throughout the 20th century. The winning team brings the competition to their country.

The day before the event, we were invited to the Pilots Pre-Race Gala and Dinner at an incredible private home on a hilltop overlooking Palm Springs. The memory of meeting Joe Kittinger, the renowned balloonist, and our extensive conversation about flying and various topics will forever stay with me. He was just a wonderful person, so friendly and welcoming to a young new pilot like me.

The following day we launched our hot air balloons while the gas balloons were being inflated for a later launch. I remember going up to about 700 feet and being maybe one-quarter mile south of the launch field when suddenly I saw one of the gas balloon envelopes come rocketing up past us out of control. Luckily, no balloons were directly above it, but we were too close for comfort, for sure!

As I recall, they were attaching the basket to the envelope when something went terribly awry. The envelope was almost full of helium but had no load, so when it got loose, it shot up over 10,000 feet in a matter of minutes! I cannot remember where or if they ever found it. The rest of the event went off without further incidents, and Joe Kittinger turned out to be the winner. This was his third consecutive Gordon Bennett win.

~   ~   ~

The day after my final desert flight on May 19th, I departed on my motorcycle for Michigan and home. I recall nothing about the ride, so it must have been uneventful, which is surprising. On May 29th, I flew two paid passenger flights for Capt. Phogg and BCA, one in the morning in Saginaw, and one in the evening in Flint.

June began with a bang, and I jumped right into the fray. Capt. Phogg and Larry had been very busy. The Buick Tour, while officially over, had helped to turn BCA into a much larger concern in more ways than one.

When I returned to Michigan from California, I did not go back to an office at Capt. Phogg's House in Grand Blanc but to a brand-new, beautiful "balloon port" on 10 acres in Fenton, about 10 miles south of Grand Blanc.

The two-story building had a large showroom and a loft with two bedrooms and a bathroom for pilots. The offices were under the loft/bedroom area, and an attached garage and workshop had four double-deep bays with 16-foot-tall automatic commercial garage doors. Built on a rectangular 10-acre grass field to launch balloons on, it was most likely the largest and most impressive hot air balloon business showplace anywhere! Capt. Phogg and Larry proudly showed me around, and I was awestruck. I also met Ron Pethick that day.

Ron was about 14 years old then, and his family lived across the street. A shy and polite young man, he always responded with "yes sir" when given a task. His dad had taken some flight lessons years ago with Capt. Phogg. Ron worked at the new balloon port, doing anything that needed to be done.

The story goes that during construction, Capt. Phogg would stop by in the evening to check on progress. (Capt. Phogg was a successful insurance salesman, and ballooning was a part-time sideline for him.) He always found the job site and the building under construction clean and neat, which impressed him. One day he arrived early and discovered a young kid sweeping the building's floor.

Capt. Phogg introduced himself to the kid and said, "So you must work for the builder?" The kid replied, "No sir, I don't." Puzzled, Capt. Phogg asked him why he was there sweeping, and the kid said, "My dad always told me that if I saw a job that needed to be done, just do it, so that is what I am doing." Capt. Phogg was so impressed that he hired him on the spot. That kid was Ron Pethick, and the rest, as you will learn, is history.

The Balloonatics

~ ~ ~

The next day, Larry and I had a meeting with Capt. Phogg at the new balloon port. I recall Capt. Phogg saying, "Well, boys, here we are. We have this incredible new balloon port. Now, what are we going to do with it?"

The Buick Tour was basically over, but BCA owned all the equipment, including two Buick Olympic–logoed balloons and two fancy Balloon Kakoon chase vehicles. Capt. Phogg also had a contract with Kellogg's and a Tony the Tiger balloon, which was a light-blue balloon with Tony the Tiger's face painted on it 40 feet tall on both sides, and a new balloon shaped like Tony the Tiger's face had just been ordered. He had a small contract with the local Anheuser-Busch distributor to fly and train their people in the new Michelob balloon. He also had people calling and asking for balloon rides. These provided a good start, but Capt. Phogg said that this would not be enough to support the new balloon port, Larry, myself, and Ron. We needed a plan and now!

Larry said he would head up a commercial division to sell corporate contracts, promote the Buick balloons directly to Buick dealers across the country, and work with Capt. Phogg to promote the Tony the Tiger balloons and convince Kellogg's to invest more into that program. I told Capt. Phogg that we should start actively and aggressively marketing balloon rides for sale. This would generate quick and substantial ongoing cash flow, just like I saw others doing during our travels on the Buick Tour, particularly in California.

Capt. Phogg liked our plan, and we ran with it. He gave me a budget of $10,000 for advertising, and we bought a new AX-8, four-passenger balloon for the ride program. The first year, we charged $125 per person for balloon rides. Larry got to work selling commercial jobs. Ron was still in high school and worked part-time keeping the place clean, mowing the 10 acres with his tractor, crewing for the balloons, and any other odd job that needed to be done. Things really got busy!

~ ~ ~

The Fenton, Michigan, area is a beautiful place to fly balloons. It is a rural area only 40 miles northwest of downtown Detroit, so we had a large population base to draw from for our ride business. There are over 50 lakes in a 10-mile radius and tons of wetlands in between. There is farmland, mostly flat, with some rolling terrain in certain directions. Deer and other wildlife are everywhere. I came up with the phrase "Aerial Nature Walk" to describe the balloon ride experience.

In June, Larry and I flew 26 flights, including six commercial jobs, using three different commercial balloons. That month, we also had 20 paid rides and a few pilot training flights, plus several student pilots in training.

~ ~ ~

Our commercial arm was doing well, and I remember several of our jobs during the month of June. For one, we attached the client's banner to a balloon that we then tethered on the top of a five-story parking garage over the entrance to Cobo Hall in downtown Detroit, where a big convention was being held. Luck was on our side with calm winds, allowing us to complete a four-hour tether. I tethered the original Tony the Tiger balloon in Franklin Park, Illinois, and then flew it in Battle Creek, Michigan, that month. I piloted the Michelob balloon from downtown Flint, Michigan, to launch a riverfront concert. Then I tethered it in St. Ignace, in the Upper Peninsula of Michigan, for a prestigious car show that was held annually. I also flew the new Tony the Tiger–shaped balloon for two hours, doing five landings and takeoffs while taking many passengers on short flights over the beautiful Fenton countryside.

In July, we flew 29 flights, with me flying 19 of them. All my flights were paid passenger rides or pilot training flights. Larry flew the

The Balloonatics

Tony the Tiger–shaped balloon in Philadelphia, Pennsylvania, where he became becalmed over the city and had to land in a tiny opening in the middle of a fenced and locked auto junkyard. Fortunately, he recovered the beautiful new balloon with no apparent harm, deflating and packing it among all the junk and dirt. He then flew Tony at the World Championship in Battle Creek, Michigan, although he did not compete in the event.

~ ~ ~

I remember two interesting flights, both in the Michelob balloon doing pilot flight training (training on what not to do, it seems). On July 16th I took several of the Ryan Distributing employees for a flight. One of them was a student pilot taking his first lesson.

We took off in the morning from the balloon port in Fenton and headed southeast toward Detroit. Everything was fine until the wind got stronger and we couldn't find a place to land. We kept trying but missing landing spots as the winds were getting squirrelly. Soon we were over the northwest suburbs of Detroit in the very well-to-do area of Bloomfield Hills. I did not know it at the time, but we were flying over Cranbrook Institute, a prestigious private college prep boarding school with science and art museums.

We were moving along at about 15 miles per hour and flying treetop level when I saw a parking lot that I thought was big enough to land in. All we had to do was clear a two-story building and drop fast into the parking lot, I figured. There was a ball field before the building off a bit to our right as we approached that was full of kids who stopped their soccer game to watch us.

As we quickly approached the building, the wind shifted us sharply to the right, directly toward the center, taller part of the building that I later learned was the Cranbrook Observatory. It was round, three stories tall, and had a domed copper roof. I applied both burners full on to clear the copper roof, but we ran smack into it with the bottom of the basket and bounced off it with a loud thud and a gigantic roar from all the kids on the field! We then flew on with the basket swinging back and forth, a bit shaken, but no damage done except for a nice dent in the copper roof.

Things were looking bleak. Our fuel was very low, the winds were getting faster, and our path was taking us farther into congested areas heading straight for downtown Detroit. As we raced over a subdivision, I saw a small front yard and ripped the top out at treetop level, about 50 feet above the ground. We crashed through some tree branches and smashed hard into the middle of the lawn 60 feet from the front door of a large, expensive house in a very exclusive Bloomfield Hills neighborhood. A woman came out of the door and was taken aback to see us and our enormous black balloon deflating and covering her front lawn. After she saw we were all okay, she started praising the Lord, and I joined her in that!

The next day at the balloon port, I received a call from a professor at Cranbrook inquiring about the balloon incident at the observatory. I confessed, freaking out and wondering if I had badly damaged it. After an agonizing minute, the "professor" burst out laughing, and I heard it coming from Capt. Phogg's office. He got me on that one! I heard nothing more about it.

~ ~ ~

I had another interesting flight in the Michelob balloon that July. We launched from downtown Flint to kick off a riverfront concert by the band Spyro Gyra. I was taking another Ryan Distributing employee, Suzie, for her first lesson. It was very windy during inflation, with the winds whipping around the tall buildings that we had to clear from our launch site in a parking lot.

About eight people helped to hold the basket while I heated the balloon. Our intention was to ensure that we had enough lift to shoot out of there and clear the surrounding buildings. I didn't realize that four additional people were pulling on the crown line attached to the top of the balloon. When I felt ready, I instructed the basket holders to let go.

The four on the crown line almost got lifted off the ground. Once they released, we shot up like a rocket and were almost pushed to the basket floor by the force. We cleared the buildings by a mile and went up almost that high before we knew it! Mike Ryan, the owner of Ryan Distributing, watched from the riverfront and described the balloon as a deformed pancake shooting into the sky. The rest of the flight proceeded flawlessly.

~ ~ ~

Throughout August of 1985, the weather in Michigan was fantastic for balloon flying. I piloted 29 flights, with most of them being paid passenger flights and seven of them student pilot lessons. We concluded the month with another successful Capt. Phogg Balloon Classic event. Larry took off once more with the new Tony the Tiger–shaped balloon, heading to the US Nationals in Indianola, Iowa (not as a competitor), and then the Coney Island Festival in Cincinnati, Ohio.

I remember one student pilot lesson flight that month. As noted in my logbook, Sharon Carmichael and I flew in her balloon, with her husband, Dave, chasing us. We flew into downtown Flint on a Saturday evening and had a high-wind landing in a small park on the north side in a rough area of town.

After we landed, we were at once surrounded by at least fifty locals, most of them teenagers, and no Dave to be seen anywhere. We kept trying to call him on the radio but got no response. The crowd was getting rowdy, and Sharon and I were getting concerned when I saw a very large guy walking toward us. He was smiling, which looked good, so I walked up to him and said, "Hey man, could you help us out here, please? Our ground crew is late finding us, and we need to pack this balloon up. We will pay you $20 or a case of beer if you could help us do that."

He said sure, and I said, "Can you please keep everyone back while we get it ready? Then when our crew gets here, they can help us pack it up if they wish." When Dave finally arrived, we got the envelope bag out of the truck, and about 20 people from the crowd, including the "Big Guy," helped us pack it up and load it in the truck bed.

I then rode in the truck bed with the "Big Guy," who was now my best friend, to a party store a block away. We bought him a case of beer and gave him $20, then drove him a few blocks back to his house with many thanks along the way!

~ ~ ~

It is very difficult to fly balloons without crew members, so we recruited by putting flyers around town that advertised free balloon rides for crew members. If you crew for us 10 times, you earn a free ride. One of our crew that year was a beautiful gal, about 10 or 15 years older than me. She had a stunning body and dressed to show off that fact. She started coming out to crew often and was a big flirt, which suited all of us guys just fine.

We all became enamored with her and, as guys do, talked about who we thought she was interested in. She and I stayed behind one evening after the passengers and the rest of the crew had left. We then retired to the back room with another bottle of champagne. She told me she wanted to join the mile-high club, to which I eagerly replied, "Me too!" I arranged our mile-high flight soon thereafter, with Ron as our only crew member to keep it on the down low.

It was a warm summer morning when we took off and headed

south. I ascended to about 6,000 feet. As we were engaging in our mile-high adventure, a large passenger jet plane flew by us pretty close. We laughed and said we hoped none of the passengers in the plane had binoculars!

After we returned to the balloon port, refueled the balloon, and put it back in the garage, she went home. I started my day in the office answering the phone, selling rides, and so on. In the afternoon I got a call from a guy claiming to be from the FAA—the Federal Aviation Administration. He asked to talk to the balloon pilot who was flying a red, white, and blue balloon at 5,500 feet 15 miles south of the Flint Bishop Airport that morning.

I stammered that it was me, and he said some passengers in that plane had filed an official complaint with the FAA about what they had seen in that balloon basket. He said I needed to come in to talk with the local FSDO (Flight Standards) chief! I asked what they saw, and he replied, "Enough to file a complaint, and my boss wants to see you as soon as possible!"

I was getting nervous when once again I heard laughing coming both over the phone and from a nearby office. I had been tricked once again! Ron later confessed that he told Capt. Phogg about our flight and couldn't resist also telling him about the jet flying by.

~ ~ ~

Another funny flight happened that summer, again involving the Michelob balloon. Mike Ryan, the owner of Ryan Distributing, was flying with a group of us. He was in training and doing a solo flight in his black Michelob AX-8 105,000-cubic-foot balloon. It was breezy, and I was flying paid passengers along with Larry and one other balloon.

Mike and another balloon landed in a big open field as we flew over them at about 300 feet. The first balloon landed normally in the windy conditions. It tipped over and dragged about 30 feet after the pilot ripped out the top to let the hot air out of the balloon. The Michelob balloon touched down close to where the first balloon had stopped, but it just kept on dragging along and was not deflating.

I looked down and saw the fully inflated envelope on its side, dragging along, with Mike running alongside it, trying to grab the red deflation line. He failed to secure the deflation line to the basket before takeoff, leaving it out of reach upon landing. The balloon dragged along for quite some time with Mike running along next to it.

Eventually he got hold of the red deflation line and pulled out the top, stopping most of the balloon's forward motion as it dragged into the tree line at the end of the big field. Luckily, there was no damage to the balloon envelope. Like my first solo fight, the almost-new wicker basket got scuffed up, and Mike's pride was also damaged.

~ ~ ~

September came, and I flew 19 flights while Larry flew seven. Again, most of my flights were paid passenger flights or student training flights. Larry flew in St. Louis, Missouri, for the Forrest Park Balloon Race with the Michelob balloon. According to his logbook, he landed in a rough area in the city, and a 12-pack of beer saved the day. He also flew the Tony the Tiger–shaped balloon in Omaha, Nebraska, for a Kellogg's-sponsored event on the 29th.

I took the Tony-shaped balloon to the National Balloon Rally in Statesville, North Carolina, September 20–22 and won the event while flying four paid passengers every flight. Cindy accompanied me for crew and companionship. Cindy was a teacher I had met a few months prior when I brought a balloon to an elementary school. They had hired us to educate the children about various types of manned flight.

The Balloonatics

Tony the Tiger-shaped balloon.

Cindy and I had an instant connection. I asked her out, and we started dating soon thereafter. We also had local crew members the event assigned to us, and we all became good friends during the event.

The event paid us to bring the Tony-shaped balloon and sold rides for us to fly as well. (Kellogg's did not sponsor us at this event.) To make the trip profitable, we relied on the paid rides and the fee the event paid us to attend. Thank God the weather turned out perfect! I flew six flights, all full of riders, flying 24 paid passengers. I also won First Place during the event! The first-place prize was two round-trip airplane tickets to anywhere in the continental USA.

During the first day of flying from the Statesville airport, an FAA inspector paid me a visit. He requested my paperwork and was upset that the balloon had a Standard Airworthiness Certificate. The new Tony-shaped balloon was a standard balloon but was modified with protrusions to make it look like Tony's face, with two 12-foot-tall ears sticking out near the top and a protruding nose and chin. The inspector did not understand how the FAA could have issued a Standard Airworthiness Certificate for it, but there was nothing he could do since all my paperwork was in order. We suspected the local balloon manufacturer had sent him to disrupt us because he immediately targeted me and Tony, inspecting no other balloon.

I also remember a big issue at the awards ceremony. I had brushed the top of a tree with the bottom of my basket while coming in toward a target during the first competition event. After the flight, several pilots came up to me and informed me they had witnessed the infraction. However, they decided not to report it because it neither affected my flight path nor aided me in reaching the target.

At the end of the event, when I was announced the overall winner, they changed their opinion. I remember several of them surrounding me, demanding that I forfeit. Feeling upset and unsure, I left the awards ceremony tent.

Outside, I saw Tracy Barnes (founder of Barnes Balloons) standing

The Balloonatics

there with a small helium advertising blimp tied to his belt. He had started making and selling helium advertising products after selling his hot air balloon manufacturing company. I told him the story and will never forget what he said. It went something like this: "Suppose Mario Andretti was declared the winner of the Indy 500 but had made a slightly illegal pass during the race. Would he forfeit? Go claim your prize, young man!" I thanked him, said it was an honor to meet him, and then walked back in the tent to accept my prize and First Place award.

~ ~ ~

In October we all headed to the Albuquerque International Balloon Fiesta. Larry took and flew the Tony-shaped balloon in its "new" chase vehicle (one of the two former Buick balloon chase vehicles). I rode my motorcycle and flew for Kinnie Gibson's Albuquerque Fiesta balloon ride concession. After Fiesta, I rode to Palm Springs for the winter to fly for Kinnie and Ron again in the desert.

That year I took the southern route to ride to Albuquerque and avoided the freezing temperatures I had experienced the year before when I took the northern route, I-80 to California. All was great until I got to I-40, west of Oklahoma City. It rained and was cold for three days straight.

I had poor rain gear, and after about 100 or 150 miles, I was soaked through and freezing. Luckily, there were inexpensive motels along the way, and they all provided a gas-fired wall heating unit to heat the room. I hung all my wet clothes and set my boots in front of it and cranked up the heat. Everything was dry in the morning, and I could continue on my way. This routine continued for three days until I reached Amarillo, Texas, where the rain finally stopped.

Stopping in Amarillo, I got a hotel room and walked to a nearby honky-tonk bar for dinner and drinks. I remember sitting at the bar, eating, when a lovely lady arrived and took a seat a few stools away. Eventually, I made contact and conversation and sat beside her. Everything was going well until about thirty minutes later when her girlfriend arrived and took a seat.

She was a tough-looking woman, and it became obvious they were more than just friends. I realized this wouldn't work out as I had hoped. They invited me to go dancing, and I rode in their car to the dance hall. I remember little after that, but somehow I managed to return to my hotel room and woke up the next morning with a massive hangover. The road was still ahead, so I had to just get on my bike and ride on to Albuquerque in the much-appreciated sunshine.

~ ~ ~

The weather for the Fiesta was great. We flew every morning, all nine days. I flew 69 paid passengers in a brand-new six-passenger Raven balloon that Kinnie had bought for his ride business in Palm Springs. On three of the mornings, we did two flights with six passengers, landing and switching out fuel tanks, then taking off again with six new passengers.

Back then the Fiesta was like the Wild West of ballooning. The field was dirt, and anyone could buy a space around its perimeter, build almost any type of stall, and sell just about anything they wanted. Kinnie and Sheri had been going for a few years and would buy a 10-foot-by-10-foot space, build a stall, and sell balloon rides. Many others did likewise as there was no official ride company.

There were also small encampments of people hawking their wares and balloon rides along the roads leading into the Fiesta. These crude assorted stalls built from wood sold all the things you would find at any large festival, including balloon rides.

The day before the Fiesta was to begin that year a big storm blew through and destroyed most of those shoddily built stalls, including

Kinnie and Sheri's. Everyone had to scramble to clean up the field, salvage what materials they could, and buy new materials to rebuild for the next morning!

~ ~ ~

One flight sticks in my mind because of the events at the landing. I had six passengers on board flying from the Fiesta Field in the morning. The winds picked up during the flight, which resulted in a tip-over drag landing. Just to clarify, a tip-over landing is when the balloon and basket tips over on its side as we are dragging to a stop. It is a lot of fun as long as everyone in the basket follows my instructions to bend their knees, hold on tight, and stay in the basket.

I landed in a large desert field where the ground was hard, almost like a parking lot. With no obstacles, it was a perfect place to land fast-moving balloons. Many balloons had already landed in front of me, and more were on their way. Pilots before me aided the landing balloons. To do this, you position yourself to jump onto the back of the basket as it comes in to land, thus adding your weight to the basket to help it stop. A few people helped me land. Then I helped my passengers crawl out of the tipped-over basket as we all laughed, enjoying the exciting adventure.

Once my passengers were situated, I turned to help other balloons land. Seeing one approach, I hurried to a strategic spot for touchdown. It was one of the new solo system balloons that was being premiered at the event. This was a tiny, one-person balloon with a gondola that resembled a plastic garbage can. I grabbed the gondola and jumped on from behind as it touched down. I was surprised to see that the pilot was the world-famous balloonist Don Piccard! He was laughing as we tipped over and started dragging along the hard-packed desert floor.

As we dragged along, I was half on and half off the "garbage can" gondola and very close to Don, who was inside it. Casually, he looked up at me and asked if I could pull the red deflation line as he couldn't reach it. Looking down, I could see it was dragging along the ground and just within my reach. I grabbed it and pulled, which opened up the top and brought us to a stop. I rolled off the garbage can and Don rolled out of it, both of us laughing after a fun and exciting desert drag!

~ ~ ~

Albuquerque back in 1985 was one huge party, man! The Holiday Inn was the official hotel and party central. It hosted an annual Toga Party in a vast tent in the parking lot.

The Toga Party was epic! Hundreds of people wore all kinds of homemade togas, many like the ones my friend Debbie and I wore, which were made of hotel bed sheets. Debbie was a friend of Kinnie and Sheri's and crewed for us during the Fiesta. She and I had a ton of fun together, including at the Toga Party, where we drank and danced with the crowd till the wee hours. Later, we went back to my hotel room for more drinks and fun. Before dawn, we returned to Fiesta Field for another sunrise flight.

One character I fondly remember was Larry, one of Ron Frusher's friends and crew members. Larry was a police officer back in Palm Springs. He was ridiculously funny and was always pulling pranks. Hidden beneath his toga was a large fake penis with a bright, lit-up head that he could flash on and off.

Whenever he spotted an attractive woman, he would flick the light on and off. If they inquired about it, he would lift his toga and expose the large, illuminated fake penis. He also wore a helmet with a flashing red light and a very loud siren. Whenever he wanted a beer, he would turn on the helmet. The siren wailed, red lights flashing. The crowd and long line to the bar would part for him like the parting of the Red Sea!

Thinking back, it's hard to believe some of the crazy things we did. I remember meeting a gal who crewed for us the first day there. She

The Balloonatics

was a beautiful blonde, about 10 years older than me. She took me to her house later, where we partied naked in her hot tub while snorting lines. Yes, it was the eighties, and cocaine was all the rage.

I was sharing a hotel room with a crew member. About halfway into the nine-day Albuquerque extravaganza, we met some pretty young ladies in the hotel lobby. They were cowgirls and were participating in a horse show and rodeo that was also taking place at the time. We got to know each other very well in our hotel room.

I remember he and his girl in one bed and me and my girl in the other one, three feet away, going at it. I would have preferred more privacy! I still have a letter my cowgirl wrote to me later that year when she had gone overseas in the military.

After each flight, we would refuel the balloons, and then many of the balloon teams would return to the launch field and begin another gigantic party that would last all day. Hot tubs in pickup trucks were just one of the crazy things happening. One team had a semi-truck with a trailer that had several hot tubs on it. Yes, it was an incredible experience for a 26-year-old single guy. Full of sin and debauchery, for sure.

~ ~ ~

My last flight in Albuquerque was on October 13th. We—Ron, Kinnie, Sheri, our crew, and I—then left for Palm Springs, California, with me on my motorcycle. This season, Ron and Kinnie rented a small three-bedroom house in the city of La Quinta in an older neighborhood of working-class folks. There were lots of young families, and we were just around the corner from Bill and Nina Henry's house. I could look out my bedroom window and see their house and their balloons on trailers in the driveway. Our place had a two-car garage, just like the country club house from the last season. However, unlike the country club house, there were no restrictions or uptight neighbors complaining about trucks, motorcycles, or balloons in the driveway.

We kicked off the season with our first flight on October 20th flying for Doug Grimes in Del Mar and drove from the desert over the mountains to the Pacific coast. They had a large group joining us. There were about 10 or 12 balloons at the launch field, which was only a half mile from the Pacific Ocean.

Having never flown there or so close to the ocean before, I was apprehensive. I met Doug the season before when he came to the desert to help fly a large group. He was a great guy. Prior to the flight, I asked Doug what I should do or look out for and what to expect. He just said, "Follow me, and you will be fine." So I did. He took off and ascended to about 1,000 feet, and I followed. I realized we were flying out to sea at that altitude.

We were over the ocean, and he stayed up high, going farther out to sea. I panicked a bit but could not show it. My passengers were concerned as well. I told them I was following the very experienced pilot ahead of us going out to sea and he knew what he was doing. It was an incredible sight; the views were spectacular. Finally, Doug descended swiftly after what felt like an eternity and a long distance from shore. He did a 180-degree turn and flew under me back toward shore. I followed him in, and we landed back at the launch field, or very close by, as I recall.

We all met up back at the launch field with the group and had our traditional champagne toast. Unlike the rest, we were the only ones to fly out to sea. They all stayed low and flew inland, so Doug and I waited a while for them to return to the launch field. I asked Doug, "Why the hell didn't you tell me about flying out to sea?"

He just smiled, chuckled, and said, "I told you to follow me, and you would be okay. You did, and you were. Wasn't it great?"

I said, "It would have been greater had I not been almost crapping my pants for the first half of the flight!"

After the morning Del Mar flight, we quickly returned to the desert for an evening flight. I flew seven more passenger flights that

October. On November 2nd we traveled to Perris, where Sheri had booked six paid passengers for me to fly in the morning. I did a one-hour flight and landed back at the launch field with the "box" winds we all enjoyed that morning.

After we landed and the passengers disembarked, Sheri informed me she had two jumpers ready to fly up to 5,000 feet and parachute down. I had never done that before and was apprehensive about it. I thought my fuel was kind of low for another flight.

She assured me it was easy and instructed me to ascend to 6,000 feet, then descend quickly. While descending, instruct them to jump before reaching 5,000 feet; dropping their weight would cause the balloon to level out. You can then drift down slowly, she said, using hardly any fuel. After a minute of digesting this, I decided it made sense.

I did it just as Sheri instructed and landed back at the launch field again 30 minutes later with plenty of fuel left. It was fascinating and insane to see people jump out of your perfectly good balloon. As I watched them fall, it seemed like they waited way too long to open their chutes, but they knew what they were doing. They all landed back at the launch field and came up to the basket when I landed to thank me for taking them up for their first balloon jump. That afternoon, we returned to Del Mar to fly there again, and this time, we all flew inland.

The rest of November, I flew 15 more passenger flights in the desert and one in Temecula. In December, I flew 18 passenger flights all over the desert.

1986

January was very busy, with 27 flights in the desert. There were several flights that I noted in my logbook that month. The first one I remember vividly. It was January 1st, and about 20 balloons with a sizeable group of passengers took off from Dan Glick's field and flew up the valley toward Palm Desert and Palm Springs.

It seemed like any other afternoon flight as we floated slowly up the valley. About 20 minutes into the flight, Ron radioed that I needed to land. I also heard several pilots in nearby balloons yelling at me to land ASAP! I glanced up the valley and saw a wall of dust rapidly approaching us.

At that exact moment, the balloon abruptly turned around and we were quickly heading in the opposite direction, back from where we had just come. Luckily, there was a large, recently mowed alfalfa field ahead. I watched five or six balloons land there as I approached fast and landed there as well. We all had a fast tip-over drag landing, but were lucky we got down when we did because the wind increased steadily over the next few minutes until it was blowing about 25 or more miles per hour.

The dust storm engulfed us, and we then got dusted as we frantically packed up the balloons as fast as we could! Later, I asked one of the more experienced desert pilots what caused the dust storm. I don't remember his explanation, except that he said it was rare. He advised me to be on the lookout for it in the afternoon and land immediately if I see a wall of dust.

~ ~ ~

For the second flight, on January 7th, which I remember and have noted in my logbook, we experienced a very windy landing with a bunch of balloons that morning when we flew farther south toward the Salton Sea than I had ever flown before. I remember following about eight balloons down the valley that morning as the winds kept increasing. The desert down where we ended up landing was very rough, with scrub bushes everywhere and very few open spaces. The other balloons were ahead of us and were all flying very low looking for a good spot to land. One by one, they started landing in front of me in a cloud of dust as their baskets contacted the desert floor and they dragged through the scrub bushes.

I landed right next to one of them, and it was very exciting as we bounced off of or dragged through many three- to four-foot-tall scrub bushes before coming to a stop after about a 100-foot drag. My four passengers and I, covered with desert dust, slowly crawled out of the overturned basket, which was made more difficult because the basket was resting in the midst of a bush. The pilot who landed closest to me came over right away and helped us while asking if everyone was okay. Everyone was fine, although a bit shook up. We dusted ourselves off, and then the champagne flowed as we toasted a flight we would not forget.

~ ~ ~

I don't remember the January 12th flight recorded in my logbook, but my notes are interesting: "a demo flight with Canadians who had plans for a 40-passenger tethered gas balloon." I also noted that I flew in a Thunder 160 balloon. I wish I remembered it. The only Thunder 160 I remember from back in 1986 in the desert was Dan Glick's, so we must have flown with him. The reference to this specific brand of hot air balloon and a large, tethered gas balloon is a very interesting coincidence that will be revealed later in this story.

On January 24th, I recorded a flight to 7,000 feet with Kelly, whom I had met the previous summer in Michigan. We had become close, and I used one of the two airplane tickets I had won at the Statesville National Balloon Rally to fly her out to visit. We enjoyed a fantastic week in the desert. She flew multiple times and supported ground crew duties for other flights.

We took some awesome road trips together while she was visiting as well. One was to the Salton Sea. We drove completely around it and stopped at the Mud Pit Flats, where there are all these little vents with hot gases and moisture pouring out of the ground. They formed little hills of mud and look like tiny volcanos spitting bubbles of gas! We also took a drive up the San Jacinto Mountains to the little village of Idyllwild, where there was snow on the ground. It is a beautiful area.

~ ~ ~

There is a date noted in my logbook, January 28, 1986, that people my age will never forget. We had just completed a beautiful morning flight and were driving back in the chase vehicle after having breakfast. Ron Frusher was driving. I was in the back seat with his cousin Jeff and a few others. Jeff was training to be a balloon pilot. He was also very interested in space and was trying to get into NASA.

We were excitedly listening to the launch of the *Challenger* space shuttle on the radio and cheering it on as the announcer described the liftoff. Then all went silent as we heard the announcer trying to describe what happened next. Joy and excitement swiftly transformed into tense anxiety, then grief. Jeff was the first to cry.

~ ~ ~

In February, my parents came out to visit, and we enjoyed numerous sightseeing road trips. One of these was to the Palm Springs Tramway, a must-see. After driving a few steep miles from Palm Springs up to the Tram, the ride begins at the Valley Station at 2,643 feet. You then ride up a sheer mountain face through five climate zones to the Mountain Station at 8,516 feet above sea level.

In less than 15 minutes, you travel from the Sonoran Desert to a snow-covered alpine forest. The transition is incredible! But you had better bring your snow clothes if you want to enjoy it.

My dad had recently bought a new video camera. Back then they

The Balloonatics

weighed about 10 pounds, and you held them on your shoulder. He took lots of video footage of our adventures, including the balloon ride over the desert I took them on. I wish I could find those old videos; they are hilarious, with my dad's constant narration adding to the fun, but alas, I haven't found them yet.

~ ~ ~

I flew 19 passenger flights in February and noted on several of them that we "picked grapefruit." The Coachella Valley is an agricultural haven. I found this description of the valley online at Wikipedia:

> The Coachella Valley is an arid rift valley in the Colorado Desert of Southern California in Riverside County. The valley may also be referred to as Greater Palm Springs and the Palm Springs Area due to the historic prominence of the city of Palm Springs. The valley extends approximately 45 mi (72 km) southeast from the San Gorgonio Pass to the northern shore of the Salton Sea and the neighboring Imperial Valley, and is approximately 15 mi (24 km) wide along most of its length. It is bounded on the northeast by the San Bernardino and Little San Bernardino Mountains, and on the southwest by the San Jacinto and Santa Rosa Mountains. ...
>
> As of 2010, the valley produced agricultural products worth about $600 million. The valley is the primary date-growing region in the United States, responsible for nearly 95 percent of the nation's crop. ... Other agricultural products cultivated in the Coachella Valley include fruits and vegetables, especially table grapes, citrus fruits such as lemons, limes, oranges and grapefruit; onions and leeks; and peppers. The valley floor served to grow bounties of alfalfa, artichokes, avocados, beans, beets, cabbage, carrots, corn, cotton, cucumbers, dandelions

(salad greens), eggplant, figs, grains (i.e. barley, oats, rye and wheat; plus rice fields kept wet or moist in the Salton Sea area), hops, kohlrabi, lettuce, mangoes, nectarines and peaches, persimmons, plums and prunes, pomegranate, potatoes, radishes, spinach, strawberries, sugar cane, tomatoes, a variety of herbs and spices, and other vegetable crops. The Coachella grapefruit originated in the region.

~ ~ ~

We often had numerous balloons flying together in the evening. The wind on these flights would usually take us up the valley from Dan's field over hundreds of acres of citrus groves owned by large corporations. A fun activity on these flights was a fruit-picking competition. Flying at treetop level, passengers would pick the fruit, watched by migrant workers who enjoyed seeing us float by.

At the end of the flight, the passengers would count their fruit and keep what they'd picked. Pilots and crew would then meet at one of our favorite restaurants, and the balloon that had picked the most fruit had their dinner bought by the rest.

~ ~ ~

In March, I flew 22 passenger flights, including the maiden flight of a new Raven AX-9 six-passenger balloon that Sheri named Haley's Comet, and several flights mention that we "boxed" Dan's Field, meaning that we took off and landed there by using different winds at different altitudes to fly away then fly back. Also, several flights landed at the Thermal Airport, where the Goodyear and other blimps would be "parked" (*moored* is the proper term) in the early mornings before taking off to film some of the big PGA golf tournaments that

The Balloonatics

were held at the many prestigious golf country clubs in the valley. We would try to land next to them, hoping to find the pilot or chief crew members there so we could try to barter for a ride trade.

Ron and I continued to go to the Red Onion for the free food buffet as often as we could, as it was very good and got busy later with lots of pretty ladies. Since I had such a great time the previous St. Patrick's Day there, I went again this year. I drove the same Toyota pickup, this time ensuring all the lights were operational.

Again, Ron did not join me; I went solo. This time I met up with a group of gals who invited me back to their place around midnight. No flight was scheduled the next morning, so I had a free night and day. I accompanied the ladies to their location. It was only about a half mile from the Red Onion, so we all walked.

The party at their apartment was fun, and more people kept joining as the night wore on. About 3:30 a.m., I had had enough and decided to walk back to the truck and sleep there. On that short walk back, the police pulled up beside me and inquired what I was doing. I told them in no uncertain terms that I was walking but must not have been very nice in my reply, or perhaps my walking was not quite up to their standards.

Anyway, next thing I know, I am pushed up on the side of the squad car, handcuffed, and taken back to my familiar old haunt from last year, the Indio County Jail drunk tank! Charged with drunk and disorderly! Hell, I was just walking. I knew I was too drunk to drive. I was being responsible, but I ended up in jail anyway, for the second St. Patrick's night in a row! I was mad and showed it in the tank, but the next morning they just let me go with no charges. It was the final time I saw the inside of a jail cell or a squad car.

~ ~ ~

April came, and I only flew 13 rides as the weather was changing and the season ended with the last flight on April 27th. I remember one flight that month. It was an evening flight and was very hot. It also got windy. I came in to land in the desert following several other balloons. As I watched them touch down and drag along the desert floor for quite a way, I decided to try something new.

I leveled off about 10 feet above the ground. As we started crossing a big scrub bush that was about four feet tall and 20 feet in diameter, I ripped out the top of the balloon, and we plopped straight down into the last five feet of the big bush. We gently dragged through it and stopped in an enormous cloud of dust. The landing was much smoother, and we did not drag 100 feet like the others did because the bush checked our fall and stopped us from dragging along. However, the cloud of dust from the bush left us all coughing and choking and looking like the Pig Pen character in Charlie Brown! I never tried that maneuver again.

~ ~ ~

It was time to go back to Michigan. This time I would not be riding my motorcycle home as it would be in the bed of the pickup truck I had recently bought in Los Angeles. Capt. Phogg asked me to find a long-bed pickup with four doors and no dual rear wheels. The four-door pickups available in the Midwest back then all had dual rear wheels.

I found a nice used one in Los Angeles for only $2,500. Capt. Phogg wired me the money to buy it and bring it back to be used as a balloon chase vehicle in Michigan. I loaded my motorcycle into the truck bed and headed home on April 28th.

About 100 miles later, in the mountains of California, the truck started sputtering. I had to pull into the next town and find an auto repair facility. Fortunately, I found an open one, and they could look at it immediately. They discovered a clogged fuel filter, replaced it, and I continued my journey.

The Balloonatics

The very next day, it broke down in the Arizona desert. This time I had to hitch a ride to the next town 20 miles down the highway to find another auto repair facility and have it towed in. Again, luckily, I found one in the tiny desert town and got it towed in before nightfall.

I got a cheap motel room, found the town watering hole, and told my sad story to whoever would listen. The next day they fixed the issue, and this time it was a lot more expensive, but I was back on the road again, looking forward to finally making it home.

I made it all the way to southern Illinois just north of St. Louis when all hell broke loose! Suddenly, at 75 miles per hour, something made a loud snapping sound in front and the truck started swerving back and forth. I was just able to bring it under control and pulled over onto the shoulder but kept going at about 10 miles per hour because there was an exit only about a mile ahead.

I barely made it around the curve on the exit ramp at 10 miles per hour. The truck did not want to turn. At the end of the exit ramp, I saw a truck stop and was just able to wrestle the truck to the service area. They said they could not look at it until the next day. I found a cheap motel room across the street and went to the nearest watering hole to drown my sorrows.

The next day, the mechanic told me that the frame had separated in the truck's front, and it would take him a week to get the needed parts and fix it. I said I couldn't wait and asked if there was another option. He said if I drove it really easy, he could patch it up enough to get me home.

I called Capt. Phogg—for the third time now—to ask for money to fix our "new" truck. He was now wondering what the hell kind of lemon I had bought! He agreed it would be best to limp it home so his mechanic at home could fix it.

I then drove the remaining 400-plus miles at 45 miles per hour down the freeway with my hazard flashers on, upsetting thousands of drivers who had to go around the "idiot" going so slow! I was amazed that the police did not pull me over for creating a traffic hazard. I finally made it back, and we had the truck fixed. We had no trouble with it thereafter. We installed a lift gate on the back and used it for many years to come.

~ ~ ~

When I returned to the balloon port in Fenton, Michigan, that May, things had already gotten very busy. Larry, Capt. Phogg, and Ron had been holding down the fort. Larry had flown 15 total flights so far that spring before I returned, with most being pilot training flights, one a paid passenger ride, and three for Kellogg's flying the Tony balloon in Battle Creek. On one of the Tony flights, he noted they flew over the nudist camp outside of Battle Creek. I remember a lot of talk about that camp and some funny stories of balloons landing there.

Jumping right into the fray, my first flight was on May 7th, flying two paid passengers and taking Ron Pethick along for some pilot training. My logbook also says that Kelly and her daughter crewed for us. We must have been short on crew that day, because her daughter was a toddler in a car seat then.

I flew 10 flights that May. Eight of them were paid passenger rides, one was a tether at the Azalea Festival on Grosse Isle, and my cousin Dennis came and helped, and one was a pilot training flight for Ron with my uncle Joe accompanying us. It had been years since I last saw Joe. We had grown up together like brothers, as he is only two years older than me. Taking him for that ride was very special. We did a "splash and dash" on Lake Copneconic, and later we went out and reminisced while drinking at a few bars.

~ ~ ~

The Balloonatics

In June, Larry and I both flew 17 times, mostly paid rides but also a few pilot lessons for Ron Pethick and one for Sharon Carmichael. The Capt. Phogg Classic event was again held at Crossroads Village on June 20, 21, and 22, and the weather gods allowed all flights to take place once again. Also, my logbook notes that June 17th was the maiden flight of the new Michelob Light balloon. Ryan Distributing now owned two Michelob balloons, one black and the new one silver.

I was told the fabric contained silver dust to make it shine, and it truly did shine! It was also VERY heavy. The Black Michelob balloon was an AX-8, 105,00-cubic-foot, four-passenger plus pilot envelope, while the new Michelob Light was an AX-7, 77,000-cubic-foot, two-passenger plus pilot envelope. However, the new silver balloon's fabric was so heavy, it weighed as much as the larger black one. This limited the passenger capacity to usually only one unless the ambient air temperature was cold.

~ ~ ~

Something else happened June 14th. The previous summer of 1985, Larry had come back from lunch at a local restaurant called Jimmy G's in Fenton and told me about this cute waitress with an awesome butt. He suggested we go there soon and meet her.

I always embraced such challenges, so we took action the following day. She was there, and I really liked her. Her name was Michelle. I returned there frequently when she was working. We hit it off really well. Being the idiot I often was around the ladies, I never asked her out properly. I just gave her my Balloon Corporation of America business card and said come out and crew for me sometime. That never happened, and then I left for Albuquerque and Palm Springs.

On June 14th, 1986, Larry gave Scott Burdick a pilot lesson. He had started training Scott earlier that year, before I had returned. I was scheduled to give a flight lesson to Sharon Carmichael. Scott was a photographer who owned BH Photographic with his brother-in-law, Dave Hodgkin, who was Michelle's brother. They had been the official photographers for the Capt. Phogg Balloon Classic for several years. As my luck would have it, Scott was married to Karen, who was the older sister to that cute waitress with the impressive butt. Michelle came out to crew for Scott's lesson along with her sister Karen.

I was thrilled to see Michelle again and was upset that Larry was doing the pilot lesson for Scott and not me! As I recall, there were one or two other balloons and pilots, including Capt. Phogg, who flew with us that day. After the flight, we all returned to the balloon port for the traditional post-flight champagne ceremony. Then, as usual, after all the paying passengers left, the party began. We had to finish all those half-empty bottles of champagne and then open some more, just because!

At some point, a bunch of us were sitting around my desk in the balloon port showroom passing a bottle of champagne around and telling stories of our flights. I was sitting behind my desk, and Michelle was sitting across from me with several pilots and crew members sitting beside her. Michelle was wearing tight jeans that had zippers on the outside of both legs, going from the ankles to almost the waistline.

Capt. Phogg was sitting next to her and asked her what those zippers were for. She made some funny remark, probably something like, "To make it easier to get out of them." Well, next thing you know, Capt. Phogg started to unzip one zipper at the ankle up to her knee, while the guy on the other side of her did the same.

I wanted in on the action and was jealous because I really liked this young lady. So I decided to rescue her from those two rogues. I motioned for her to meet me under my desk. She ducked and crawled under, and I did as well.

I gave her a big kiss and said let's get out of here. She said okay, and we left. We went to Flint and had dinner at Filglio's, which was a nice Italian restaurant. She ordered fettuccine Alfredo, a dish unfamiliar to me. After dinner, we went back to the balloon port and had more fun.

I told her I really liked her and wanted to see her a lot, but I had other girlfriends who I also wanted to see. She agreed and said she felt the same. (Later she told me she thought that was a strange thing for me to say on our first "date.") We started seeing a lot of each other from then on, and she began to crew for me. I took her up on flights whenever I could; heck, she only weighed 98 pounds!

~   ~   ~

July was busy. I did 29 flights, and Larry flew 27 times. Most were paid passenger rides, and there were a few pilot lessons. On July 21st and 22nd, Buick contracted us to fly one of the Buick Olympic balloons over the Buick Open PGA Golf Tournament in Grand Blanc, Michigan, and Larry flew those commercial flights.

I have a few notes in my logbook about some flights that month. The first one was a flight in Flushing, Michigan, from the country club there. A well-to-do family who belonged to the club paid for the flight. They were having a party and just wanted the balloon to fly away; they did not pay for any passengers to fly. Ron and one crew member came with me, and I was to give Ron a flight lesson. I believe he was 16 at the time.

After we inflated the balloon and Ron was about to jump in, two gorgeous young gals who looked like twins and looked very much like Michelle came up and begged to go for the ride. I told them that passengers were not part of the contract. They told me it was their dad who had paid for the balloon. I had met him earlier, and he was standing there giving me the okay.

The weather forecast was for the winds to pick up, so I was concerned about taking them up if it got windy and said so. The dad agreed. So Ron got in, and we took off. The weather turned out perfect, and we had a nice leisurely training flight and a soft landing. All the while, I was kicking myself for not taking those two beauties along with Ron and me! (Funny, the things you remember.)

Another logbook entry shows I flew the maiden flight of our new Raven AX-9 six-passenger-plus-pilot ride balloon. The ride business was really taking off now, and we had to fly three to five balloons often to handle all the passengers. We only had one four-passenger and several two-passenger balloons. The new six-pack really helped because now we could fly two balloons and take 10 passengers. Finding crew and pilots for three to five balloons was difficult and costly, so this was a much-needed addition to the ride program.

~ ~ ~

The other logbook notation was about a pigeon. I remember this one like it was yesterday, though it happened on July 31st, 1986. I was flying the new six-passenger balloon loaded with passengers on a morning sunrise flight. It was a beautiful morning, and we were flying low over the countryside toward Grand Blanc.

Everyone was loving it, when suddenly, a pigeon started dive-bombing the basket. It literally was diving at us like an attack bird, just veering away at the last second before it could crash into the basket. It did this several times, with all the passengers ducking as it dove at them repeatedly.

It stopped for a minute or two, but then I heard one passenger yell, "Here it comes again!" And there it came again, two or three more times. Then came the strangest thing I have ever seen. That crazed pigeon flew around us in circles a few times and then landed on top of the balloon! Balloon fabric is very strong but also very thin, so I could see the outline of that nutty bird as it landed and walked around on the top of the balloon.

It walked around for a while as the passengers and I all looked up in amazement, and then it just kind of settled in for the ride. All I

The Balloonatics

could figure was maybe we had flown close to its nest as we were treetopping earlier, when it first attacked, and now since it was a chilly morning it found that it liked the hot balloon as a resting place to recover from its attack.

That pigeon stayed put for the entire rest of the flight, and about 20 minutes later, when we landed, it was still there. Our crew arrived. I had told them on the radio of our attack, and they could not believe their eyes. We deflated the balloon, and as it slowly fell over on its side, the bird was still there riding it down. I actually had to shoo it off before we packed up the envelope, and before it finally took off at my insistence, it pooped, forever leaving its mark so we would never forget the attack of the crazed pigeon!

~ ~ ~

Most balloon flights could not take place without a ground crew. It is possible to launch and fly away with a small balloon all by yourself. But it is a lot of work, and since the balloon flies with the wind, you usually end up far from where you took off, so getting the balloon back home becomes an issue.

We were lucky back in the seventies, eighties, and nineties because we almost always had plenty of crew willing to help. I do not know why, but it just seemed to get harder after that. Capt. Phogg sponsored a local Boy and Girl Scout troop, and we received lots of help from the scouts and some of the scouts' parents, and that worked out well. Now that I had built up the ride business, we needed more crew as we were scheduling way more flights, even on weekday mornings.

The crew were all volunteers who worked for rides—after 10 crews, they earned a ride. They could take it themselves or give the ride away as a gift to someone else. Capt. Phogg had started a Crew Club, which consisted mainly of the scouts and parents, plus some friends and balloon groupies who had shown up along the way. We needed more crew, though, and decided to expand the club. Capt. Phogg came up with the name "Capt. Phogg Balloon Platoon."

I promoted it in the same manner that I promoted the ride program. I wrote a press release and sent it to all the local newspapers, radio stations, television stations, and so on, and got some free press that got the phones ringing a bit. I placed a few inexpensive ads in the local papers, and with that and word of mouth, we ended up with about 50 members who paid $25 each to join the club.

With their membership, they received an official "Capt. Phogg Balloon Platoon" golf shirt with the official "Capt. Phogg Balloon Platoon" logo on the front and back, an official "Capt. Phogg Balloon Platoon" pin, and a membership card with 10 spaces on the back for pilots to sign and date each time they crewed. As with the volunteers previously, every 10 times they crewed, they earned a ride.

We had monthly crew training meetings, and one of the original Buick Olympic balloons that we had rebuilt with no artwork was named the Club Balloon. We also had elections to elect a president and secretary, and it became one big family! Several of the members got their pilot's license, and several weddings directly resulted from the couples meeting through the club! At least one of those couples is still together after all these years. Alan and Beth Clark met through the club, and Alan started working for BCA soon after and took many pilot lessons. They are still good friends of ours to this day.

~ ~ ~

In August 1986, Larry flew 20 flights. Three of them were commercial jobs, one in Detroit with the Black Michelob balloon, and two in Battle Creek with Tony the Tiger. The rest were training or paid ride flights in Fenton. I flew 24 times, all local paid rides and a few pilot lessons.

On August 1st my logbook says, "state land had to carry balloon out in the dark." I remember that one. I had landed in a nice spot 100 feet from the road that the chase crew was on, and I saw that there was a two-track coming into the field from the road just north of where the crew was. Thick young woods separated our landing spot from the road, and it was getting dark.

I radioed my crew to find the two-track into the field, and they informed me that there was a locked gate and a sign that said "State land—no motor vehicles." They came back to the road they originally were on only 100 feet from where we had landed and walked in through the thick young trees. There was no way to get the balloon system out through those trees.

While we were trying to figure out what to do, all my passengers walked through the trees to sit in the van without me even noticing. Meanwhile, Alan walked a half mile to the house that was at the other end of the field and found we could get the balloon out that way, but we could not drive out to it. We had to carry it out.

None of the passengers offered to help when we told them what we had to do, so Alan, a crew member named Royston, and I had to carry it out ourselves. We would alternately carry the very heavy basket 10 to 20 feet, set it down and carry the envelope to it, and repeat. We first lightened the load by carrying the burners and propane fuel tanks through the thick woods to the van. It took us over an hour to carry everything out.

The passengers were not happy campers, having to wait in the van that long. I was not a happy camper because not one of them offered to help! Four of them were not much older than me and in good condition, and they could have helped. The other two were older, and I did not expect them to. Anyway, we got back late, did our champagne ceremony back at the balloon port, and all felt better thereafter.

~ ~ ~

One more that I remember was a lesson for Don Campbell. We took a local radio celebrity, Johnny Burke, and his wife up for a ride and a live remote radio broadcast. I had built and continued to promote the ride program through paid advertising and garnering free press with an aggressive press release and follow-up campaign. I would write press releases every month about some new idea or event or ride offering, mail them to all the news outlets, and follow up with phone calls inviting them all to go for a ride.

Johnny was one of the many who took me up on those offers. He and his wife were wonderful people, and Johnny helped us promote the rides and the Capt. Phogg Balloon Classic for many years. This flight turned out to be breezy, and we had a fun, windy, bouncy tip-over drag landing that was enjoyed by all and was good training for Don.

~ ~ ~

A hilarious flight that summer involved the Michelob balloon and the first solo flight of one of the Ryan distributing employees we were training. A bunch of balloons took off from Capt. Phogg's BCA, with Larry and I and one or two others flying paid passengers on an evening flight. The weather was perfect, with calm surface winds and a nice wind of 5–6 miles per hour at 500 feet and above. We flew east toward Lake Copneconic, which was only about one mile from the balloon port.

The student flying solo in the Michelob balloon took off last and was following the other four or five balloons. I took the perfect opportunity to do a "splash and dash." The calm conditions make touching down in the water and then taking off again easy and fun. You can set the basket down on the water and pretend you are a sailboat and let the gentle wind "sail" you across the water. All the other balloons did the same, so there were four or five balloons sailing ever so slowly across the lake.

The Balloonatics

The solo student, of course, decided to join us. He came down quick and realized it, so he poured tons of heat into the balloon and overburned, rising back up again about 200 feet. Trying once again, he came down too fast, but this time he did not realize it until it was too late. He poured tons of heat into the balloon just before he hit the water with an enormous splash!

He hit the water so hard, in fact, that the entire basket tipped over on its side and went completely underwater, and the skirt of the balloon came down far enough to touch the water. Luckily, he had put just enough heat into the envelope right before he crashed into the lake that it lifted the basket out of the water and brought it upright and sitting pretty, just like the rest of us.

He, however, came up shaking like a soaked dog after being completely submerged for a few seconds. The pilot lights for the burner were extinguished, and he was panicking! We all laughed hysterically after seeing him come up and realizing that he was okay.

Meanwhile, he realized he had to relight his pilot lights before the balloon cooled down and deflated on the water. He had lots of time but did not realize that and kept trying to relight the pilot lights with his soaked strikers. We used the same type of strikers to light our pilot lights that you might use to light your gas grill—ones that create a big spark when you pull the trigger. When soaked, they do not spark.

As luck would have it, I had just read an article in the Balloon Federation of America's monthly newsletter on how to remedy this exact scenario. It seems this sort of thing had happened before. The article said if your strikers get wet and will not spark, all you have to do is position the business end of said soaked striker over the main jets of the propane burner, open the blast valve that releases the propane that feeds the burner, and the propane will instantly freeze the water that is soaking the flint, thus drying it off. It will then create a spark again.

I was close enough to the soaked student pilot and his soaked basket that I first yelled over and calmed him down and then relayed the striker's drying instructions to him. He frantically performed the operation a few times before finally—*voilà*—a spark and relit pilot lights! Then he sheepishly thanked me and again poured heat into the envelope to take off from the lake and his humiliation.

He never told us how the rest of his flight went, but I remember him coming back very late after all our passengers were long gone. He walked in with his tail between his legs, still dripping water out of his shoes. We felt sorry for him, so we all helped him take apart his soaked flight instruments and radios to dry them out.

A few years later, that pilot earned the nickname "Major Voltage" when he hit power lines on New Year's Day. It happened during the Rose Bowl game while Michigan was marching down the field to score the winning touchdown. He flew through the lines while trying to land. Thank God no one got hurt, but I was told sparks were flying.

Unfortunately, his misfortune also resulted in a power outage for about 10,000 local homes and businesses. The local paper identified him as the culprit the following day. He received nasty threats from many University of Michigan football fans who missed the thrilling ending of the Rose Bowl and were without power on that chilly January day for quite some time. From then on, the two Michelob balloons were prohibited from flying on New Year's Day.

~ ~ ~

I was still living in one of the bedrooms up in the balloon port's loft when I returned from the bar late one evening. I decided to take a shower. As I was washing my hair, I heard someone storming in yelling, "Hands up! This is the police!" They opened the shower door, and I saw through my shampoo-stinging eyes two state troopers with guns drawn and pointing directly at me!

I exclaimed something like, "What the hell is going on?" They responded they had received a call from our alarm company reporting a break-in at the building. I said, "I did not break in; I live here." They decided I probably did not break in to take a shower and lowered their guns. Capt. Phogg had put in a new alarm system, and I had forgotten about it.

It was then decided that I probably needed to find my own place to live since things were going pretty well and I could now afford to do so. I agreed, and soon I was living on Lake Copneconic about one mile east of the balloon port. There was a small trailer park on the southwest side of the lake, owned by a delightful couple. The trailers were old and small but in good condition. I got one that was right on the lake next to the boat launch. It was tiny, but it was all I needed. It had lots of windows and was in excellent condition for its old age. And the rent was only $175 per month, including utilities!

~ ~ ~

September came, and Larry only logged six flights, with two being in St. Louis during the Forrest Park event flying the new silver Michelob Light balloon. I flew 21 times, 16 being local paid rides and training flights and five back in Statesville, North Carolina, defending my title from the year before at the Statesville National Balloon Rally.

I returned to the Statesville National Balloon Rally, which took place September 19–21. They paid us to attend again with the Tony the Tiger balloon, and again they filled me up on five flights with four paying passengers each flight. And again, the weather was perfect; we flew all five flights! This year, however, Michelle, her sister Karen, and her brother-in-law Scott came as my crew. The same local family from the year before was assigned as our local crew. I remember their young son asking me where Cindy was—the teacher he remembered who was my crew the year before. Apparently, he had grown fond of her at the previous year's event and was sad that she had not come back.

We had a blast at the event, and several things stand out in my memory, the first being the day before the event started on Thursday when we drove into town and could not find our hotel. We stopped and asked a local we saw on the road, and he gave us a long, drawn-out explanation on how to get there and kept saying it was a little bit "mis-deceiving." So that became our new word for the event every time something was a bit, well, "mis-deceiving."

One other funny thing happened when we were walking back from the field to our hotel after a successful evening flight and long post-flight champagne celebration. Karen copied the water balloon launcher we had seen some people using back at the field by taking off her bra and using it to launch small rocks in the parking lot behind the hotel. Michelle joined in, and it was just hilarious watching them sitting on the ground with their bras somehow attached to their feet and trying to see whose bra could shoot the rocks the farthest! They were double-shot bra launchers!

~ ~ ~

The flying was great, but the afternoons were very hot. Tony the Tiger again knew how to find all the targets, and I was in the lead going into the last flight, which was a fly-in to the airport to drop your bean bag on the X target. I remember that flight. It was hot. I was flying into the airport toward the target at about 800 feet, which gave me a great line to the target. Then I heard and saw a smaller balloon coming up under me real fast, much faster than he should have been, and much faster than the rules permitted for safety reasons.

I quickly realized that I had to climb as fast as I could to avoid him flying right up into our fully loaded basket. A long burn raised the envelope temperature to over 310 degrees. Raven envelopes had a maximum temperature rating of 250 degrees. Going over that called for an inspection of the envelope if the temperature monitors sewn onto the top of the envelope read 275 or above. We had to inspect Tony after that flight.

I finally started up, and we avoided a collision. However, the higher altitude brought me into a wind direction that was not ideal. I got really pissed off at that pilot for making me do that! Because of that evasive maneuver, I ended up descending toward the airport runway, about 100 yards to the right of the target.

I cursed that reckless balloon pilot all the way! (Under my breath, of course, but I pointed out to my passengers what had happened and that it most likely cost me the repeat championship.) I descended and decided to land on the runway 100 yards away and drop my marker there. When I came down over the runway, the air was still, and we just hung there for what seemed like a minute 10 feet over the runway on the center line.

We heard the announcer on the loudspeaker all the way in, telling the crowd, "Here comes Tony. He is in the lead coming into this flight." As we got closer and the announcer saw we were going to miss the target, he started saying, "Oh well, it does not look so good for Tony today."

I remained hovered 10 feet above the runway, then got a slight movement toward the grass at the other side. We then started ever so slowly moving sideways right down the edge of the runway toward the target! I held my altitude right there about 10 feet, and we kept creeping toward the target. In about five minutes, we had gone straight back down the runway toward the target and only had about another 50 yards to go. The announcer noticed, and he said, "Look at that! Tony has not given up. He seems to have a steering wheel in that basket and is steering right toward the target!"

It was an incredibly exciting next 10 minutes. The announcer got the crowd excited, and they started cheering us on. That crazy slight breeze on the surface kept inching me toward the target. Then it changed, but still in the direction down the runway. We crossed the runway to the other side but were still making headway and ended up in line with the target, about 100 feet away.

I knew that if I went up about 100 feet, the wind would take me right toward the target at that point. I ascended to about 100 feet and flew directly toward the target, descending to about 30 feet over the target with the announcer and crowd roaring their approval! I dropped my marker but was not happy with where it landed and was not sure if it would be good enough for a repeat win. The announcer kept saying, "How did he do that? He must have a steering wheel in that thing!"

After the flight, we refueled Tony and learned that I had indeed won the event again! What a thrill that was, and we all celebrated big time after that last flight! I won a five-day cruise for two and promised Michelle that we would take it together soon. After the awards ceremony, the event organizer told me he did not think they could justify paying us again to come and win the event. Sadly, we never went back.

~ ~ ~

After we returned from Statesville, I flew four more paid passenger flights in Fenton, and then we got ready to leave for Albuquerque once again.

The week before we left for Albuquerque, I met Jennifer. Larry and I were out at some bar in Flint just having a beer or three. I saw this incredibly beautiful lady walk by us. She sat down just a few seats away at the bar from where we were sitting. She was with a lady friend, and they were chatting away.

I told Larry that she was stunning and looked just like Tyra Banks, the famous model. He had not noticed her, but when he looked, he concurred. I went over and started talking with her. She was friendly, and we talked and laughed for a long time. I got her phone number.

I called her the next day and asked her out to lunch. We met at a restaurant and talked again for a long time. She worked part time as a fashion model and full-time for General Motors at one of the the auto factories in Flint.

When I told her I flew balloons, she said it sounded like fun. I told her we were going to Albuquerque next week, and she said she had never been there. Half kiddingly, I told her I had a round-trip ticket left over from last year when I won the Statesville National Balloon Rally and would be happy to give it to her if she wanted to join us.

She said she would consider that, thank you very much, and she would let me know as soon as possible. She called me the next day and said she could get the time off from work and would love to join me there. Wow, that was unexpected! But I was committed at that point.

Later that week, Larry and some of our crew drove the Tony the Tiger chase vehicle and balloon, and I drove our AX-9 ride balloon in the former Buick Balloon Chase vehicle with some crew to fly rides again in Albuquerque. We all checked into our rooms in Albuquerque on October 4th at the official hotel, the Holiday Inn. Jennifer flew in the next day.

The weather was not good that year for the Fiesta; we only flew four of the scheduled nine days. It actually snowed one night, and we all woke up to 4–6 inches of snow covering all the balloons, trailers, and chase vehicles in the parking lot! I flew 25 paid passengers, so the trip was a bust financially for BCA.

Jennifer got to fly on the last flight, as we only had five paying passengers. She always dressed to the hilt, and although I informed her about ballooning and Albuquerque and how to dress for it, I believe she had no such clothes. She wore heels all the time, and in them she was over six feet tall. I remember many people doing double takes as we walked around the balloon field that morning before and after the flight. I was not the only one who thought she was Tyra Banks!

We had a windy drag landing, and her foot and ankle got caught and wedged between a fuel tank and the basket. I had to help her get unstuck. She was a trouper and did not complain, but her foot and ankle were a bit bruised up.

Jennifer and I spent most of the Fiesta in the hotel room. Several of the crew members, as well as Larry and Capt. Phogg, said afterward that the only time they saw us was those four times that we flew. We had a fantastic time just "partying" in the room, as I recall, and once again there was as much "snow" flying inside as well as out.

One time Ron Pethick and another junior crew member, Mike, came to our room to visit. Jennifer and I were drinking and snorting lines. She was wearing a low-cut nightgown. When she bent over to do a line, Ron's and Mike's eyes about popped out of their heads! I was not an exemplary role model for those two young guys.

That year I did not return to the California desert to fly for Ron and Kinnie. Ron Frusher had gotten his commercial balloon pilot's license that summer, so he was planning to do all the piloting for their company in the desert. The timing could not have been better, as I needed to stay full time in Fenton and run the ride program I had started, which was growing larger every day.

~ ~ ~

In 1984, BCA had balloon ride revenue under $5,000. In 1985, the first year I started promoting Balloon Rides for BCA, the revenue was over $36,000. As of October 1986, we had more than doubled the previous year's total ride revenue, and I had a big Christmas Gift Certificate advertising and promotion campaign planned. I had my inexpensive lakeside rented trailer home and now planned to make Fenton, Michigan, my full-time residence.

I was being compensated for running the ride program with a whopping salary of $500 per month, $20 per passenger that I flew, and 10 percent commission on all ride sales. If I could achieve my goal of $100,000 in ride sales and fly 350 passengers myself, in addition to my salary, I would make a whopping $23,000! That seems like a pittance now, but back then it was not bad for a young single guy. I did not really consider it work at all but play, and I was loving it! Also, my living expenses were extremely low. Had I been fiscally responsible, I could have saved a good part of it.

~ ~ ~

After we drove back from Albuquerque, the last two weeks of October in Michigan blessed us with fantastic ballooning weather! I flew 10 flights and Larry six; we flew 71 paying passengers in those two weeks. And that was just us. We also subcontracted passengers out to several other pilots because we could only fly 10 passengers between us.

I was in for a big surprise that October on my birthday. We had hired one of our crew members from the crew club, Kim, to work in the office. She was a nice younger gal, maybe 18. We got along very well and flirted with each other all the time.

She threw a surprise birthday party for me at the end of October. She invited all the members of the Capt. Phogg Balloon Platoon, all our pilots, and anyone else she could think of, which included Cindy, Kelly, and Michelle. Luckily, she did not know about Jennifer, or I would have had four girlfriends at my surprise party!

I was extremely surprised, to put it mildly! Kim was just loving the drama and enjoyed seeing me squirm, trying to negotiate this dilemma. I had not known she was so devious!

In the end, everything turned out better than anyone could have expected. Cindy and Kelly could see that I was much more interested in Michelle. They both left early, and I never saw much of either of them after that night. I felt bad about it because they were very nice ladies. I truly liked them both very much!

November flying in Michigan is usually few and far between, and it was no different that year, with me only flying three times and Larry once. December was the same as usual. I flew twice, and Larry did the same. The Christmas Gift Certificate sales went great and kept me busy on the phones and mailing out gift certificates. I sold over $10,000 worth! Our total ride sales in 1986 was over $94,000.

~ ~ ~

In December, we received an invoice from the Albuquerque Balloon Fiesta for $1,000. It included a photo of our AX-9 ride balloon that I flew there in October four times. I had forgotten to remove the banner promoting Balloon Rides in Fenton from the balloon. I should have known to do so, but just never gave it any thought.

The banner said "Balloon Corporation of America—Rides" and the phone number. Denny (Capt. Phogg) called the powers that be at the Fiesta and convinced them we had made a big mistake, and we were sorry. They ended up dismissing it, thank goodness! We already had taken a big revenue loss on that trip since we only could fly four times.

Shortly after, Denny said to me that while he was looking at that photo with the banner, he realized we needed to "brand" our ride program. The obvious name should be simply "Capt. Phogg Balloon Rides." Balloon Corporation of America—Rides just did not cut it, and he was 100 percent correct.

Capt. Phogg had a strong reputation in our area and was synonymous with ballooning. Denny was a great salesman and promoter and had been flying and promoting ballooning in the area for about 20 years by then. "Capt. Phogg Balloon Rides" was the perfect name for the ride program.

That name recognition would help us stand above the very few competitors we had at the time and any more to come. Denny trademarked the name. It is still in use as of this writing in 2023 by the company who bought the franchise in Fenton, Michigan, where you can to this very day go for a "Capt. Phogg Balloon Ride."

1987

In January 1987, Capt. Phogg, his ex-wife, Laraine, Larry, and I flew to London, England. Denny had been working on a new project, manufacturing hot air balloons. We were going to Oswestry, England, to visit the Thunder & Colt balloon factory.

Before we left, Denny took Larry and me to a local Kmart store that back then sold just about everything we needed to get outfitted for the trip. He bought us all matching winter coats, boots, hats, gloves, and other warm-weather gear. We planned to meet some of the Thunder & Colt folks at the annual Icicles Balloon Meet the first weekend of January. The ongoing meet is known as the world's longest continual balloon meet.

We flew into London and rented a car. Walking to the car lot, I had the keys and asked, "Who wants to drive first?" Larry said he would, so I gave him the keys. We all squeezed into the tiny Ford Fiesta, barely fitting with our luggage. We sat there for a minute. "Here," Larry finally said as he gave me the keys. "Looks like you decided to drive after all."

Unknowingly I had sat down in the driver's seat, which would be the passenger seat in the United States. Driving out of the parking lot, I almost got into an accident right away! I turned into the oncoming traffic going the wrong way in the wrong lane, which would have been the right way in the correct lane in the good old USA! Soon I got the hang of it, and off we went.

~   ~   ~

Our first stop west of London in Bristol was the Cameron Balloon Factory, where Denny had arranged for a tour. Don Cameron himself graciously greeted us and gave us the tour. The amount of activity there was incredible. I remember little, except that we were highly impressed not only by the balloons and the factory but also by the hot-air airships, and I think they were also constructing a gas airship. With limited time, we toured briefly before heading to our hotel for the Icicles Meet, located west of Bristol.

The Icicles Meet hotel had an ancient feel, like the quaint town it was in. The English breakfasts at the hotel were fantastic, with tons of different breakfast meats, eggs, potatoes, tomatoes, and more. We sure needed the winter gear we had brought, since it was freezing, with a smattering of snow on the ground. The meet had a laid-back vibe, and I was invited to fly with two other pilots on the first morning.

The flight was spectacular over the old English countryside. We flew over many beautiful buildings and ancient castles. When the pilot began looking for a place to land, it took quite a while before he said he was landing in the field ahead. I was concerned, as that field ahead was nothing but mud, not very big, and had power lines running along the back end of it. He came in too late and began his descent into the back quarter of the field, heading for the power lines.

I almost jumped out! I literally came within two seconds of jumping as I thought we were going to hit the lines. That would have hurt, but not as bad as the lines, I thought, and if my 200 pounds exited, they would most likely then clear the lines. We were about 10 or 15 feet off the ground when, at the last moment, the pilot poured on the heat and I realized we would clear the lines, but not by much!

Ascending, we were carried left by the wind. The pilot vented hard to get into the next field, which had power lines running in our direction of travel. We were roughly 200 feet left of them at this moment. I thought, *This is good. He will land here.* A two-track trail was running along the lines, which would make an easy retrieve.

We came in nice, and at about 20 feet above the ground I expected him to pull the parachute top and land in the windy conditions. Instead, he burned, and we ascended again! About half a mile later, we crossed a road, and he landed right in the middle of a big dairy cow farm in the cow patties, scattering the cows and all! I could not believe it! Why had he done that? The farmer was unhappy, but I just stayed out of that mess and helped pack up carefully, trying to avoid as much manure as possible.

Later, we went to a local pub where they'd brewed their own beer for centuries. They called it "Weed Killer," and the signs on the wall advertising it said, "Weed Killer—It gets to the Roots." It really did, too: two pints and you were hammered! I told the story of my harrowing flight. I believe it was Chris Kirby from Thunder & Colt who had arranged for me to be on it. Chris must have chastised the pilot later, as he came up to me the next day and apologized for his poor performance.

~ ~ ~

Our next stop was Oswestry to visit Thunder & Colt. We set out Monday morning after the Icicles meet ended. Despite being just 150 miles north, the winding, narrow two-lane roads through tiny towns made the journey feel eternal, but it was truly enchanting. We were charmed by such beautiful scenery and ancient architecture along the way. We longed for more time to explore the countless incredible sights and towns.

The journey to Oswestry lasted the whole day. We stopped a few times to eat and change drivers. When we arrived at our bed and breakfast lodgings, we thought something was wrong. Remember, this was before GPS, so we were using maps and arrived at what looked like a castle! The vast land was enclosed by a fence, with an open gate adorned by a castle-like archway. We had to drive over a cattle bridge grate at the entrance, and we soon discovered why—the grounds were filled with hundreds of sheep.

We drove up the long and winding narrow road leading up to the castle and entered the huge front entrance doors. The place was ancient and just fantastic! I now think of it like the buildings in the movies of Harry Potter. The owners were a nice British couple who welcomed us and showed us to our sparse second-floor rooms.

Walking through the place was like stepping back in time 500 years. They informed us that breakfast would be served whenever we woke up and showed us the dining room as well. Turns out we were their only guests, as winter was not the tourist season. We were tired and decided to call it a night after having dinner at the recommended place in town.

Larry and I were in one room, while Denny and Laraine were in another down the hall. Larry and I woke up at sunrise to a freezing room. We could see our breath, and the wind blowing through the cracks around the ancient windows made the floor-length curtains billow about.

When we used the toilet, we discovered that there was no hot water either. We walked down the hall, knocked on Denny and Laraine's door, and walked into their room to find them huddling in bed with every blanket they could find over them. Both were fully clothed, with their winter coats and hats on! Their room was colder, with bigger windows, and curtains blowing like a flag.

We all went down for breakfast and found the entire castle was freezing. Denny chatted with the owner, who said it's normal to turn off the heat and hot water overnight and turn it back on in the morning. Denny objected, causing a brief argument. Eventually, the owner reluctantly agreed to ensure heat and hot water throughout our presence. From that point on, the owner always appeared gruff toward us.

~ ~ ~

We had a meeting scheduled at the Thunder & Colt factory at 9 a.m., so we left early and arrived around 8:30. A cheery receptionist greeted us and directed us to the small conference room to await our meeting.

The Balloonatics

She said she would let us know when the owner and president, Per Lindstrand, was ready to meet with us.

Another man, slightly older than Larry and me but younger than Denny, sat at the table in the conference room. He had longish, brownish-blond hair and a beard; he looked up as we entered and said hello. I remember walking up to him and introducing myself and shaking his hand as we all then said our introductions.

His name was Richard Branson. We had never heard of him. I said, "I see you are studying a balloon piloting book. Are you learning to fly balloons?" He said yes, he was a student pilot of Per's. We briefly engaged in small talk before he returned to studying.

A few minutes later, the receptionist called us out to meet with Per, and she was just giddy, exclaiming, "You shook his hand, you shook his hand!" Puzzled, we exchanged glances, questioning the fuss. It became clear later when Per told us about his plans to fly the Atlantic with that young entrepreneur. Per then gave us a tour of the factory and showed us the capsule and envelope they were building for that first-ever trans–Atlantic Ocean hot air balloon flight.

I do not remember a lot about our meetings with Per, Chris Kirby, Paul Dickinson, and his partners and employees. I know they treated us very well, and we thoroughly enjoyed our time with them. Negotiations went well, and we returned as USA Thunder & Colt distributors and future manufacturers.

~   ~   ~

One of my memories is of the trip we took with several of the Thunder & Colt guys to Wales, which is not far north of Oswestry. They took us to a tiny 900-year-old pub for lunch. We had to duck to walk in, as the doors and ceilings were very low. We were told that people were much shorter 900 years ago. The only place I could stand straight was at the 900-year-old wooden bar. It was so worn down that balancing a glass was difficult. We saw more incredible sights, but this ancient pub stands out in my mind.

I also recall the night Larry and I went out to the local bar that was recommended to us by one of the younger Thunder & Colt employees, someone about our age. We enjoyed local beer, danced, and met two local ladies who invited us to a speakeasy after the bar closed. This was interesting, as it was in someone's large house, and half the bar ended up showing up there after we arrived. It seemed like the whole town, including the police, knew about it, but they left it alone. We stayed briefly, then were invited to the ladies' flat with a few others.

One of the ladies was physically impaired and walked with crutches, and the other one seemed a bit odd, but they were both lovely and fun to be around. We ended up at their flat with a small group sitting around smoking hash and drinking some more.

Soon we realized it was extremely late and decided we had to get back to get some sleep. I remember driving back to our bed and breakfast castle VERY carefully in our little rental car, almost getting lost but somehow finding the way. As we entered our room, the sun attempted to peek over the horizon.

After a short sleep, Denny woke us up by pounding on our door, urging us to hurry. We devoured a bit of breakfast and went to the Thunder & Colt factory. I remember several of the guys there pointing at us and snickering as we arrived.

Later, when we were having lunch with a group of them, one of them spoke up and asked, "So how are the cripple and the nut doing?" and they all broke out laughing! Turns out some of them had also been at the bar and saw us leave with those two ladies, who apparently had quite a reputation around town. We never lived that one down.

Unfortunately, I remember little more about this wonderful trip, but I recall we had a fantastic time and our hosts at Thunder & Colt treated us like royalty. We really felt like we had formed a great bond and a start to a mutually rewarding working relationship and partnership.

The Balloonatics

~ ~ ~

We returned home and got to work at once. Capt. Phogg tasked Larry and me with calling every member of the Balloon Federation of America and introducing ourselves as the new Thunder & Colt distributors, soon to be manufacturers. As I recall, the BFA membership roster back then comprised approximately 4,500 members, so we had our work cut out for us. We stayed late trying to reach every member in the evening, which meant a late-evening call for us to the Pacific time zone. Calling everyone took months, leaving behind a trail of voicemails.

The reception we got varied widely and sometimes was downright hostile! The balloon camps were divided based on loyalty to their familiar brand and flying experience. It was crazy, but we had been like that a couple of years before, and even more so in the seventies when Larry and I learned to fly in Raven balloons. Denny had been one of Raven's first and longest-standing distributors. The folks at Raven and most of the other Raven distributors, dealers, and loyalists were the most vocal in their hostilities to our introductory phone calls! Our new venture sparked numerous conversations and generated immense interest. We never knew what to expect when dialing a number, so a friendly voice on the other end was a welcome relief.

~ ~ ~

That January, flights were typical of Michigan in the winter: few and far between. Larry flew zero times, and I flew twice. One of my flights was a lesson, and my logbook says we did 12 landings. Great training for Ken Baird, Andy's father. February flying weather was, as usual, just a bit better, with me doing three flights and Larry only six.

Larry flew at the Toledo Winterfest twice. He did two pilot training flights. He also flew two press flights in Fenton, flying our local newspaper reporter on one and the local TV station reporter on another to promote the ride business. I arranged these flights through the press releases that I was regularly mailing out, inviting the press to come out and experience ballooning.

My three flights comprised two pilot training flights and one commercial job with the Michelob Light balloon in downtown Flint. I tethered on a tiny bit of grass during an event and then flew away for a half-hour free flight with Michelle. Ron crewed for us, and I remember having to launch out of there real fast to clear all the buildings, and then we had a great winter flight. Packing up that heavy, thick silver fabric after the flight took forever in the just-below-freezing temperature.

~ ~ ~

Michelle and I were always together now. I had only seen Jennifer a couple of times since Albuquerque. Jennifer had told me she was looking for a husband and wanted to move back to her home state of Mississippi, start a big family, and work at her family's restaurant in Mississippi. I was not that guy for her, and we agreed to go our separate ways.

Michelle and I became inseparable, and I realized I was really in love with her. In February, we took the cruise I had won in Statesville. It sailed out of New Orleans and was a small, older cruise ship called the *Bermuda Star* that only held about 450 passengers.

The cruise was wonderful, and we called it the "geriatric" cruise because it was 90 percent senior citizens. We were by far the youngest passengers on the ship. Michelle said yes when I proposed to her on the cruise, after she had previously said no when I first asked her the past summer. When we sailed back into New Orleans five days later as a happy newly engaged couple, we walked up on deck and wondered what was going on.

The Balloonatics

The city was going wild. We asked a crew member who informed us it was the beginning of Mardi Gras. By chance, my parents were at a conference in New Orleans, so we met up with them, shared the exciting news, and joined the chaos! I remember we had only walked a few blocks when a parade was going by with a group of Hare Krishnas in it. I joined in with them, dancing down the street. Michelle must have been wondering what she had gotten herself into! Later, we decided on January 1988 for the wedding, just under a year away.

When we returned from the cruise, the March weather was bad. Larry only flew one paid passenger flight. I flew one paid ride—my logbook says "Great Winter Flight"—and one pilot lesson, and I took the Buick Olympic Balloon to Crown Buick in Winston-Salem, North Carolina. There I flew one free flight and did one tether. We both continued to call through the Balloon Federation of America's membership roster and finished that task by the end of April. April weather was not much better, as I flew only six flights and Larry only two.

~ ~ ~

One issue I have always had problems with was going in too many directions at once. My dad always told me, "Stick to your knitting," which basically meant concentrate on and complete the task at hand before going on to another one. I often head off on another project before completing the one at hand. This happened with a new idea of mine, the Grand Traverse Resort Balloon Ride Program.

Michigan is home to the Great Lakes and truly is, in my humble opinion, one of the most spectacular places on earth. Because it is home to 20 percent of the world's fresh water, you are never more than six miles from a body of fresh water or 85 miles from one of the Great Lakes. One of the true gems is the Traverse City area and its two enormous bays off Lake Michigan. Traverse City is known for growing the greatest number of sour pie cherries in the United States and is billed as "The Cherry Capital of the World." Torch Lake, which is just a few miles northeast of Traverse City (and is not one of the five Great Lakes), is rated as one of the 10 most beautiful lakes in the world.

I had learned about a huge new resort being built just outside of Traverse City from articles in the newspapers and travel magazines I used to advertise Capt. Phogg Balloon Rides. The area was the largest and most popular tourist area in Michigan. There were no other balloon ride companies anywhere close by.

I knew it would be an incredibly beautiful place to fly, although I had not flown there yet, and I thought it would be the perfect place to expand Capt. Phogg Balloon Rides. (The program was really just getting started, so I should have concentrated on continuing to build it first before any thought of expanding.) I had begun negotiations with the management of the new Grand Traverse Resort (referred to as GTR from now on).

We came to an agreement, and the program began in the summer of 1987. The resort would sell and help promote the rides from their concierge's desk and promote it through other publications and ads that they ran regularly. They got a percentage of the ticket price of $175 per person. (We also raised our price in Fenton to $175 that year.)

We flew from the GTR property in Acme, Michigan, right next to the resort. The place is all first class and beautiful, 17 stories tall with a gold glass exterior. On the top floor is a five-star restaurant and bar that offers incredible views of the entire area. It proved to be the most beautiful and challenging area to fly that I ever encountered. Water dominates, with Lake Michigan and the bays dictating sudden weather shifts.

I began by taking the general manager and her staff on the first flight from GTR on May 1st, 1987. An "equipment mistake" delayed the flight by one week. I had traveled 150 miles from Fenton to the resort the weekend before with a crew member, Royston, to do the flight. We stayed overnight, and the next morning, the weather was perfect. I called the general manager around 4 a.m. to wake her up with the good news, and she called the rest of her staff. We all met at 6 a.m. in the GTR lobby for our preflight briefing.

Everyone was so excited, especially me, as it was also my first flight in the area. At the launch site, Royston and I began to set up the AX-9 Raven six-passenger-plus-pilot balloon. Excitement filled the air, and some passengers showed signs of first-time jitters.

As Royston and I laid the basket over on its side, opened the top of the envelope bag, and pulled out the load blocks that attach to the basket, I panicked! I realized something was not right. The envelope's colors were wrong. Additionally, there were only two load blocks for all the cables. This big basket required a four-point hookup with four load blocks.

Due to our haste, we had neglected to double and triple check the equipment loaded on the truck the day before. We had brought an incorrect envelope that wouldn't attach to the basket. I was in shock and embarrassed beyond belief!

That spring, Ron Pethick was assigned the job of equipment manager. The day before our departure for GTR, he used the Hi-Lo to transfer the basket and envelope from the industrial racks to the garage floor. He then backed the truck next to them and came in and asked me to help him load them on the truck. I was in the middle of something, so I rushed out to help and then ran back in without paying attention to what I was loading.

The envelope bags were all the same. The only differences were in size and weight. I should have noticed that the 77,000-cubic-foot envelope bag we loaded was lighter and smaller than the 140,000-cubic-foot one we should have loaded. However, I paid it no mind, figuring Ron was in charge of this and knew what he was doing.

I used that excuse when I broke the news to my excited passengers. "My new equipment manager sent us up here with the wrong balloon envelope," I said. "We cannot fly. I am so sorry and so embarrassed!" They all were very gracious, and some actually said they were a bit relieved. I did not get my head chewed off by the general manager as I thought I was going to!

We rescheduled for the next weekend and retreated to Fenton with our tails between our legs to load up the correct envelope next time. Poor Ron got blamed, and he felt terrible. I told him and Denny that it was really my fault because I was the pilot, and ultimately it was my responsibility to double check that I had all the correct equipment before I left for any job. Then Ron and I went out to the garage and used permanent markers to label each envelope bag. We also put a tag on each one, clearly marking what balloon was in each envelope bag.

~ ~ ~

The next weekend, we returned to GTR with the correct balloon envelope, and on May 1st we had a fantastic flight with the general manager and her staff. This flight completely sold them all on the balloon ride program. On May 6th, I flew six of the concierges who would be selling the rides from the concierge's desk in the resort's lobby. We again had a fantastic flight, this one windier than the first.

We landed 15 miles away on the southeast side of Torch Lake. We flew over the lake, and I saw a big hayfield in my path that looked like a perfect landing spot. Michelle was my crew and had another concierge riding along with her as a navigator. Unfortunately, that person did not tell Michelle that she had to work that morning. During the chase, she informed Michelle that she needed to go to work and asked her to drop her off so she could hitchhike back.

Michelle was now on her own. I radioed her that we were going to land on the southeast side of Torch Lake. She glanced at her map and headed north on the road on the west side of Torch Lake. Turns out she was a bit "directionally challenged." Had she continued on the road she was on, which ran east and west along the south side of the lake, and then taken the road north on the east side of the lake, she would have been right there when we landed.

Her wrong turn forced her to drive north along the lake's west side, then around the north side and down the east side to reach us. Torch Lake is 19 miles long, running north and south. She spent an hour searching for us, so we waited in the field for a while after landing. Michelle recalls there was a song on the radio playing with the lyrics, "I'll never do this again."

I walked up to the farmhouse where we had landed. They were very nice and excited about the amazing new event on their property. Using their phone, I called in our location to the "lost balloon" number, and Michelle found a pay phone on the north end of Torch Lake to do the same. It was not a big deal, as we all were reveling in the beauty we had just experienced and discussed the events of the "miraculous" breezy landing as well.

It was indeed the most miraculous thing that ever happened to me on any landing. The hay was about three feet tall where we landed, and just after we touched down and started our 100-foot drag in the wind, I noticed the disc in our path. The disc had been hidden in the field by the hay, but now I saw it and was instantly horrified! We were dragging with the basket tipping over at 10 to 12 miles per hour straight into a 20-foot-long, two-and-a-half-foot-tall steel disc that is used to plow the fields! I started both praying and saying out loud—and asking my passengers to say it with me—"Left, left, left, go left!!!"

When we were about 25 feet from crashing into it, having slowed to about six or eight miles per hour, we miraculously curved around it to the left, then curved back right, and ended up on the other side of it about 50 feet later! It was as if a giant hand had reached down and pushed us around the thing! Passengers didn't know why I had told them to think left until we crawled out of the basket and retraced our path.

There was a clear path of tamped-down hay starting about 50 feet before the disc heading straight for it. Around 25 feet in front of the disc, the path veered left around it, only to veer back right and end up 50 feet directly behind it! Hitting the disc probably would have caused injuries, likely ending the program.

~ ~ ~

After that tenuous beginning, the program began in earnest. I made several more introductory flights with GTR personnel, and on May 24th I flew our first paid passenger ride from GTR. The next morning, on the 25th, I found out how unpredictable things could be up there on Grand Traverse Bay.

I was flying four more GTR personnel on a comp introductory flight, and the forecast was for normal light winds out of the southwest. These were the prevailing winds for the area and was the best direction for flight. As soon as I launched that morning, we flew straight for the 17-story GTR tower instead of away from it. The winds were going almost 180 degrees opposite of the forecast.

Today, balloon pilots commonly utilize a small helium-filled balloon (called a pi ball) to assess wind patterns before flying. Not doing that then was a major mistake, especially with the vast bodies of water in the bays to the west-northwest of GTR. I had to blast both burners full on to clear the tower, which I barely did, passing it by about 200 feet north of the top of the tower.

A passenger captured a great shot of the balloon's reflection in the gold glass of the tower as we passed too closely. We took off west-northwest over the East Bay, and I radioed to Michelle that our flight path was going in the opposite direction than planned. She had to go the other way around the bay, on the south side, and wait for further directions.

The Mission Peninsula is a jewel of land only about three miles wide on average, stretching almost straight north for 18 miles and separating the East and West Grand Traverse Bays. The East Bay is approximately five miles wide where we were crossing, and the West Bay another six miles wide. My immediate goal as we flew out over the East Bay was to land on the peninsula.

As we flew on over the big water, I kept looking north, which went on and on forever, it seemed, into Lake Michigan. I kept looking to make sure we were heading farther west than north. Had we started veering farther north, I might have had to radio Michelle to call the Coast Guard.

We continued to fly at a good pace, mostly west, so I was not too concerned. Within a short 15 minutes, a male resort employee expressed an urgent need to pee. There were four guys, including me, and one gal in the basket, and we all laughed. I said over the side if you must, so he did.

As we approached the peninsula, I noticed we were moving along at around 10 to 12 miles per hour and decided I needed to find just one open field to stick a landing in. All we saw as we sped over the three miles were trees and vineyards. Cherry trees and grape vineyards cover the Mission Peninsula.

I radioed Michelle and instructed her to head to the west side of the West Bay, then go north along the shore. This time she had a local who stayed with her, so she was doing well. We flew across the West Bay, continuing on a good west-northwest track.

As soon as we crossed over the road on the west shore, there appeared a nice landing field that was shielded from the wind by tall trees. I dropped in, and we did a nice stand-up landing. The passengers said it was great, but they would rather have flown over land as we had been over water for over 90 percent of the flight! I heartily agreed with them.

~   ~   ~

On the 29th I flew a press flight to promote the rides from the Grand Traverse Resort with several press outlets. The next day we were all over the news, including a large front-page photo and article in the largest newspaper, the *Traverse City Record-Eagle*.

Meanwhile, back in Fenton, Larry had been flying paid passenger rides and pilot training flights. He also returned to the Alabama Jubilee event in Decatur, Alabama, where we had gone with Dr. Hall years ago. This time he took the Buick Olympic Balloon and did a three-hour tether on May 22 and a 1.5-hour free flight May 23rd.

~ ~ ~

Sometime around the last week of May, I met Jeff Geiger. He was a local, born and raised in the Traverse City area. Jeff had just returned from Palm Springs, California, where he had been training and had received his hot air balloon pilot's license. He had returned home with a balloon to start his own balloon ride company. We were both surprised, caught off guard, and I am sure he was not happy that we had just started our division of Capt. Phogg Balloon Rides two weeks earlier!

This was uncomfortable for both of us, to put it mildly. We both now had competition that we had not expected or planned for. He named his company Grand Traverse Balloons. On June 4th, Jeff and I flew together, and in the two balloons we took up a bunch of airport control tower employees from the local Cherry Capital Airport. I also flew a local reporter and cameraman from the local television station, TV 9&10. On June 9th, I flew another press flight with more local newspaper reporters and a TV camera man.

Michelle had been with me all along as my crew chief since we began the GTR program. BCA rented a two-bedroom apartment two miles south of GTR for the pilot and crew to live in, and she was being paid to crew. We had just started the program and were not flying every day, so Michelle took a job at the resort as a waitress in the five-star restaurant at the top of the tower, called the Trillium. When not flying, I was busy promoting the program. Michelle was waitressing midday for lunch so she could be available to crew early mornings and evenings for our flights.

Since we now had two locations, we also needed another pilot. I reached out to my buddy Ron Frusher in California, and he agreed to come spend the summer in Michigan flying for us this time. Ron flew with Larry in Fenton to start the season. Later, he flew on and off in Traverse City while I worked on commercial jobs with the Buick and Tony the Tiger balloons. Michelle stayed in Traverse City to crew for Ron Frusher when I was not there. She also continued to work as a waitress at GTR. She was and still is a very dedicated and hard worker!

The Capt. Phogg Balloon Classic took place June 13th and 14th and again was a success with good flying weather, but it was the first one I had missed since we started going back in 1976. I was in Traverse City watching the wind blow and only flew three times before Ron Frusher came up and relieved me. Larry was busy in Fenton flying rides and lessons and working on the Capt. Phogg Classic, helping to organize it and flying in it.

~ ~ ~

We also took delivery of our first Thunder & Colt 160 in June, a 160,000-cubic-foot envelope with a large T-partitioned basket (like the one I flew in with Dan Glick in CA a few years before). Larry flew it on its maiden flight on June 19th with Capt. Phogg and several other pilots. He also tethered Tony the Tiger in Grand Rapids at the Gerald Ford Museum on June 22nd and flew the T&C 160 again on June 23rd with five paying passengers and Capt. Phogg. The logbook says, "1st splash and dash lesson in 160, didn't go well."

They billed the 160 as an eight-passenger-plus-pilot balloon. Its T-partitioned basket had wicker walls inside, dividing it into three sections. One section was designated for the pilot and fuel tanks, while the other two were designated for up to four passengers each. This was a new and novel concept then. The size of the basket amazed most balloonists.

We regularly flew eight passengers plus pilot in the 160s back then but soon realized that such a load was pushing the limits on an envelope of that size. Unless the ambient air temperatures were cool, you would have to fly the balloon very hot, and they did not last too long that way. Soon, we realized that we needed to increase the envelope size to 180,000 cubic feet, but that didn't happen until a few years later.

~ ~ ~

Mid-June I took the Buick Olympic Balloon to Middletown, Connecticut, sponsored by Town & Country Buick. Ron Frusher went to Traverse City to fly from GTR. Town & Country Buick had several big promotions centered on the Buick-sponsored Hartford Open Golf Tournament at the TPC Golf Course in Cromwell, Connecticut, about five miles north of the Town & Country Buick dealership in Middletown. Alan Clark came with me as my crew chief. Ron Pethick was to fly in to relieve Alan later in the week. This trip turned out to be quite an adventure and certainly had its ups and downs!

Alan and I drove to Middletown, and on June 18th we tethered in the morning for two and a half hours at Town & Country Buick in the parking lot. We arrived the day before and met the owner/general manager, George. As usual, we had to convince him that tethering was no fun, and he could garner a lot more press coverage from flying. He said he wanted to see how both worked.

The evening of the 18th, I free-flew from the dealership with two of the employees who had helped us tether that morning. Ideal winds allowed me to fly and land at the TPC golf course in Cromwell, where the upcoming Hartford Open was to take place. The weather did not allow a flight again for a couple of days. On the 20th, we took the balloon to the University of Connecticut to tether it for the Special Olympics there.

Again, we had a few days' weather delay, during which George continued to treat us like royalty, taking us out to dinner and constantly asking if there was anything else we needed or something he could do for us. We received great treatment from everyone there! On the 24th and 25th, I once again flew from the dealership parking lot with employees. On one flight, George joined me, and three times in a row, the winds again allowed me to fly to and land on the TPC golf course. After the third time, the golf course general manager asked me to stop doing that. He said he did not want us landing there during the tournament.

George began flying with me on every subsequent flight. He also told me he wanted to get his pilot's license and buy a balloon for his dealership! I was genuinely excited about the prospect and the potential commission I could earn on the sale. George bought a logbook, and we logged several hours of flight time during the next four flights we took over the TPC course during the Hartford Open the 28th and 29th.

On the morning of the 28th, we conducted two quick 30-minute flyovers. Later that evening, we flew over the TPC again and continued for another hour. As the breeze picked up, we covered a substantial distance, and I informed George that it was time to land soon.

We started looking for landing spots, and after a while he said we'd better land before we cross the road about a mile ahead of us, because after that road there was nothing but forest and Dead Man's Swamp for miles and miles. We located a landing spot at the final farm prior to the road. Finally, we landed between the apple trees in their orchard only 100 yards from the road before the forest and Dead Man's Swamp!

Earlier, during the lull in the action when the weather did not allow us to fly for two days, George invited Alan and me to go out for the day on his yacht, which he docked at the local Yacht Club on the Connecticut River. It was a big boat! The 40-footer accommodated six people, and we had a great time on the river. Unfortunately, we had too much fun and drank too much.

George started a game of looking for other boats with pretty girls on them. He would motor up behind them, then I would go out on the front gangplank and moon them in hopes they would respond by dropping their tops. It worked a couple of times, but a few were just pissed off. I suspect the latter had not had as much to drink as we had.

We returned to his slip at the Yacht Club somehow, having avoided being arrested, and he ordered dinner for us on the boat. We, being in the state we were in, continued to pour it on and got so drunk that we all passed out. I had totally forgotten that Ron was flying in the next morning to relieve Alan. I was supposed to bring Alan to the airport to fly home and pick up Ron.

Alan woke up first and, realizing the time, tried in vain to wake me up. It turns out that Alan was locked out on the deck while George and I had passed out in the bunks below deck. I finally heard Alan banging on the locked door and awoke. We rushed to the airport, where poor Ron Pethick had been waiting for three hours.

Alan had to wait another six hours for the next flight as we had missed his as well. I felt terrible both from the hangover and my dereliction of duty and was thoroughly and rightly chastised by Ron and Capt. Phogg. George never bought a balloon. I contacted him regularly for months, but nothing resulted from it.

~ ~ ~

Ron Pethick and I returned to Fenton, where things were buzzing! A large building addition was being planned for the production of

The Balloonatics

Thunder & Colt Balloons, US. We had two Capt. Phogg Balloon Ride locations flying passengers every day the weather cooperated. Also, the Buick Olympic, Tony the Tiger, and Michelob balloons were being flown at many events.

Larry took the Buick Olympic Balloon to the Battle Creek International Championships and flew on July 16th and 17th. I returned to Traverse City and Ron Frusher back to Fenton to fly paid rides. I flew 10 paid rides from GTR all of July, which was a big disappointment. Sales at GTR were not going as well as we had expected. Fenton's ride sales soared, and more flights were able to be flown due to better weather.

The weather reared its ugly head at GTR on July 21st. My parents had rented a house at the tip of Mission Peninsula for a week, and my three younger sisters and their spouses and kids all came to stay with them. Michelle and I drove our balloon chase van there that day, and we all spent a wonderful sunny day on the beach.

Around 4 p.m., I called the FAA Flight Service Station to get a weather briefing for the flight we had scheduled at GTR at 6 p.m. We had not flown for four days, so I was excited about flying that evening as the weather looked perfect, although hot. With a positive forecast from Flight Service, I contacted the GTR concierge's desk to relay the message to passengers: The flight is confirmed; meet us at 6 p.m.

Michelle and I packed up our stuff and started driving down the 18-mile-long peninsula to pick up the balloon trailer and go flying. We got almost to the end of the peninsula when all hell broke loose! Suddenly, the winds came up, and tree limbs started falling around us. I thought the van would blow over!

Thank God I was able to pull over into the large parking lot of a church away from any large trees and pointed the van into the wind to keep it from blowing over. It was nuts! Rain and hail soon began pelting us; it was so loud it sounded like a freight train was going through the van. Strong gusts lifted our van, almost tipping us over.

It lasted only 20 minutes, then it ended. The rain and hail stopped, the winds slowly subsided, and the sun came out! We navigated through numerous fallen trees and branches on our way to the apartment, resulting in a lengthy journey. We had to turn around twice and go a different route when trees blocked roads.

Two people lost their lives in that freak storm when their boat capsized on the West Bay. It was a miracle the death toll was not higher. If the unexpected storm had arrived a few hours later and the balloon was airborne, we might have made the list.

~ ~ ~

After my surprise wrong-way flight across both bays back in May, I started seriously looking for different places to start our flights from, depending on the actual direction of the winds. I found several and started using them when needed. One flight in August, I flew from a site in Elk Rapids, about 10 miles north of GTR, and landed in the parking lot of Tom's Supermarket, which was across the street from the entrance to GTR. I basically hugged the east coast of the East Bay most of the flight.

On August 8th, I launched from GTR and flew a fantastic flight pretty much straight east over Lake Skegemog and the vast swamp on its east side. Our fuel was running low due to a long time in the air on a hot day. The sun was setting, and I was unsure if we would cross the swamp because of calm winds.

With the sun setting, we finally crossed and found the only landing spot available. I kept at treetop level, as that was the only breeze I could find. As we crossed over the tree line into the small field, I descended, and our direction changed 180 degrees. We slowly backed up into the trees. I had the basket about 10 feet below the tops of the trees at this point, and as we slowly drifted back into them, a limb reached out and knocked off my glasses. They fell onto the basket floor.

The Balloonatics

Fortunately, a few residents of the nearby house came out to witness our landing. I yelled we needed them to grab our drop line and pull us out of the trees into the opening, which they did. We never found one of my glasses lenses. Michelle could not find us for about 45 minutes. I kept the balloon inflated for easier location, and it glowed after the sun set. She finally found us, and we packed up in the dark, fighting the mosquitoes.

~ ~ ~

August weather was better than July had been in Traverse City, and I flew 10 flights by the 13th. Then I returned to Fenton, and Ron Frusher came back up to Traverse City. On August 20th, I flew our new T&C 160 with eight passengers and loved it!

That was a game changer, being able to fly eight in one balloon, since the Capt. Phogg Balloon Rides program in Fenton was selling very well. Now we had one eight-passenger, one six-passenger, one four-passenger, and several two-passenger balloons to fly. Many times, we had three or four balloons flying 18 to 20 passengers at a time.

~ ~ ~

September was a great weather month in Fenton. With the new eight-passenger balloon plus our other smaller ones, we flew over 150 paying passengers that month. The ride sales in Traverse City were not going well, and the weather was not allowing many flights.

One of my most memorable flights took place in Fenton on September 2nd when I flew the new eight-passenger T&C with my grandmother and grandfather on board! They absolutely loved it, and I vividly remember the smiles on their faces during that wonderful experience.

Another memorable one was the maiden flight of the Fiesta America Balloon N-775TC, which we were giving away at the upcoming

Albuquerque International Balloon Fiesta. We had been promoting and selling these AX-7, 77,000-cubic-foot sport balloons and donated one to the Fiesta as the grand prize. I got to fly its maiden flight to help promote that giveaway.

In October, Larry, Denny, and a few new additions to Balloon Corporation of America took a new T&C 160 balloon, along with several other new T&C balloons, to Albuquerque. They had a large display tent to promote balloon sales and the new manufacturing facility being completed in Fenton. I stayed home in Fenton to run and fly the ride program.

We had a very successful year with Capt. Phogg Balloon Rides in Fenton. Ride sales, including over $20,000 in Christmas Gift Certificate sales in November and December, totaled over $134,000. However, the GTR program was a big disappointment. I do not recall the total sales, but I know they were way below expectations.

The T&C debut in Albuquerque, I was told, was a great success. Larry flew our T&C 160 all nine days, taking up many other balloon pilots on demo flights, and several of them placed orders for one of their own. Also, Ron Pethick earned his private balloon pilot's license during the Fiesta that year flying in the Tony the Tiger balloon with Capt. Phogg.

1988

On January 23rd, 1988, Michelle and I were married! She decided on that date so I could never forget our anniversary date, 1-2-3. I still forgot the year sometimes. It was a fantastic ceremony, with Larry as my best man. Larry and Gretchen had gotten married a few months before.

The reception was a blast, even though Michelle had asked me not to drink. I had a ton of fun without alcohol and should have taken notice of that fact. Also, one of my old high school and hockey buddies surprised me with a gram of cocaine as a private wedding gift, so I didn't really need alcohol. I am so sad to admit this. I was an idiot. Only he and I were the wiser.

We did not take a big fancy honeymoon trip but returned to my little trailer on Lake Copneconic. My logbook shows I flew a paid ride the next weekend, on January 28th. Soon thereafter, we bought a little 800-square-foot house in Burton, Michigan, and settled into our wonderful, now 35-years-plus marriage.

Michelle was working part time at Balloon Corporation of America in the office, helping with the ride program, ground crewing, and anything else that needed to be done. The flying weather must have been awful that winter. Larry and I combined logged only five flights the entire first three months of 1988.

~ ~ ~

On April 8th, Michelle and I went up to Traverse City to fly a media flight for TV 9&10 to promote the TV 9&10 Balloon Classic that was to take place in July during the Cherry Festival in Traverse City. The Cherry Festival is a huge annual event, and we had been working with TV 9&10 to start a Balloon Event in Traverse City. TV 9&10 wanted it to be first class and, as the main sponsor, paid BCA $50,000 to put on the event.

Ron Frusher did not come back to fly for us again that summer. We hired Carol Ross from Arizona to take over piloting the GTR ride program. On May 30th, I took Carol, Michelle, and Seth, who was to be Carol's crew chief, up for Carol's introductory flight from GTR, and the next day Carol and I and three new GTR concierges flew again.

I did not know that Carol had a fear of water, but she told me then, and I did not know what to say or think. Michelle and I returned to

Fenton after helping Carol get settled into the apartment we had rented for her. She ended up doing a great job flying for us up there, although the ride sales and the weather again did not live up to expectations.

~ ~ ~

Larry took Tony the Tiger to the Philadelphia Balloon Race in May. In June, the Capt. Phogg Classic took place. Two things stand out in my mind from the 1988 Capt. Phogg Classic. The first is that only one pilot flew on Saturday's afternoon flight. It was very windy, and everyone else elected to stay on the ground while a bunch of us helped launch this one daredevil and his passengers. They flew over 20 miles on a one-hour flight and had an exciting landing! The flight earned that pilot the nickname "The Human Pi Ball," after the small balloon pilots use to test the winds.

Later that evening, most of the balloons took part in an after-dark balloon glow. Unfortunately, a torrential downpour caught us all by surprise. Thunder and lightning turned it into a very exciting time as all the balloon crews scrambled to deflate and pack all the now-soaked balloons. I remember seeing large sparks flying, looking like tiny lightning bolts between the silver Michelob Light and the black Michelob balloon envelopes while they were touching just before all hell broke loose. That event was thereafter called "The Electric Soggy Phoggy Balloon Glow."

Larry again took the Tony the Tiger balloon to the Mississippi Balloon Championships the first four days of July, and this year he won the event! While Larry was in Mississippi with Tony winning the State Championship (Tony really knows how to find the targets!), the rest of us were in Traverse City for the TV 9&10 Balloon Classic held in conjunction with the annual Cherry Festival.

~ ~ ~

As usual, we lucked out, and the weather in Traverse City was perfect for every flight. However, 1988 was a terrible drought year in the Midwest, and everything was brown in July. We flew like crazy that year, but it was hot and dry and brown. The videos of the Balloon Glow at the Cherry Capital Airport tell the tale of the magical event we were able to host with the generous sponsorship of TV 9&10. (See the videos at www.theballoonatics.com.)

So many great things happened at that event I could almost write a book just about it. One of them was that Scott Lorenz sponsored the first Chinese Balloon Team to come to America. Ours was the first event they attended and the first time they flew their Chinese-built balloon in America. I remember hearing from some pilots that the balloon was good except for the fuel system, which they said was dangerous.

Another cool thing was that the astronaut Jack Lousma was a distinguished guest of Capt. Phogg. Michelle flew with just the three of them in the original Tony the Tiger balloon over the East Bay to the target at GTR. Denny let her fly the balloon for quite some time after giving Mr. Lousma some burner time first. Michelle recalls that she flew the balloon up to 7,000 feet above the East Bay! Michelle and I were the Co-Balloon Meisters and wish we had a video of the awards ceremony, which was hilarious. Somehow, we both kept putting our feet in our mouths and cracking up the room!

~ ~ ~

In mid-July, Denny, Larry, and I, along with a bunch of crew members, attended the Battle Creek International Championships in Battle Creek, Michigan, again. This time we took one of our new T&C 160s to demo as well as Tony the Tiger. I flew the Buick Olympic Balloon and was competing; I did well in scoring the first two days.

The third flight I asked for help from some "experienced" competitors, as it was a judge-declared goal and I was not sure how to find the targets on the map. I, along with several of those I asked for help and some others who were not in our group, ended up flying to the wrong targets! Although I scored very well, it did not count as the actual targets were a mile away.

I could not believe it as I flew into the intersection at what we thought was the first target and saw nothing. Oh well, so much for my great hopes of winning or even placing in the top 10. Had I scored well that day, I may have been in the money, as I scored well in two of the next three flights.

The evening competition flight on the 13th was cancelled because the winds did not calm down soon enough. All flights from the airport field were also cancelled. However, anyone who wanted to do a fly-in to entertain the crowds was allowed to do so.

Larry had arranged to fly some of his family along with three members of the US Army Parachute Team, the Golden Knights, that evening. When they gave the go-ahead to fly in, he asked me to be part of the crew. We scrambled to get everyone together and get going.

By the time we had found a good launch site that would allow us to ascend quickly to 5,000 feet and be over the airport to drop the Golden Knights, who were going to land on a target at the airport, it was getting late. By the time we hastily inflated and the balloon was ready to go, it was very late. I worked the crown line and expected to drive chase, but when I brought the line to the basket and handed it to Larry, he said, "get in." I looked at my watch; it was 8:55, sunset was at 9:20, and I said, "No, you need to go up fast now." He said, "Get in, chicken. I'll need your weight after dropping these guys," or something to that effect, so I got in, and off we went.

Larry blasted us up as fast as the balloon would go and then descended rapidly directly above the airport. The entire time since coming on board, one of the Golden Knights sat on the floor of the basket, with the other two laughing hysterically at him for being afraid of the balloon! We were amazed, and to this day, he remains the only

The Balloonatics

passenger I have ever flown with who stayed seated and scared until he jumped out. He couldn't wait, and was the first one to exit when Larry gave the okay at 5,000 feet directly above the airport target.

The time was 9:10 p.m. We were in a rapid descent when the three of them jumped, and we leveled out at about 6,000 feet. Then we began another rapid descent; we had to land in 10 minutes as the FAA was right there; sunset was at 9:20, and the rules for balloons are to land before sunset. We had a Thunder & Colt banner that was only pinned to the envelope at the four corners. It was a form-fitting banner and looked good on the balloon, but the balloon had no Velcro on it, so the four corner pins were the only fasteners holding it on.

As Larry put us into a terminal descent, I was told later by some friends watching on the ground at the airport that the envelope looked like a question mark, and the banner was flopping so much that they thought it had come off the envelope! It was amazing that it did not. Larry expertly halted our terminal descent 100 feet above the ground. We just happened to be right over a large schoolyard about one mile from the airport, where we made a nice, gentle landing at exactly 9:20 p.m.!

~ ~ ~

We spent August, September, and October flying a lot of paid rides as the drought that year continued to provide more flight opportunities than usual. I remember one flight in August on a sultry morning. We had five balloons flying, three with paid rides and two new pilots flying with us.

The "Human Pi Ball" flew a lot of the ride balloons with us. He and I were flying side by side over a decimated brown corn field at about 100 feet, moving along at about 8 to 10 miles per hour. Two deer were running along in front of us toward a tree line at the end of the field. We crossed it just behind the deer and watched the doe jump over the fence and the buck just behind her trip on the fence, go tumbling head over heels, and not get up. He struggled to get up, but to no avail. We both noted where he lay.

After the flight was done and all the passengers had left, we wanted to find the deer and see what had happened. We figured it had broken its neck in the fall and that we would find it dead. We called the state police first to see if we needed a permit to harvest it if we found it. When we told the officer the story over the phone, he started laughing and said, "Well, we do not have a balloon deer kill permit, but I would be happy to give you a roadkill permit," and then he said just to go get it and not to worry about it.

We went to the farmhouse behind which it had happened and told the owners, who gave us permission to go back and look. We found it lying in the same spot. It tried to get away when it spotted us but could not get up. We realized it had broken its neck or back, and we put it out of its misery. First, we hog-tied its legs so it would not kick us, and I slit its throat, which quickly killed it. We then dragged it out to our truck and took it to a butcher shop to have it processed. We now call that the "Balloon Deer Kill Flight."

One morning I woke up and looked outside to see the entire little front yard of our Burton house covered with "for sale" signs and toilet paper covering the entire house and both balloon trailers! I knew it was Ron's doing, but he would not admit it.

~ ~ ~

The Thunder & Colt manufacturing team again went to Albuquerque, including Capt. Phogg and the Tony the Tiger balloon. I stayed home to run the ride program, selling and flying paid rides. One great thing that happened in Albuquerque in 1988 was that Ron Pethick earned his commercial balloon pilot's license flying in the replica Virgin Transatlantic Crossing balloon with Chuck Rohr.

The Balloonatics

Another flight I remember happened October 22nd, as noted in my logbook. Larry and Capt. Phogg had been pitching the Kmart Corporation, which was headquartered in Troy, Michigan, on a corporate balloon program. They had it in the bag, so to speak, until this flight.

A group of five of Kmart's top executives and their wives came out for an introductory flight. I flew four of them in one balloon, while another pilot who had been recently hired to help promote Thunder & Colt balloon sales flew eight in the big 160. I had a fantastic flight, and my two executives and their wives loved it. We came back to the balloon port and waited for the rest of their group to arrive—and waited, and waited, and waited.

They never called in to say they had a problem, so we kept waiting. Finally, two hours later, they arrived. I saw the truck pull into the parking area. I walked out to greet them and saw nothing but very glum faces. My four passengers came out also, and after a few words with the others, all of them simply went to their cars and drove away.

Turns out they had not had a glorious adventure. The other pilot had tried a "splash and dash" in Lake Fenton that went badly and turned into a dunk and dash. It was October, and the weather was a bit on the chilly side, so being wet up to your waist was not a good thing. Then they had a hard time finding a landing site and flew on forever, finally landing at dusk, and their crew had lost them. After a long time with the balloon kept upright as a signal, the crew finally found them and packed up in the dark, fighting mosquitos, with the Kmart folks in the truck trying to warm up.

They had only brought our four-door pickup truck with a lift gate on the back and no second vehicle, so some of the passengers had to ride back in the basket in the truck bed in the cold since they could not all fit inside the truck. We never sold the contract. Larry and I were furious. Larry had put in a lot of time and effort to sell that one, and it should have and would have been a done deal had that one flight gone well.

Craig Elliott

~ ~ ~

My brother-in-law, Scott Burdick, joined us as the production manager for Thunder & Colt US. I recall sitting with Denny, Larry, and some members of the T&C production and sales team from Oswestry, discussing ideas. The topic of the Cameron Pressure Scoop came up. Cameron Balloons in Ann Arbor, Michigan, was owned by Bruce and Tucker Comstock, and was going to be our target competitor.

Cameron had patented the Scoop a few years before. T&C had gotten around the patent with a few slight modifications to the design, as the Scoop was very popular with many pilots. It really helped on windy inflations, tethers, and to keep the balloon standing after landing in a breeze as well. We were discussing names for the T&C design, as we could not call it a "scoop." Someone came up with the name "Air Tucker," and as an inside joke, that got a great round of laughter. I think the name that was eventually used was "Scroop."

The Christmas Gift Certificate sales season went great again, and the Fenton ride sales total in 1988 was just over $158,000. The GTR program was disbanded after the 1988 season. Carol Ross had done a great job flying there despite her fear of water. However, the sales just never justified the expenses of the program, and a big part of the reason for that was our competition.

Jeff Geiger was local and seemingly knew everyone up there, and with his connections in the area, tremendous work ethic, and outstanding personality, he just won out in the end. We retreated, leaving him and his company, Grand Traverse Balloons, to make a go of it. He turned it into a fantastic success story over the next 25 years!

~ ~ ~

The Balloonatics

The year ended with a trip to Florida to deliver a new T&C 160 eight-passenger ride balloon to Terry Dillard in Orlando. I not only was to drive the balloon system down there and deliver it to him, but I also had to train him to fly it. The hot air balloon insurance company Terry used for his ride business in Orlando required 10 hours of instruction in a balloon that size before they would insure the pilot to fly it. Now, anyone who knew Terry back then would know what I mean when I say this was quite a trip!

I left Fenton with the balloon in the back of our pickup truck and drove down to Orlando, arriving on December 20th. The next morning, Terry and I, along with a bunch of his friends and crew members, took a two-hour introductory flight. That evening, we flew again for one hour. The next morning, we had another two-hour flight, and the next two days, one flight each day. Then the logbook shows we did not fly again until the 31st, with one flight, and then another lull. The last two flights took place on January 3rd and 4th. In between, and especially the days we did not fly, we partied.

Terry had a few special places we would go to in the evenings. Everywhere we went, all the girls knew and loved Terry. He would give me a wad of fives and tell me they were for the girls, not for drinks, and tell me to put all my drinks on his tab! Many years later, Terry posted on Facebook a photo of one of the special places we went to before it was torn down. The building was shaped like two giant female breasts sticking out of the ground and was painted pink.

One day we went to the Orange Bowl to help a couple of pilots who were going to fly over the Orange Bowl football game. One of them was the Hooters Balloon. I helped that pilot set up, and he invited me to fly with him, which I did. We had a cool flight over the stadium and landed on a helicopter pad at Orlando International Airport.

The tower gave us permission to fly in and land short of the main runway, which was in use. That helipad was our last option. The area was just large enough for the balloon in the slow winds we were flying in. Afterward, we all went to the nearest Hooters to celebrate. On the drive home, I got a speeding ticket in Kentucky, and to this day it is the last traffic ticket I have received.

1989

One day in 1989, Ron flew a private charter flight, and five minutes into the flight the young man got down on his knees and proposed to the young lady he had brought with him. She said, "I would not marry you if you were the last man on earth." It was a very quiet flight for the next 55 minutes! Ron said afterward that he thought the unfortunate young man was a bit odd, and the gal was just along for the ride.

Denny had brought in and hired a couple of well-known balloonists, including another former world champion, to run the sales of Thunder & Colt US balloons. He also made one of them manager of BCA and Capt. Phogg Balloon Rides, which really upset Larry and me. We felt like we were being pushed out as the new guy investigated all aspects of the business and made changes we did not like at all.

Larry's logbook vividly portrays the rift between us. Larry had logged an average of over 80 flights per year the last few years at BCA. In 1989, he only flew 15 flights for BCA. He began to fly for our friend in Lansing who flew Cameron balloons and owned a company based in Lansing, Michigan, called Michigan Balloon Corporation. Larry left BCA after flying Tony the Tiger again at the Mississippi State Championships the first weekend of July. All his logbook entries after that weekend are in Cameron balloons flying for Michigan Balloon Corporation.

~ ~ ~

The Balloonatics

I stayed on at BCA for the rest of 1989 because Denny had landed another commercial contract, and he offered me the job as chief pilot for the program. I flew rides until August, when the new commercial program began. It was for Virgin Atlantic, Sir Richard Branson's new upstart airline that flew from New York's LaGuardia Airport to London's Heathrow Airport.

They were going to expand, and since Sir Richard Branson was now a balloonist, he had just flown the Atlantic with Per Lindstrand, the owner of T&C Balloons, and he loved using balloons to promote his brand. They wanted a balloon program in the United States to help promote this new expansion. Since Denny was the T&C "big guy" now in the States, he got the contract. I again was in the right place at the right time and got the chief pilot's job.

Denny bought an older, used Chase Commander for the program. It was a motorhome that was converted with a lift gate on the back and

Virgin Atlantic Jumbo III balloon.

a separate compartment to store the balloon equipment. On August 2nd, my crew chief, Jimmy, and I drove to New Jersey in the Chase Commander loaded with the new Virgin Atlantic Jumbo III special-shape balloon and all the ancillary equipment.

Denny flew in, and we all met in Clinton, New Jersey, at the Balloon America Race on August 4th. It was a hot day, and we had parked the Chase Commander on the balloon field early for that evening's flight with the 60 other balloons to begin the event. The US Promotions manager for Virgin Atlantic was going to meet us on the field.

Denny, Jimmy, and I were sitting in the Chase Commander with the air conditioning running, talking about the upcoming virgin flight of the Virgin Atlantic Jumbo III balloon and going over the flight manual. We had not yet even inflated or flown this special-shape balloon, which was basically a standard T&C 77,000-cubic-foot envelope painted to look like a cloud that had a Virgin Atlantic 747 flying through it.

The nose of the plane stuck out 40 feet or so, as did the wings and tail. There were deflation ports located in several places at the ends of all four protrusions that were sealed with Velcro. You could open them to help deflate those appendages. However, you had to remember to reseal them before inflating the balloon or else the appendage would not fully inflate and pressurize. It would then just hang there, looking like a limp wing or tail or nose.

As we were reading through the flight manual, Jimmy and I began changing into our flight clothes. Jimmy and I were in our underwear when the Virgin Atlantic US promotions manager and her female assistant walked in on us and said hello! We said hi back and apologized for our appearance, saying we were just changing. They said that was okay and just started talking with Denny, who had burst out laughing and said, "Well, isn't this a great way to meet?"

They just stood there talking with Denny, who was fully dressed, as Jimmy and I finished getting dressed. When they saw what we had

The Balloonatics

on they said, "Oh no, that will not do." One of them threw us each a pair of lightweight sweatpants and T-shirts emblazoned with the Red Virgin Atlantic logo. We said, "Cool!" and changed again, much to everyone's amusement.

The virgin inflation and flight went off without a hitch, with just Denny and me in the basket for this test flight. One wing did not fully inflate because, as we discovered after the flight while packing up, one of the Velcro deflation ports on that wing had not been sealed. It took us forever to fully deflate and squeeze all the air out of all the appendages and pack the balloon in its bag.

We got better at it every time and soon could pack it up almost as quickly as a regular balloon. We flew during the event the next two evenings, taking up the promotions manager and her assistant as well as several other Virgin Atlantic employees. Then Jimmy and I were off on an amazing adventure on the East Coast for the next two months. During the event, the Virgin Atlantic employees gave Jimmy and me the nicknames that we used for the rest of the tour. With our Virgin Atlantic logo shirts and sweatpants as our flight uniforms, they dubbed me the "Virgin Commander" and Jimmy the "Virgin Chief."

I had always envisioned New Jersey to be ugly and all built up. Getting away from Newark and the other built-up coastal areas, I was pleasantly surprised by how beautiful New Jersey is. It reminded me a lot of flying in Michigan.

~ ~ ~

Back home in Fenton, Michelle and our sister-in-law Susan Burdick were hired as promotion liaisons and logistics assistants for the program. They were busy sending out press releases, setting up press flights and interviews, and helping to coordinate lodging for us. Then they joined us for a week in New York, where we met at the Virgin Atlantic offices in Manhattan every day to plan and promote the tour.

The Virgin Atlantic office had arranged for a local artist to paint, by hand, the Virgin Atlantic logo and balloon on the Chase Commander.

The four of us stayed at a hotel in Newark by the airport. Every morning Jimmy and I drove the 28-foot Chase Commander motorhome into Manhattan and parked it on the side of the road in front of the 20-story building where Virgin Atlantic's US offices were located. The artist would arrive during the day and paint. Driving that thing in rush hour traffic into Manhattan every morning was a bitch, but Jimmy managed while I held on in the passenger seat. He was in command of the vehicle. I was in command of the balloon. We could not just leave the Chase Commander there but had to drive it back to our hotel in Newark every evening and then drive it back into the city every morning.

The girls would take a shuttle from the hotel to the Newark Airport and then take a bus to Manhattan and meet us at the Virgin Atlantic offices each morning. We all had a fun time in New York. Jimmy had a friend who lived there and served as our tour guide. Then the girls flew back home, and Jimmy and I started the tour.

We flew in many locations and at several small balloon festivals. The Manhattan Virgin Atlantic sales team arranged many flights for travel agents who were selling Virgin Atlantic flights as a thank-you to them. We tethered at the Polish Festival on Long Island, then I did one incredible free flight in Glen Cove on August 22nd.

~ ~ ~

The flight in Glen Cove was a press flight that the sales team had arranged. I agreed to it without really knowing what I was getting myself into. I had looked at the aviation maps and realized that I could legally fly there if I stayed below 1,200 feet above the ground. What I did not fully realize was that there is no place to land on Long Island except for the few parks and golf courses. Those were the only open spaces, period.

We arrived at a park in Glen Cove, and Virgin had six people they wanted me to fly. The balloon could only safely carry two plus me. My plan was to fly off for 20 minutes and land, change passengers, and do it again, doing three takeoffs and three landings. It was a morning flight, thank God, as there usually are some "steering" winds in the morning.

As soon as I took off, I got nervous as I saw nothing but houses and buildings everywhere. The park we launched from seemed to be the only open space for miles. As I ascended, I found many different directions of wind at different altitudes below 1,200 feet. I calmed down a bit when I realized that I could fly the balloon in almost any direction I wanted using all those different winds.

I flew to and landed at a golf course a mile away to complete my first passenger exchange. Then I flew back toward the park where we had launched from and found a schoolyard to do the second and final passenger exchange. From there, I flew back to the original park and landed after an incredible 90-minute flight, taking up all six passengers.

I was excited, and the Virgin Atlantic promotions folks were showering me with praise as I started the post-flight champagne celebration with the traditional balloonist prayer:

> *The winds have welcomed you with softness.*
> *The sun has blessed you with its warm hands.*
> *You have flown so high and so well*
>   *that God has joined you in laughter*
> *And set you gently back again into*
>   *the loving arms of Mother Earth.*

In my excitement, I forgot about the dangers of the champagne cork and popped it right into the left breast of one of the Virgin Atlantic promotions gals, at which she let out a loud howl of pain! What a way to ruin an otherwise fantastic morning. She was a good sport, and after a few minutes and glasses of champagne, she forgave me, but I was very upset at myself for that stupidity!

~ ~ ~

NOTE: My dad died at 9 a.m., April 8, 2023, at my parents' home in Bradenton, Florida, as I was writing this. I was there helping take care of him. Mom called me from their bedroom. It was a blessing as he had been suffering for too long. Now he could have peace. He was the best! RIP, Dad.

~ ~ ~

One funny quirk of the Jumbo Jet balloon was that it always wanted to fly backward. I would use the rotation vents to orient the 747 to fly in the direction we were traveling, and it would just slowly rotate backward every time! I finally gave up and just let it fly backward. We figured maybe it drew more attention by flying backward.

It was a very easy shape to fly since it really was just a regular balloon with four large appendages, two of which were identical and opposite of each other. It just could not climb or descend as fast because of the drag of those appendages. Also, when landing in the wind, they would make you drag farther than you would in a regular balloon since they would act like a sail. Once we figured out how to deflate and pack it up, it was not much harder to operate than a regular shape balloon.

~ ~ ~

After the fight on Long Island, we went to Connecticut. I flew two flights from Newtown on August 24th with travel agents as passengers. The first we landed in Trumbull, and the second we landed in Easton.

The Balloonatics

We then did a tether in Trumbull on August 25th, and on August 26th and 27th we flew three flights from Plainville with local press and travel agents as passengers. One of these flights ended up being the worst flight of my career.

We were doing a live remote during morning rush-hour traffic with one of the big radio stations in Bridgeport, Connecticut. A popular DJ and his female sidekick were flying with me. We flew right down the main highway, State Route 25, heading to Bridgeport.

It was a fantastic morning, with the live remote going perfectly well. Lots of calls were coming in, and people were honking their horns from the highway as we gently floated above it. I vividly remember the field I should have landed in. About 40 minutes into the flight, a perfect, large, open mowed field lay right along the highway, and I passed it up despite knowing I should land. The DJ was in the middle of describing how great the flight was, and I did not want to interrupt him. I told myself it was a bit too early to land, and we were still only about halfway to Bridgeport, so there would be more landing spots ahead. Famous last words.

About five minutes later, I realized my stupid mistake. The winds began increasing, and the pretty rolling countryside we had been flying over suddenly turned into nothing but wall-to-wall houses and buildings and power lines. I stayed low over every obstacle, looking for any place to land that came along. About 15 minutes later, I radioed the airport in Bridgeport to tell them I was going to land there if I did not find any place before I reached them. I also mentioned that my last resort would be to ditch in the Long Island Sound as close to shore as possible and asked them to please call the Coast Guard if they saw me do that.

The Long Island Sound was now only about three miles and about 10 minutes away at the speed we were traveling. I had earlier briefed my passengers on the rough landing we would most likely have: as soon as I saw any place big enough to land, I would rip the top out and slam in from treetop level. I was just about to brief them on what to do if we had to ditch in the sound when I saw a small church parking lot ahead of us.

I ripped the top out from about 50 feet above the ground, and we slammed into the asphalt as the envelope lay over onto the large oak trees that surrounded the parking lot. The basket remained upright since the trees stopped us from dragging, and I slowly helped the two passengers up. All three of us were dazed and bruised. The DJ had injured his back and was in pain, while his sidekick was shaken up but okay. I hit the side of my face on one upright, breaking my glasses and causing a cut next to my left eye. Jimmy, as usual, was on the spot at once and helped us out of the basket.

The envelope fell off the trees except for one spot where it was hung up. We had to carefully pull it off and did so with only several small tears, the largest being approximately 10 or 12 inches. We packed it up and drove back to our fancy hotel in Bridgeport and had our champagne ceremony in the lobby.

The DJ was hobbling but said he would be okay. They both said they loved the flight but could have done without the landing! They both left in good cheer and thanked me for a flight they would never forget. I heard nothing else about it, so I hope he completely recovered! I flew the balloon one time before we could get it to a repair station to sew up the rips. We used sticky-back fabric to temporarily seal them up for that flight.

I had violated a very important rule—never pass up a suitable landing spot unless you know 100 percent for sure what lies ahead—and I paid the price. I have told a much shorter version of that story many times later to passengers who tried to persuade me to "keep on flying."

~ ~ ~

After the crash landing in Trumbull, we flew a few more flights in Plainville at a great local event held at the fire station. Once again, I found out how hard it is to find landing spots in Connecticut. There are trees everywhere, and with the light winds we had during that event, landing spots are few and far between. On one flight, my passengers and I literally had to pull us through the treetops toward an open field 100 yards away.

The next flight, I had to land in a tiny backyard. One wing of Jumbo III was almost hanging over the power line that ran to the house. We had to be very careful deflating the balloon straight down into the yard and then rolling it off all the small trees, bushes, and the roof of the house while packing it up. I developed a great respect for the pilots who flew in these areas of endless trees, and they were all so welcoming and friendly to boot!

It was a real eye-opener for me to see such vast forests and wild areas so close to New York City! I was happy to see all of this. It gave me joy knowing that even on the heavily populated East Coast, we had not destroyed as much of the land as I had previously thought, at least when one got away from the immediate coastline.

~ ~ ~

While I was on the road with the Virgin Atlantic Jumbo III balloon tour, Ron Pethick was at BCA flying passenger rides. Denny had also hired veteran pilot Tom Orman to fly rides with Ron. One day they flew together in the big eight-passenger 160 with six passengers. It was a morning flight with perfectly calm winds on the surface.

They flew south over Lake Fenton and were able to land at the Owen Road McDonald's drive-thru and order coffee! They asked to have the coffee brought out to them because they could not drive to the window.

An irate restaurant manager then ran out yelling, "Get out of here!" She quickly changed her tune when she heard horns honking and turned around to see cars pouring into the parking lot to see the balloon. "Oh, sorry," she said. "I will get your order out ASAP." She hurriedly brought out eight coffees, saying, "It's on the house." Ron and Tom then took off to a huge roar from the crowd that had gathered, and the car horns were a-honking!

A few years later, when we owned Michigan Balloon Corporation, our crew member Dan drove through that same McDonald's drive-thru with our van and trailer to get coffee. He did a poor job negotiating the tight turn and caught a steel post with the trailer fender. It resulted in a big dent that we subsequently called "Dan's McDent."

~ ~ ~

August 31st was the highlight of the Virgin Atlantic tour. Sir Richard Branson had flown in to do a live national TV news interview to announce and promote the expansion of Virgin Atlantic flying from both New York and Newark direct to London. We were told that the interview was to take place at Liberty State Park in New Jersey by the Liberation Monument on Black Tom Island.

This is a great vantage point to look across the Hudson River and view Liberty Island and the Statue of Liberty. They wanted Jimmy, the "Virgin Chief," and I, the "Virgin Commander," to tether the balloon right next to the Hudson River as a backdrop for Sir Richard Branson's live interview, with the Statue of Liberty in the background behind the balloon.

We were very excited to possibly meet Sir Richard and help him create a great backdrop for his live national TV interview. We arrived early that morning, around 6 a.m. It was hot and humid with a good breeze already blowing. I was concerned about the wind as we looked over the site. Jimmy drove the Chase Commander out on the lawn after carefully walking it to make sure it was not soft or wet and was drivable.

The Balloonatics

We had just started to set up when a big white limo pulled up in the drive, and out stepped Sir Richard Branson. He was casually but nicely dressed as usual and had just a couple of people with him. Jimmy and I stopped working for a minute to watch, and I wished I had a camera to take a few photos. Looking back, I now really wish I had taken the time to take lots of photos on this tour, but unfortunately, I have very few.

We were just about to go and introduce ourselves when we noticed he was walking toward us. He extended his hand to me and said, "Hello, I am Richard Branson." I said, "Yes, I am Craig Elliott. This is Jimmy. We are delighted to meet you." I then told him we had met in Oswestry in January 1987 at the T&C balloon factory, and he said, "Oh yes, I remember!"

We spoke briefly about what was to take place, and I asked if we had placed the balloon in the best spot, which he concluded we had. He then asked about the wind. I said it was going to pose a problem, but we would do the best we could to keep the balloon up during the interview. He then asked if he could lend a hand setting up, and I said that I never turn down help.

Sir Richard Branson helped us pull the balloon envelope, basket, tether ropes, inflation fans, and so on out of the Chase Commander. He then took all four tether ropes, undid the daisy chains, and stretched them out for us to the tie-off points I directed him to. And he did not stop helping until we told him we were all set! He is just that down-to-earth and pleasant. Remember, he was there to do a live TV interview on that hot and humid summer morning. And he took the time to help us, all the while getting hot and sweaty just like we were—a true balloonist! We were flabbergasted and honored to have such a great ground crew helper.

As we three were getting the balloon ready, the TV crews arrived and set up near the drive. They came over to talk with us briefly, and then Sir Richard left us to get ready for his interview. Soon, we started inflating the balloon, and the "Virgin Chief" was tested on the crown line because the wind began blowing and gusting even more.

We inflated and stood the balloon up during the live interview. Jimmy was being blown around holding the crown line, trying to keep the envelope upright, while I tried to keep it as hot as possible without torching any fabric on live TV. The interview began, and Sir Richard mentioned we were doing a great job of keeping the balloon up in such windy conditions! At one point in the interview, Jimmy was pulled around the balloon by the crown line and ended up running right behind Sir Richard while waving at the camera! (See this video at www.theballoonatics.com.)

Thank goodness it was just a brief interview. After about 15 minutes of fighting the wind and not burning any fabric, we deflated Jumbo III. As we packed her up, to our astonishment, Sir Richard walked over again with another person and asked what they could do to help us! The four of us packed everything up in the now VERY hot and humid morning. When everything was all packed and put back in the Chase Commander, Sir Richard invited Jimmy and me to join him and his small entourage for a picnic on the grass near where we had tethered.

We then sat on blankets on the ground, ate, and had a beer or two while talking with him and his group for over an hour. What an awesome experience! I told him the story of the first time I met him not too long ago in Oswestry at the T&C balloon factory, when I did not know who he was and wondered why the secretary reacted the way she had. He got a good laugh out of that.

~ ~ ~

We did another short, windy tether that evening for 20 minutes at the same spot and then left for an epic adventure, the Long Island Sound America event. L.I.S.A. was an environmental group formed to help clean up the Long Island Sound. One fundraising and promotional event they put on back in the eighties was the Long Island Sound America Balloon Festival.

Here is a brief description of the 1989 event I found on Facebook from CT Ballooning, LLC:

> Labor Day weekend and the Long Island Sound America Balloon Festival. Launching from Taylor Farm Park in Norwalk, CT with the goal of making it across the sound and landing on Long Island. A perfect straight line is 8 miles, but that never happened. Chase vehicles were swapped out for chase boats, extra fuel & supplies were carried—and yes, over the years there were the occasional "damp" landings, boat landings and the getting-towed-to-shore landings. This was a successful year as we made it across and landed in Port Jefferson, NY.

I cannot find much else on L.I.S.A. or the balloon festival online. Anyway, this proved to be one of the most incredible flights and comic adventures—funny in retrospect, anyway—of my career. Jimmy recruited his friend Chris, who lived in New York, to join him as ground/water crew. We stayed at a very nice hotel in Norwalk, Connecticut, and the Friday evening reception was quite a big and fancy affair. It was also a sign of things to come! At the reception, each balloon was assigned a chase boat that would follow it across the sound during the flight. This was in case a rescue was needed but primarily to transport the balloon back to the launch field after the crossing.

The aim was to fly across the Long Island Sound, land on the beach on Long Island, and then have the balloon transported to the nearest dock. From there, it would be loaded onto the boat and brought back across the Long Island Sound to the dock at the launch field at Taylor Farm Park in Connecticut.

We had no cell phones back then, so using handheld radios was the only means of communication to help accomplish this difficult feat.

The balloons would launch, and then the ground/water crew would go to the dock. The dock master would tell them which slip their boat was in so they could board the boat with their boat captain and begin the chase. They assigned us one of the larger boats, along with two other balloons and crews. Our boat captain was thus responsible for three balloons and crews.

After dinner, the organizers presented everyone with all the pertinent information needed and assigned boats to balloons, so we could meet our boat captains. Our boat captain, with his white beard and hair, boat captain hat, and uniform, looked the part of a jolly old sailor. However, he was so drunk that we could hardly understand a word he tried to say. We shook hands and said see you in the morning, weather permitting, and under our breath said to ourselves, *if you can wake up!*

The next morning, the flight was called off because of unfavorable winds. To successfully cross, we required a wind speed under 10 miles per hour and in the correct direction to avoid being carried out into the Atlantic Ocean. We imagined our boat captain was probably thrilled to sleep in. Sunday morning the flight was on with perfect wind conditions, and boy, were we excited!

We arrived early and picked out an ideal launch area that I thought would give us the most press coverage, being as close to the spectator area as possible. We inflated early and sat as a static display while the other balloons inflated and took off. I stayed on the ground until all the others had launched to milk as much press coverage for the Virgin Atlantic Jumbo III balloon as possible, then was the last to launch. I flew solo in case it was a long flight and put all four 15-gallon propane tanks in the basket, which turned out well because I used almost 10 gallons before I finally took off. Also, I figured if I had to ditch in the water and had four empty tanks in the basket, it would float quite well!

When I took off, the task at hand became obvious and a bit intimidating! Straight across the sound was eight miles, but any other way except back where we launched from was just open water with no

The Balloonatics

land in sight! I told myself that I was sure going to love having that boat under me. We had done a radio check before launch, and when I radioed my crew again, they said they were heading for the dock to board the boat.

I was following all the other balloons slowly across the sound, solo, and it was a genuine thrill watching all the balloons and boats chasing after them. A few minutes later, Jimmy called on the radio in a panic and said our boat had left without them! He said he had gone to the docks, and it was gone. The dock master called the boat captain and ordered him to return, and they were waiting for him.

Approximately 20 minutes later, Jimmy called again and said that they were finally on the boat, heading out to find me and the others. He relayed to me that the boat captain, still drunk, was extremely unhappy about having to come back for them. Jimmy said they had gotten into an argument, and all was not well between them. The captain said he had waited for a long time and figured they had gone out on another boat.

As I floated across the sound, it seemed to take forever. I never went much over 500 feet above the water since the direction was good down low and all the other balloons ahead of me were doing the same. I never saw my chase boat, although Jimmy radioed they had me in sight. It was very peaceful. I was enjoying the slow, serene float across the sound as I saw it was going well and Long Island was getting closer and closer. Approaching Long Island, a few boats appeared, waving and cheering me on. Soon I could see some balloons that had launched first landing on the beach on Long Island.

I was a mile or more behind the first balloons. As I got closer to shore, I saw the beach was not very wide, and there were lots of docks and boats moored to them all along the beach with areas of open beach between them. To my left, farther east, the beach was more open, and to the right, or west, it was much more congested with docks and boats. I followed the same path as the other balloons but noticed that my balloon and the closest balloon ahead of me were the furthest to the right as we approached the shore.

Soon I began watching the other balloons landing on the beach to the left of us. As we both came onto shore and tried to land, docks and boats in our path thwarted us. I came in and had a very tall sailboat mast directly in my line. I had to power over the sailboat mast at the last minute and had no chance of dropping in after it to the very narrow beach behind it. Then it was nothing but big houses, wall to wall, along the beach. The other balloon in front of me had the same result, and we had to keep flying.

I radioed Jimmy that I was flying inland to find a landing spot, and I think he was able to confirm that, but I do not recall for sure. So the two of us flew on and got lucky in just a few miles to land at Willow Creek Golf Club, one of the very few open areas to be found. My landing was by the first tee and the 18th green, just off the road next to the clubhouse. Imagine how surprised the golfers and staff must have been to see a Jumbo Jet–shaped hot air balloon drop in on Long Island! Who in their right mind flies a hot air balloon on Long Island?

There was just enough room to deflate the envelope with half of it on the green and in the sand traps. The golfers and staff were gracious and not busy in the early morning, so everything was well. I tried to reach Jimmy on the radio, but it didn't transmit far on the ground, so I couldn't get in touch. Alone, I packed the envelope as no one offered to help, with few staff and golfers around. It differed from most landings, which draw a large crowd. It took me a while to pack the envelope.

As soon as I finished, the other balloon pilot who had landed near to me on the golf course arrived with his balloon on a boat trailer pulled by a local in his pickup truck! I wish I remembered his name, but I do not. Anyway, the other pilot came to help me, and we loaded Jumbo onto the boat trailer with his balloon. Then the helpful local guy drove us back to the docks. Most of the boats had already loaded all the other balloons that had landed on the beach and had left the dock.

The Balloonatics

I kept trying to radio Jimmy to no avail, and when we got to the dock, my drunk boat captain gruffly said to me, "It's about time. We have been waiting for you again!" As I kept trying to radio Jimmy, both balloons were loaded on the boat with several others before I knew it. The captain and everyone else on board were yelling for me to get on as they were leaving. I kept protesting, asking where my crew was, and they kept saying that my crew had already left in another boat since they knew you were on your way here. I did not believe them and kept protesting. I finally had to get on the boat after the drunk captain started the motor and was going to leave without me.

So off we went back to Norwalk without my crew. I was upset but figured Jimmy probably had had enough of the drunk captain and it made sense that he did not want to ride back with him. The worst part was that I had not brought the post-flight cooler with me! Jimmy had it, and to my astonishment, no one else on the boat full of four or five balloons and crews seemed to have anything to drink except water. (I was sure the boat captain was personally supplied though.) I wanted to have a big post-flight drinking party on the boat ride back after that epic flight!

About 10 minutes into the boat ride and about half a mile from the docks, I noticed a small speedboat coming toward us from the shore, and it soon was right behind us. They were waving frantically at us, and I soon saw it was my crew! I yelled and ran to the boat captain to stop and let them aboard, and he reluctantly did so. My joy at seeing them was met with their discontent. In fact, they were furious and let me know it by not even talking to me except a passing "f— you" as they boarded the boat. I was shell-shocked. What did I do? Then I realized they had been left behind both at the beginning and at the end and blamed me for the latter.

Silence filled the long boat ride as they ignored me and my questions. It was a very sad ending to an otherwise excellent adventure. Back at the docks, we loaded Jumbo back into the Chase Commander in silence, except for me apologizing and trying to explain myself and what had happened. The ride back to the hotel was no better as they gave me the cold shoulder.

Jimmy didn't speak to me until the following day. He explained that upon reaching the Long Island dock, they flagged down a police car and persuaded the officer to assist in their search for me. They had no luck locating me. Upon their return to the dock, they were left behind yet again. They frantically searched and found a speedboat owner who agreed to chase us down. Better communication equipment would have helped. Jimmy forgave me, and we left the next day for our next assignment.

~ ~ ~

Unlike the Buick Tour, where we crisscrossed the United States and drove for days on end from job to job, we only had to make short drives during the Virgin East Coast Tour. Most of the jobs were within a 50-mile radius of New York City. One drive was to the City of Brotherly Love, which I knew well from my earlier flight over the airport with the Buick Olympic Balloon five years before.

On September 7th we tethered Jumbo III on the famous "Rocky" movie steps of the Philadelphia Museum of Art. This was in conjunction with the "Best of Philly Party" the city was hosting. There was barely enough room for Jumbo III, but the weather gods smiled upon us. We were able to pull off a tether lasting one hour and 45 minutes—or rather, a static display of Jumbo III. It was breezy, so we kept Jumbo III tied down tight and got a ton of attention.

We had no time to rest as we headed off to the Pennsylvania State Championships Balloon Race in Williamsport, Pennsylvania. The next day, September 8th, we did a press conference tether for one hour. Then Jumbo III was the Hare Balloon for the first flight of the competition that evening. I flew a 45-minute flight as the Hare Balloon, and the

The Balloonatics

next day flew a one-hour flight with local travel agents as passengers. On September 10th, we tethered Jumbo again at the event for an hour.

We left the next day for Far Hills, New Jersey, where we met the infamous balloonist Denny Fleck, who worked for the famous and flamboyant publisher Malcolm Forbes. What a great guy! We had a few travel agent flights scheduled in the area, so we called him up and went to his balloon port, where he welcomed us with open arms. We had a few beers while he showed us around his wonderful balloon barn with all of its great equipment and iconic chase vehicles.

The weather was fantastic, and we flew three flights with him on Sept 12th and 13th. We were able to fly many people by doing passenger exchanges. Each of the three flights had a duration of one and a half hours, with four landings recorded for each flight. We had a wonderful time with Denny Fleck and his crew. These were to be the last East Coast flights for the tour.

The next couple of scheduled flights had to be cancelled because of inclement weather. We took advantage of the break and went to Atlantic City for a few days. I won $500 playing roulette on the last day, then took Jimmy and some friends out to dinner. Then we drove back to Michigan to pick up Michelle and Susan as our next stop was to be the Albuquerque International Balloon Fiesta.

~ ~ ~

I have not yet mentioned that Jimmy and I were two peas in a pod when it came to partying and drinking. My poison mostly was beer, and Jimmy was a vodka guy. He said he liked vodka for two reasons. One, it mixed well with orange juice, and two, it was hard to smell on your breath. He always had his thermos of "coffee" with him, from morning to night. Jimmy could drink all day without anyone realizing it unless he truly let loose. He only did that when he didn't have to be in control or drive.

Personally, I've always had an issue with controlling my drinking. Usually, once I started, I could not stop. In just a few hours, it became obvious I had overindulged. This was okay at a party. I was sociable and fit in well with the other partygoers, as there are always a few of us who like to overdo it. Anyway, Albuquerque was to Jimmy and me the biggest party in the world!

Michelle and Susan's exceptional pre-promotion efforts ensured a busy schedule of press flights. We flew seven out of the nine days. On four days, we flew morning and evening flights, completing 11 flights during the Fiesta plus the night glow. We were all over the local newspapers and TV news every day. Several other pilots came up to me toward the end of the Fiesta asking what the heck we were doing for promotion, because every time they turned on the TV or opened a newspaper, there we were! Capt. Phogg had brought the Tony the Tiger balloon once again, and we flew together almost every flight, sharing the spotlight.

Reflecting, I find it astonishing that we managed all this, given our frequent and heavy drinking. Jimmy helped me out at the Annual Balloon Night Glow after I had forgotten about it and had drunk way too much all that day. I could barely help with the inflation of Jumbo III, and Jimmy did the Glow with me sitting in the Chase Commander, watching. It's sad reflecting on everything I missed back then. So many mornings I was looking forward to my "hair of the dog" champagne toast.

Ron Pethick likes to tell the story of the morning they could not find me in my hotel room. After frantically searching for me, he found me passed out in the passenger seat of the Chase Commander with a half-drunk fifth of vodka between my legs. Believe it or not, I remember that one. Ron yelled at me, "Craig, we have been looking all over for you! It is time to go fly, man!" I woke up and said, "Okay, let's go!" Ah, the wonders and stupidity of youth!

I remember one night Ron and Justin Fortney, who was a good

The Balloonatics

friend of Ron's and a great crew member, Michelle, and I, were partying in our hotel room. Justin started jumping on our bed like it was a trampoline. There was a set of large bull horns mounted on the wall above the headboard, and as he jumped, he lost his balance. He ended up grabbing the bull horns and yanking them off the wall. We all laughed; however, I was worried about getting a bill for the damage. I decided to fill the holes in the wall with my white stick deodorant, and I was quite pleased with my patch job.

Ron then came up with the idea to mount the bull horns on the front of the big Cadillac that Bruce Bussey used as the chase vehicle for the Cadillac-sponsored balloon he flew. We got some wire and did a fine drunken job of mounting them on the chrome grill of the big black Cadillac late that night, incognito. Bruce loved it and reinforced our sloppy mounting job to make sure the horns stayed on the Cadillac balloon chase vehicle throughout the Fiesta and beyond! I never got a bill from the hotel for those bull horns, surprisingly.

~ ~ ~

I must note that as I was writing this manuscript in April 2023, I learned that one of our ground crew heroes, Justin Fortney, died at only age 50. RIP, Justin! Michelle and I attended his funeral on April 29th.

~ ~ ~

After the fantastic success of Jumbo and Tony at the Fiesta, Jimmy and I were on cloud nine. Our next and last scheduled job on the tour was in Miami, so off we drove to Florida, hoping we could extend the tour. The Miami job was a tether job for ASTA, the American Society of Travel Advisors. They put us up at a posh hotel, where Jimmy and I enjoyed our free time at the incredible outdoor pool and bar.

Because of the windy conditions near the convention center on the ocean where the event took place, we could only complete two one-hour tethers, on October 25th and 26th. As a result, we had plenty of free time during the four days we spent there. We met another infamous balloonatic, Chuck Rohr, there and had a good time with him as well. Chuck introduced us to another balloonist named Bob, who told us about the International Zephyrhills Parachute Get-Together held each year in Zephyrhills, Florida. Bob talked about his idea of offering balloon jumps at the event. I was intrigued.

And then the fantastical Virgin Jumbo Tour ended. Jimmy and I were sad. It was an incredible journey and had gone by so fast. Before I wrote this book, my memory of it, like the Buick Tour before it, seemed to last forever. In my memory, both lasted for years. I was quite shocked when I went through my logbooks while writing this book and saw how short they both really were!

~ ~ ~

We drove back to the beautiful balloon port in Fenton, Michigan, and on October 29, 1989, I flew Jumbo one last time on a farewell fun flight. I told Denny about the idea of doing balloon parachute-jumping flights at the Zephyrhills Parachute Get-Together, where parachutists from around the world gathered in November and December. We thought about it and decided to give it a go. I would bring one of our T&C 160 eight-passenger balloons and try to make some money. Also, it sounded like another fun adventure to me!

A week later, I drove down with our 15-passenger van and trailer carrying the balloon to Zephyrhills and met with Bob. He was in his late 40s, I would guess, with a full dark, scraggly beard and longish dark, scraggly hair, a big beer belly, and every bit the look of a hillbilly biker. He had an old, beat-up pickup truck with an old, small Barnes balloon in the back.

The Balloonatics

We decided to take a reconnaissance flight in his balloon to scope out the area, but he told me his balloon was old and porous so I should go solo, and he would chase me. So, I did, and yes, his old balloon was not in the best shape, but it flew okay except for using a lot of fuel even with just me in it. I got a good lay of the land on the flight and saw that it was a very flyable area with lots of wide-open farmland, except to the east of the airfield where the event was held. The beginning of the Upper Hillsborough Wildlife Management Area was about a mile or two east. This area was the beginning of nothing but trees for miles and miles.

So, we set up shop, so to speak, with a handmade sign on the side of the basket advertising balloon jumps. We parked our van and trailer in what we figured was the most advantageous spot at the Zephyrhills Municipal Airport and waited for all the skydivers to appear in earnest. Dan and Denny had an arrangement that I was not involved in, or at least, that I do not recall. Dan was the organizer and crew chief, so he got a cut of the revenue.

As I recall, we priced the balloon jump rides at $125 per person. One thing none of us realized was most of these jumpers—and there were hundreds of them there—were camping out at the airport and had come with very little money. They could take the old cargo plane the airport was using to drop them for only $15 a jump.

So, although we had lots of interest, we made ZERO sales on the first day. We went back to our shared little cheap motel room, and I called Denny to report our progress. We realized we had to reduce our rate to get enough sales to fly the big balloon. The next day we reduced the rate to $75 per person and made some sales.

On November 18th, I made my first Zephyrhills Parachute jump drop flight with five paid jumpers. Multiplied by $75, that came to $375—hardly enough to justify flying the 160, but better than nothing! They all wanted to jump together, and I said why not try it? We had to drop them over the airport. It was quite a challenge to figure out the winds, find a launch site that would allow me to fly the balloon toward the airport, arrive there at approximately 6,000 feet, and then bring it down into a terminal velocity descent of 1,200 feet per minute right over the airport. At an altitude of approximately 5,000 feet, they would jump on my command. We wanted to give them a nice long free-fall opportunity, so releasing them at 5,000 feet was the goal.

We had lots of "steering" in the mornings, so it was the best time to go, and this morning was no exception. I had to go very high to get in position, and at about 5,500 feet while in a terminal decent of approximately 1,200 feet per minute, they all jumped out. What happened next was interesting and a bit more than I expected.

The large T-partitioned basket passenger side, when unburdened of all that passenger weight, jerked up violently, and my pilot side—with me and all the weight of the fuel and fuel tanks—tilted down immediately at such an angle and so abruptly that it startled me. I quickly jumped over the partition into the passenger side to level the basket floor out a little. The balloon immediately reversed course and started a very rapid ascent, with the variometer pegging the rate of climb at over 1,200 feet per minute. I ascended to over 12,000 feet in a matter of minutes.

Once my adrenaline stopped pumping so fast and the balloon stabilized at around 13,000 feet, I looked around and marveled at the view. I could see the Gulf of Mexico and thought I could also see the Atlantic Ocean! I could see forever, that is for sure! Lucky for me, the wind was very calm even at that altitude, so I just sat there waiting for the balloon to descend.

I waited and waited and vented heat a bit more and a bit more. The bottom of the envelope was limp, so I did not want to vent much more for fear of the mouth closing off. The balloon eventually started descending, and I just let it go carefully, watching and adding heat to keep the mouth from closing off. It took forever to get down, but it was a calm, peaceful ride, and I actually enjoyed it!

The Balloonatics

I eventually came down into almost calm conditions on the ground and gently landed in a farm pasture I had descended almost straight down into! The landowners were nowhere to be found. The gate to the field was open, so Dan just drove in, and the two of us took our time and packed it up. We drove back to the airport after leaving a thank-you note for the landowners. Back at the airport, we had a fun celebration with the five jumpers, and I told them I would not do that again! From then on, I'd allow a maximum of only three people to jump all at once.

The next day, I flew six jumpers and was able to position the balloon over the airport and get it into a terminal descent two times, both times dropping three jumpers. Talk about luck with the weather: we just had perfect conditions, without which this would have been very difficult, if not impossible. When Dan and I got back to the airport after packing up the balloon, one jumper, who was from Germany, came running up to us as we pulled in, all excited. He was yelling, over and over, "You should have seen it, man! I almost bounced; I almost bounced!" Turns out his main chute had malfunctioned, and he had great difficulty getting rid of it. He was finally able to pull his reserve chute at the last minute, at about 300 feet. Luckily, it deployed—barely in time to save him. He was just ecstatic about it, and that, we thought, was just nuts!

~ ~ ~

That night, Dan and I went out to a local bar after we had eaten dinner. Dan liked to play pool. He started playing while I sat at the bar having a beer. The bar was a local biker hangout and was a bit rough. I was minding my own business drinking at the bar when a rough-looking older guy sat next to me and harassed me, asking what the hell was I doing there all alone. Guess I looked out of place. I said I was not alone. My buddy was over there playing pool, and he said something like, "Oh, is that your fat girlfriend?"

I tried to ignore him and said, "Hey man, I am just sitting here minding my own business drinking my beer."

He then said, "Well, watch this." He stuck a finger in his left eye socket, extracted his glass eye, dropped it in my beer, and said, "What do you think about that?"

I said, "I do not think I want to drink that beer now, thank you." I got up, walked over to Dan, and said, "Let's go." He protested, and I grabbed his arm and said, "We are leaving now before I get into a fight with that asshole at the bar." So we left without a fight, thank God, as I think we would have been outnumbered.

~ ~ ~

The weather was windy the next two days for ballooning, and Ron Pethick arrived to relieve me in Zephyrhills. I picked him up at the airport and showed him around, familiarizing him with the operation. On December 21st, Ron and I took up four jumpers and two German guys who were not jumpers but wanted to go along for the entire ride. We dropped all four jumpers at once at 5,000 feet over the drop zone while in a terminal descent. The four of us then shot up to about 10,000 feet and had a fantastic view.

I noticed we were heading for the forest and wildlife area and pointed it out to Ron. All we could see were trees for miles and miles in the direction we were going. We started a terminal descent and kept it going all the way down, leveling out about 15 feet below ground level. With a tremendous thud, we slammed into the ground about a quarter mile from the edge of the forest in a big clearing. The two passengers were okay, although a bit shook up at the hard landing. Ron and I were happy to be down!

I flew out the next day, and a couple of days later, Ron packed up in the middle of the night and left without telling Bob. Turns out they were not getting along well and not selling many jumps or riders. Ron called Denny, and they decided it was time to cut our losses and run. I felt bad about the dismal results, but we gave it a good try, and it was an interesting adventure for sure!

~ ~ ~

When I returned, I decided to find a "real job" and quit working for Balloon Corporation of America and Capt. Phogg. The Virgin contract would not be renewed. Denny had given a new guy the title of general manager over BCA, and just like Larry had, I felt like I was being pushed out as well. I do not think Denny meant it that way, but that is how we felt.

They decided I would no longer receive my measly $500-per-month salary or my 10 percent commission on all ride sales. However, they still expected me to be in the office answering the phones and selling the rides. The new manager said I needed to be more aggressive and fly more often. I recall him saying that I should not cancel flights just because the National Weather Service has a good chance of thunderstorms in the forecast. Instead, he said, bring the passengers out and then make the call on the field. I did not agree with his aggressive approach. The new deal was that I would only be paid when I flew, and the pay was going to be $30 per passenger flown, period. I quit. I walked away from Balloon Corporation of America and the Capt. Phogg Balloon Ride program that I had started and away from my cushy hot air balloon pilot job that I enjoyed so much. I did not know what I was going to do, but I just could not stay there and accept their new offer.

Nineties

1990

In early January 1990, I took a job at A-1 Transmissions, which was only a mile from our home in Burton, Michigan. I sold wholesale rebuilt transmissions to auto repair facilities and helped the owner run the shop. Michelle started going to school full time at the University of Michigan–Flint to pursue physical therapy. Also, as I mentioned earlier, Larry had been flying in the Lansing area for Michigan Balloon Corporation. Larry told us that the owner was considering selling the business. I was very excited at the prospect of owning and running our own balloon company. Over the next two months, we negotiated and came to an agreement to purchase Michigan Balloon Corporation/Lansing, and we moved it over to our little house in Burton. It all happened so fast!

We conducted all of this in secrecy, or so we thought. However, somehow Denny caught wind of it and called me into his office, which I believe was in February. He outright said he had heard of our plans, and I denied it. I felt bad about lying to him and still do today. We had become good friends over the years, but it all seemed to have fallen apart. I figured this was business, and I did not want him to know our plans and thought it was none of his business. On April 22nd, I flew the first paid ride for our new company, American Balloon Promotions Inc., d/b/a Michigan Balloon Corporation/Flint.

The Balloonatics

Michigan Balloons

It all happened very fast, but I already knew how to market and sell balloon rides, so I just copied my own script and had at it. Michelle and I ran the company out of our tiny little house in Burton. I had negotiated and secured a fantastic launch site at Seven Lakes Vineyard in Fenton. This little gem of a vineyard was the perfect place to launch from and return to after the flight, using the wine tasting room for the post-flight champagne celebration! I could really sell this combination and right away got a ton of free press, flying lots of press people the first year.

With the purchase of the company, we acquired two Cameron balloons with enclosed trailers and all the support equipment. One was a Michigan Balloon, a 120,000-cubic-foot, five-passenger balloon with artwork of the State of Michigan on one side and the state bird and state flower on the other side. The other was a new eight-passenger, 180,000-cubic-foot balloon, which was named Big Blooming Balloon because it had artwork of Michigan wildflowers all around it. This gave us an instant balloon fleet to fly passengers. I had never flown a Cameron balloon, but I soon began to love them.

We worked on Ron Pethick to come join us, but he resisted and stayed with BCA. I continued to work at A-1 Transmissions that first summer as we were just building the new balloon business, and Michelle helped me run the office for Michigan Balloon Corporation/Flint. We started out working from our home, then decided we needed an office outside of the house—why, I do not know. My boss and friend who owned A-1 Transmissions, Larry Franzel, had an office for rent at the transmission business and offered to rent it to us for a good rate, so we moved the business office there.

Not too long after, I was working late at the office after a flight, and when I left, I forgot to lock the doors. When Larry came in the next morning and found his transmission shop unlocked, he had a fit and kicked us out. We had to move everything back to our house. It was a costly move and a ton of extra work in the middle of our flying season. All the phone lines that had just been moved from the house had to be moved back along with all of our office supplies, but in the long run it saved us money and it was much more convenient working from home. No internet or websites back then so all sales were done over the phone and then we mailed everything to the customer using the good old US post office.

Our sales started off slowly since our advertising was just coming out and we had just started. I only flew two paid rides in May. In June, things took off. I flew Rick Sylvain, who was the travel writer for the *Detroit Free Press* newspaper, and his mother on June 25th. Four days later, on June 29th, I flew Jim Murand, who was the editor of *Michigan Living* magazine. Both those publications back then were huge, with over one million in circulation each.

Both Rick and Jim wrote feature articles in their publications that resulted in our sales soaring. Ron soon took notice of how often we were flying, and after much persuasion in August, we convinced him to join us. We had a good first year and flew lots of passenger rides every month, with only a few in November and December, as usual. I do not recall what our final numbers were, but I know we were thrilled with them for our first year.

1991

We began our 1991 flying season March 10th. I flew two paid passenger flights in March and two in April, then five in May. In June, we started flying a lot.

We started July with two flights in Traverse City for Jeff Geiger and then flew a ton of passengers back at home. On August 4th, we did a photo shoot with the Michigan Department of Transportation. They contracted my brother-in-law David Hodgkin of BH Photographic to photograph our Michigan Balloon over Seven Lakes State Park. That photo ended up on the back side of the 1993 Michigan Department of Transportation State Road Map.

~ ~ ~

We had an excellent year flying passenger rides from Seven Lakes Vineyard, though we also spent a ton of money on launch fees and using their expensive champagne for our post-flight passenger celebrations. Additionally, we would often buy additional wine in their tasting room once we had consumed the champagne. Many times, we had passenger groups who liked to party as much as we did, and we always accommodated them. We had a key to the vineyard, and that was dangerous.

One time after all our passengers had left, Michelle, Ron, and several crew members and I were finishing the last of the beer and wine. One of the crew members was Justin Fortney, one of Ron's best friends. Justin was a big guy, about six foot one and 300 pounds, and he was leaning up against the tasting room bar when Ron suddenly said, "I love you, man," and jumped up into Justin's arms, wrapping his arms around Justin, who was about half passed out. Justin, after being pushed backward against the bar with Ron's body hanging on to him, rebounded and simply fell forward, body slamming Ron to the floor with a tremendous crash. The entire building shook! Ron was literally crushed, and as Justin rolled off him, Ron just lay there for a minute moaning in agony and saying, "Oh, why did I do that?"

~ ~ ~

Our little house in Burton was a 20-minute drive north of the Vineyard. The Big Blooming Balloon was in an enclosed trailer. The trailer had

The Balloonatics

Michigan Balloon photo featured on State of Michigan map. Photo by David Hodgkin of BH Photographic.

a heavy top-mounted lift system for moving the basket and envelope. We parked it and our old Suburban chase vehicle in our driveway, which was barely wide enough to back it into. Our driveway butted up to our neighbor's driveway with nothing separating the two. I had to be very careful not to smash our neighbors' car when backing our trailer in. In our quiet neighborhood in Burton, we kept the Michigan Balloon in another enclosed trailer we parked on the road in front of our little house.

Initially, we only had one chase vehicle, and Ron had a Suburban. Ron lived in Fenton, so he had to drive 20 minutes to our house to pick up one trailer with his Suburban every time he flew, bring it back after the flight, and then drive home. We also had to refuel the balloons with propane after every flight. I negotiated a good price with a gas station between the Vineyard launch site and our home. The owners of the gas station were a delightful couple who gave us a key to the propane station so we could refuel anytime, day or night. We kept a refueling logbook in the propane pump house and paid them every week. After those late nights of partying at the Vineyard, we first had to stop and refuel the balloons before taking them home. It resulted in long nights and short sleeps when flights were scheduled for the next morning.

One weekend, Larry and Gretchen had been at her parents' property in Norwood, Michigan, which is north of Traverse City. As they were returning home to Fenton, driving south along the west shore of Torch Lake, Larry had to find a bathroom. Larry saw a sign for a bar, and they went there. They ended up at the Dockside Bar, which is located right on the mouth of the Clam River where it flows into Torch Lake. Larry went to the bathroom. The place was for sale, and they became the new owners. It all happened very quickly, so now Larry and Gretchen had to move up north to run the bar with his new partner.

Gretchen was thrilled about that because her parents owned that lot on Lake Michigan, and she had been spending her summers up there since she was a child. So Ron and I now handled most all of the flying for Michigan Balloon Corporation (MBC).

~ ~ ~

That summer, we flew at the Springfield Oaks Balloon Race and learned something that would haunt me for the next 10 years. One of the other pilots introduced me to a new pilot, and he introduced him as "The New Capt. Phogg." His name was Eric, and it turned out that he had just bought the Capt. Phogg Balloon Ride business—yes, the one I started in 1985—from the original Capt. Phogg, Denny Floden.

I was not at all happy about that. I had hoped and figured that Denny would just shut down the business when he was done with it. I knew he did not want to continue running it. He was too busy and making too much money selling insurance and investments to run the balloon business.

The Balloonatics

The Thunder & Colt Balloon Manufacturing deal had not worked out so well for him. Thunder & Colt had moved out of his building, and the building was for sale. Learning that someone purchased the ride business I had built upset me, and I treated the new guy, Eric, poorly. I told him sarcastically, "Don't quit your real job." Little did I know that he already had, and he would soon be my major competition.

~ ~ ~

After a night of flying and staying late at the vineyard, Michelle and I went home and slept after refueling the balloons at the gas station. About an hour later, our phone rang around 2 a.m., and Michelle answered it. She woke me to say the police were on the phone saying our balloon and trailer were in a wreck. I said it was a prank call and told her to hang up, so she did. The phone rang again, and this time Michelle told me I'd better listen, as it sounded like this was not a prank call.

The person at the other end said they were with the Fenton police and that Ron had crashed his white Suburban towing our white enclosed balloon trailer. He said Ron was fine, but the Suburban and trailer were not. He wanted us to come out and identify the trailer. I asked what it looked like; he described it to me and I said, "Yes, that is ours." I asked if they could smell propane, and he said no. I said then there was really no reason for us to come there in the middle of the night. He said they would tow it to an impound yard then, and we could come to recover it in the morning.

The next morning, we went, and the trailer was in awful shape. The balloon was fine, but the trailer was totaled. I'd never liked that trailer anyway and was happy when the insurance company paid it off and we could now find a more practical one. That trailer was the reason Ron crashed. It was very top heavy, with the lifting system installed on the roof. Ron had been driving home on a narrow two-lane road, and the trailer wheels went off the road, catching in a rut, which started it rocking back and forth. Ron could not recover and ended up in the steep ditch, rolling over the entire rig. He was unhurt, so everything was fine in the end. We borrowed a flatbed trailer from a friend for the balloon for the rest of the season, and all was well. We had a very successful second season flying passengers, and I quit my job at A-1 Transmissions that summer to concentrate on our new successful business.

We realized we needed to do something in the off season to make money since flying balloons in Michigan is so seasonal. Trying to get by all winter on our Christmas Gift Certificate sales and the few flights we usually could pull off from October through April would be tough. So I called my buddy Ron Frusher in Palm Springs, California, and we worked out a deal for us to bring our Big Blooming Balloon out there for his winter season. He would subcontract us out for his overflow flights, and we could be available to all the other companies out there to do the same. Since we were going to go there, it only made sense to first go to Albuquerque and fly rides during the Fiesta again. Michelle was thrilled about this. She had never spent the winter in California like I had, so we made it happen.

~ ~ ~

Fiesta had changed a bit since the Wild West days I remembered, and you no longer could just rent a 10-by-10 space along the perimeter of the field, build a booth, and sell rides. There now was an official ride concession, and this was the only entity that could legally advertise, sell, and fly paid rides from the Fiesta Field. Sid Cutter's famous World Balloon Corporation from Albuquerque was that official vendor. We applied to be one of its subcontracted ride companies and were approved. On September 29th, I flew our last two flights of the season from Seven Lakes Vineyard, and we then packed up and drove to Albuquerque.

The Balloonatics

The event began October 5th, 1991, so we only had five days to pack up and get there. Ron Frusher had bought a used four-wheel-drive, full-size Ford van and a flatbed trailer for us to use as our new Big Blooming Balloon chase vehicle. All it needed was passenger seats. It had been used to haul motorcycles out in the desert and therefore had only the driver's and passenger front seats. I bought four used rear bench seats in Michigan for a good price. We loaded them in the back of the little Toyota pickup we had bought earlier that year, along with a bunch of other equipment, and covered it all with a tarp that was strapped and duct taped over everything. We hauled a small trailer behind it that was also overloaded with stuff. The rig reminded us of the Beverly Hillbillies' truck from TV! A friend hauled the Big Blooming Balloon in his truck for us. And off we went to Albuquerque.

We arrived on Friday the 4th and checked into our hotel. There was no time to get any rest. We had to fly the next morning for the first day of Fiesta, but first we had to install those four seats in the van and load the Big Blooming Balloon and all the other equipment in the van and trailer. Ron had brought tools, and he and I set up shop in the hotel parking lot. Two local volunteer crew members had been assigned to us, and they met us in the parking lot to introduce themselves.

Valerie and Manny turned out to be wonderful people and crew. We were blessed to have them. They ended up staying with us all afternoon and into the night, talking and helping us get everything ready for the next morning. Installing those four seats took longer and was more difficult than Ron and I expected. Since the van was originally a cargo van, we had to drill holes through the floor and bolt all the seats down, which doesn't sound difficult until you attempt it. We finished well past midnight, utterly exhausted. Valerie and Manny introduced us to pizza with green chilies, which was served as dinner for all of us along with some local beers while we worked feverishly to finish the grueling job.

Saturday morning, October 5th, came way too early, but we were ready to go and flew two flights, taking up 16 paying passengers to start the Fiesta out with a bang! We would take off with eight passengers plus me and have another eight in the van with Michelle, while Valerie and Manny followed in the little Toyota pickup. I would fly for 45 minutes or so and then land, and the crew would arrive with two full propane tanks and the other eight passengers. The crew would have to bring me the two full tanks from the truck, and I would switch out the two mostly empty ones for the full ones (the balloon carried four 15-gallon propane tanks and approximately two would be used during a 45-minute flight) while the crew was carefully helping the passengers to switch out at the same time. All the while the balloon was fully inflated standing upright. It was easy if the wind was calm but exciting if there was much of a breeze!

The weather once again blessed the Fiesta with nine good days in a row, and we flew 99 passengers on those nine morning flights. We also did one late afternoon/evening flight where we took up Valerie and Manny and a bunch of other friends and helpers. Michelle went back to the World Balloon tent on the last day to ask for at least one more passenger so we could fly 100, but alas, they had given all the passengers they could give us, and that last morning we flew 12 passengers. Some days they only gave us eight passengers, and on other days they gave us 16, but overall, we received a nice check to cover all the expenses and kick-start our season in Palm Springs.

~ ~ ~

Of the 10 flights we flew during the Fiesta in '91, one will never be forgotten. I remember trying for a long time to find a landing spot on this flight and finally was able to line up for one. I had to drop in quick to make it. Several other balloons had already landed in this overgrown field, so I figured it would be a good place to land, even though it looked rough. I came in fast and barely cleared the power lines on the leading edge of the field. As I was landing, a bunch of the people on the ground were yelling for me not to land there.

I had to land at that point and was confused why they were saying not to since a bunch of others, including Ron Frusher, had already landed there. Ron and several others helped me land by jumping on the side of the basket. Ron then told me that this was not a good place to land after all because the entire field was fenced in, and the gate was locked. They were trying to figure out how to get access to the field. They all suggested I take off and find a better landing spot. I should've stayed or had passengers exit as fuel was running low. Instead, I made a poor decision and took off again with all my passengers on board.

We flew off for about a mile, heading toward the zoo and the surrounding fields. Several other balloons had landed there, but there was one power line feeding a bunch of light poles in a line in my flight path. One balloon that had landed on the other side of that line of light poles was close enough for me to yell out while holding my drop line, asking them to help.

Turns out that balloon belonged to pilots I knew, Terry Dillard and Paul Woesner. Paul came running to help, but no one else did, to my chagrin. Paul was fast and was soon under me. I was just a bit too close to the line of light poles to land, but I figured if Paul could grab my drop line and help direct me just a bit farther away, I would be good to land.

Unfortunately for Paul, we were flying faster than he could run, and soon after he grabbed the line, he was pulled off his feet. He gallantly held on, dragging across the field on his back as I yelled to him to please hang on! Paul, a veteran pilot, held on as we dragged him across the grass until we could safely land. When we landed, the balloon was rocking back and forth, and a gust of wind blew the envelope onto one of the light poles. I watched in horror as the top of the pole pushed into the balloon as it continued to lean into the pole. Just when

I expected it to rip open, the envelope miraculously rebounded off the pole. I ripped the top out, and it deflated safely away from the pole, falling over the other way.

As it turned out, the flower artwork on Big Blooming Balloon saved the day. The exact spot where it contacted the pole was the only place on the entire envelope where the fabric was three layers thick with overlayed artwork—thank God! If it had contacted the pole almost anywhere else, it would surely have ended up impaled on that pole. The thick three layers of fabric saved the day for me. Paul did as well, and I still owe him for that and for his new sweater that was ruined during his long drag as a human balloon anchor! Everyone was safe and sound, including the balloon, and the passengers had an exciting tale to tell. I will forever kick myself for taking off again after my first landing.

~ ~ ~

On another flight I remember, it was windy as we took off from the Fiesta Field. The balloon and basket had dragged to the end of the tie-off rope, which was attached to the van. We used a quick release attached to the basket carabiners that attach the basket to the envelope. That meant that the quick release was above my head and the passengers' heads. I never thought much about that. On this occasion, when I pulled the release to take off, the tension made it very difficult to release. I jerked on it real hard to get it to release.

Unfortunately, this action caused my hand and the metal quick release to snap back into the basket while the tie-off rope snapped back toward the van. I always made sure to clear the area between the van and the basket before I did this so no one would get hit by the rope. This time, however, that was not the problem. When my hand and quick release snapped back toward the basket, they both hit one of my passengers on the back of her head! And to make it worse,

The Balloonatics

the passenger was a sweet elderly lady. I felt instant mortification and disbelief as I realized what I had just done.

At that moment, there was nothing else I could do but safely take off and fly the balloon off the field. She let out a howl of pain and almost fell to the floor of the basket! All I could do was apologize profusely. I had no ice or anything to offer her except my water bottle and apologies. She said she was okay but was in obvious pain and had a nasty headache throughout the entire flight. That was the worst I can ever remember feeling during a flight. I just kept apologizing over and over till she said there was no need to do so anymore; what was done was done. She was okay at the end of the flight but had a bad headache and welt on the back of her head, and I just felt horrible!

~ ~ ~

I remember one non-ballooning incident that I am also not proud of. It happened on the Tramway. Ron Frusher, Michelle, and I took the tram up the San Jacinto Mountain to the nice restaurant at the top and had dinner one evening. I, as usual, drank too much, and on the way down on the tram I passed gas terribly. It just came out before I even realized it!

Knowing how uncouth it was in such a small, enclosed space with a bunch of people we did not even know, I was instantly mortified. Michelle heard it, and her reaction was to say out loud in an upset tone, "Craig," which led, about 10 seconds later, to one of the other tram riders saying in a very disgusted tone, "Who is this Craig guy anyway?" I was too buzzed and embarrassed to say anything, but they all knew. Fortunately, the guy didn't hit me for my rude behavior and spoiling their otherwise beautiful nighttime tram ride down the mountain.

Our last flight at the Fiesta was October 13th, and two days later I logged my first flight in Indio, California, where we flew 16 passengers in two half-hour flights. We did the same on the 17th, 18th, and 19th. There must have been an enormous group in for that week. Michelle and I rented an apartment in Bermuda Dunes that was very nice, with two pools on the property, and close to where we flew. Many times, we would fly over the apartment.

On November 16th, I logged a flight with Kinnie Gibson during the Indio Polo Field Race, which was the beginning of the enormous event they now have there. I remember Kinnie and I flying into the field toward the target, descending fast, and stopping just one foot above the ground over the target as Kinnie dropped his baggie in the center of the X!

1992

We flew only 40 flights in the desert that season from October 15th, 1991, through April 12th, 1992. We supplemented that meager income with our new rentals. We had purchased and begun to rent out what we called "Cold Air Advertising Balloons" and our "Inflate-A-Tent," a cool-looking big, new, round inflatable tent that looked like the top of a multicolored hot air balloon. Before we left for Albuquerque, we mailed out a ton of postcards advertising the Inflate-A-Tent for rent in Southern California and Las Vegas to auto dealers and the like. We sold a few jobs. Michelle and I traveled to Las Vegas several times to set up the tent in Vegas and around Southern California while we were there. We had brought it with us in our little Toyota pickup along with all the van seats and other equipment.

Jeff Geiger from Traverse City had also come to fly in the desert with his balloon. He actually camped out the entire time on the balloon field owned by John Zimmer, who was the "top dog" out there

The Balloonatics

at the time with the busiest company, Desert Balloons. This was the same field that Dan Glick had originally owned. We spent a lot of time with Jeff going on exciting excursions in his four-wheel-drive pickup in the desert and mountains.

One day Jeff called us to say he was going parachute jumping and would land at the wash near Jefferson Street. The wash was a large, dry riverbed that only had water in it when it rained. If it rained a lot, which it did only occasionally, the wash turned into a raging whitewater river. We frequently landed balloons in those areas, as did the parachute companies. We often landed at Jefferson's wash, so we knew exactly where to go and drove over to watch him parachute in.

As a beginner, he did a tandem jump with an instructor securely strapped to his back. We watched as they floated in and then crashed into the wash with a thud. The instructor must have messed up a bit as he basically pile-drove Jeff into the sand in the wash. Jeff was hurting and limping after that one! We could relate, as we also occasionally made mistakes and landed a few feet below the ground sometimes. Apart from not flying enough, we had a wonderful time that season in the desert.

The desert experienced a huge rain event that winter. The washes turned into raging rivers and washed out many roads that crossed them, including the one closest to our apartment. The rain also created a beautiful blooming of the usually dormant desert flowers, and it was a beautiful sight to behold thereafter!

~ ~ ~

On April 12th, Michelle and I packed up and drove the two vehicles and trailers back to Michigan. The "new" red four-wheel-drive van and trailer hauled the Big Blooming Balloon, and the little Toyota pickup and trailer hauled the Inflate-A-Tent and various other gear. We also brought back with us Bill and Jim, two crew members from the desert. Ron Frusher had hired Bill and Jim to crew, and we became good friends with them.

Both were college athletes. Bill played basketball, and Jim was a football punter. They were both tall, around six feet, six inches, making them great crew members! They had never been to Michigan and decided it would be an enjoyable experience to come and spend the summer with us and work as our full-time crew. My logbook shows our first Michigan flight of the season on April 28th.

We had done a mailing to school districts promoting hot air balloon school programs and had a bunch of bookings for them that spring. We would take Ron Pethick's little T&C 56,000-cubic-foot balloon and tether it at the school while educating the kids on lighter-than-air flight. Bill also started taking flight lessons in his effort to become a pilot. Due to his legal blindness, Jim couldn't. How he could be a football punter I could never figure out. His vision allowed him to crew competently, but driving was not within his capabilities.

~ ~ ~

In June 1992, I logged my 1,000th hour as a hot air balloon pilot in command, which was a big milestone back then. We had another successful season flying passengers, renting our Inflate-A-Tent and Cold Air Advertising Balloons and promoting our company.

~ ~ ~

Sometime that year I learned that "The New Capt. Phogg" had bought a building on Grange Hall Road just one mile from the Vineyard where we flew and was running his ride business from there. The company was called Balloon Quest featuring Capt. Phogg Balloon Rides. This again upset me as half of my passengers came from west of the Vineyard where we flew from, and they now had to drive past our

The Balloonatics

competition to locate us. They installed a big "balloon ride" sign out on the main road just one mile from us. Many of our passengers were getting confused and stopping at his new location, thinking he was us.

It was even more of a problem back then than it would be now because there was no GPS or Google maps guiding our passengers directly to our location. They had to read and follow our directions from the information we had mailed them (snail mail from the US post office). Often, they would see his sign and figure they were there! Many of our passengers started arriving late to our location after stopping there first. I was furious! We now had to inform all our passengers that we were not on the main road, Grange Hall. We were off on the back dirt road at the Vineyard, one mile away. I believed he had picked that location on purpose and really resented it.

~ ~ ~

On August 12th we flew a radio personality from the local CK 105 Flint radio station, Ian Richards, and his new wife, Mary. Ian, an Englishman, had recently arrived in America. He was causing quite a stir on the radio while building quite a following with his fun personality and British accent. I flew them in the Michigan Balloon with two other paying passengers, and Ron flew alongside us in the Big Blooming Balloon with eight more paying passengers. Ian took a great video of this flight that you can watch at www.theballoonatics.com.

This marked the start of a lasting friendship, and we collaborated on numerous promotions in the following years. One of the funniest and most memorable on-air bloopers that helped him gain fame happened during his first week on the air. He was introducing Janet Jackson's new album, *Black Cat*, which had just come out. The album cover showed Janet Jackson naked with a real, live large black panther lying on her, covering her private parts. He announced, "And from her new album, here is Janet Jackson and her big black pu—." Immediately the station manager ran in and yelled, "What did you just say?? Tell me you did not say that on the air!" Ian didn't understand, and the uproar shocked him. You see, in England back in the 1990s, the word "pussy" meant only one thing, a cat. The station manager explained to Ian the faux pas. Ian felt shocked and embarrassed. Immediately, he went on air to apologize and explain to his audience what had just happened.

~ ~ ~

In September, Michelle and I attended the first Midland Balloon Festival in Midland, Michigan, sponsored that year by Re/Max. We took Ron's little T&C 56,000-cubic-foot balloon in our little Toyota truck, and I flew it three times in the event. We went for fun, but competition and prizes were additional incentives. One competition I flew was a "fly into a target" event. Just a few balloons ended up making it close to the target which was located at the main event site.

There was a sizeable crowd surrounding the target. As I descended toward the target, the crowd erupted in cheers and the announcer called my name, motivating me further. It was quite exciting, and my heart was racing as I got close, only about 20 feet off the ground. I realized I was going to have to throw my baggie about 50 feet toward the center of the target as I passed it to the left. I twirled it by the end of the attached three-foot-long streamer to get more distance out of my throw. The crowd really started cheering as I twirled my baggie. Right when I was ready to launch it, the thing got tangled in the cables above my head!

The crowd's enthusiastic cheering at once turned to a disappointed "ohhhh no," and my heart sank as I reached up to untangle the baggie. I untangled it quickly, but it took me farther from the target. In desperation, I just threw it overhand as far as I could, and the crowd returned to a cheer in response to my final throw. I believe I placed third or fourth on the task, which was disappointing. I could have won if not for the baggie mishap. The inaugural event was a great success anyway and has continued annually up to this day.

~ ~ ~

On October 3rd, I logged the first flight of the 1992 Albuquerque International Balloon Fiesta, flying 14 passengers. Valerie and Manny again were crewing for us, but this time we arrived with the red four-wheel drive van ready to go! We flew eight total flights and 95 passengers, so again we had a good financial start to our journey west for the winter. Michelle and I rented the same apartment in Bermuda Dunes for six months, and I flew the first flight of that season in Coachella Valley on October 17th. We had to return to Michigan that year. Why, I cannot remember. Ron Pethick and Justin Fortney flew to Palm Springs on a jet plane to fly and crew the balloon, and Michelle and I flew back to Michigan.

I flew a few passenger flights from Fenton, Michigan, in November, including one that I will never forget! On November 14th, I took four passengers for an early winter flight. The weather was beautiful in Fenton, but a dark, ominous sky was looming about 15 miles north of us over the Flint area. I observed it for a long time and decided it was heading east and should not affect us.

We launched into those nice skies and began the snow flight from hell! The winds took us toward Holly, and about 30 minutes into the flight it got overcast suddenly. I felt the basket shake, and we got hit with some turbulence. I wanted to land, but we were not over any suitable landing spots. Then it got worse, and snow started falling heavily—big snowflakes all around us—as the winds got crazy and blew us this way and that.

We were heading south toward Grange Hall Road and quickly crossed over it toward some open fields, where I really wanted to land!

I descended and was blown away from the field I wanted to land in. Then we encountered a strong downdraft, causing a rough crash into a cluster of fortunately small trees. They were right on the edge of a stand of 100-foot-tall trees. We bounced back into the air and literally went 180 degrees back to the north over those 100-foot-tall trees that we had just crossed over a minute before.

There was another small open field on the other side of those tall trees. We just cleared the tall trees. I ripped out the top, and we crashed again into that field. This time, we stayed there as the balloon deflated.

We were all very glad to be on the ground, and the snow was really coming down now. The field where we ended up was close to a dirt road. Michelle was right there to come help us pack up the envelope, which was quickly getting covered with several inches of wet snow. The passengers videotaped the flight and sent us a copy. It can be viewed on the website. It does not really look as bad on the video as it was in person, but it does show an interesting balloon snow flight!

On November 28th, we did another flight with Ian Richards and CK 105 live radio broadcast from the balloon, and that was the last flight of 1992.

1993

Michelle and I flew back out to the desert, and Ron and Justin flew back to Michigan. I logged my first desert flight of 1993 on January 21st. In February, a new friend from Michigan, Mark Sheppard, who had just bought a new Cameron balloon from us, brought his new balloon and his wife, Jackie, out to the desert to finish his flight lessons.

This kept Michelle and me busy, both flying passenger flights and giving Mark his lessons. It was a ton of fun, and we had some nice, memorable flights together with Michelle and Jackie flying along with us on several of them. Regrettably, they departed within weeks.

The police had pulled them over and told them they had to have a California commercial license plate on their vehicle to operate a balloon business, and they insisted they had to have a business license and business insurance as well! The police refused to listen to or believe their explanation about taking flying lessons. They threatened to impound their vehicle and balloon, so they just left and finished out their lessons back home in Michigan.

I flew 44 flights from January 21st through March 24th, so it was much busier than the year before out in the desert. And once again we brought our Inflate-A-Tent. We rented it out to auto dealerships in Las Vegas and around the desert area, including a 10-day rental at the Indio Date Festival. Michelle and I took a trip out to Phoenix during those three months and bought an old Raven 210,000-cubic-foot balloon. We needed another large passenger balloon for our Michigan ride operation. I saw an ad in the Balloon Pilots Newsletter that the Phoenix Balloon company was selling two of its older big balloons, still in good flying condition, for only $5,000 each!

We drove out and flew in one of them while a ride operator from another state flew in the other one. They were identical, and we both ended up buying the one we flew in. We made the deal the next day. We loaded the balloon basket in the back of our little Toyota truck and put the envelope in the basket. It barely fit with the basket riding at an angle, since one side rested on the wheel well. The little truck was almost bottomed out from the load, but it did not complain and brought it back just fine.

We drove it back to our apartment in Bermuda Dunes and unloaded it into a parking spot in the parking lot outside the apartment and covered it with a tarp. We were happy with the purchase and were looking forward to flying two eight-passenger balloons together back in Michigan. The first time I inflated it back home, a lot of desert dust rolled down the inside and out of the mouth of the envelope. Someone said, "Oh my God" as it fell on us in the basket, so we named it "Oh My God."

Once again, Jeff Geiger came to fly in the desert that winter and rented an apartment close to us. Again, we enjoyed the desert and mountains with him, going on many four-wheeling excursions when not flying. When it was time to drive back to Michigan, Jeff helped us out tremendously by towing our little pickup behind his truck back home. We had two big balloons and the Inflate-A-Tent to bring home and also rented a U-Haul to get everything back. Bill and his girlfriend, Nina, drove the U-Haul back with us to be our full-time paid crew for the 1993 season in Michigan. We had quite the balloon caravan driving home that year!

~   ~   ~

The first flight back home that season was on April 22nd in Ron Pethick's little T&C 56,000-cubic-foot balloon. Ron had bought it a few years before, and we used it for lessons and private charters with the little Toyota pickup as the chase vehicle. This flight was the first lesson for Mark VanBenschoten. Mark was an accomplished fixed-wing pilot who flew fixed-wing charter flights for a van conversion company owned by a ballooning friend of ours, Craig Bye.

We had just sold them a new Cameron balloon with the company name and logo on it, "Debut Automotive," and they hired Mark to fly it and promote the company. Mark and I had a lot of fun during his training, and he completed it later that season and got his "lighter than air" endorsement on his license. Mark told me during his training that flying a balloon was harder to learn than flying fixed wing. The lag time from the pilot's action to the balloon's reaction was the reason, he said.

Later on, Mark and a friend circled the globe in a two-passenger Cessna airplane. He had told me of that dream of his, and he

The Balloonatics

accomplished it, taking several months with many refueling and sightseeing stops along the way. Now that sounds like an incredible adventure!

We did more school demo programs that spring and early summer and enjoyed another successful passenger flying season. We also kept busy with the Inflate-A-Tents and Cold Air Rooftop Advertising Balloon rentals. On June 3rd we again flew our radio friends Ian Richards and Mary, along with Mary's parents, for a ride. Ian continuously promoted us on the radio. We got together with them many times and became good friends. Ian, Mary, and I were big drinkers; Michelle was not, but she put up with us and laughed along with our shenanigans.

~ ~ ~

At the end of August, Michelle and I loaded up the little Toyota pickup with Ron's little T&C balloon and inflation fan in the truck bed. Both Inflate-A-Tents were towed in a trailer. We drove to Buffalo, New York, for the first Uplifting Buffalo Balloon Race. Thankfully, both of our Inflate-A-Tents were rented for the event, justifying our attendance.

Our excitement stemmed from the opportunity to fly over Niagara Falls, the main attraction. Carroll Titsworth, an accomplished longtime balloonist and pilot instructor, worked for many years with the FAA to make this happen, and it finally paid off. It was exhilarating to be involved. Arriving early, we set up our Inflate-A-Tents side by side at the main event launch field. The weather forecast for the entire event was fantastic. A local crew was assigned to us, and we had a wonderful couple, Pat and her husband (whose name I can't recall). On Friday, August 25th, I flew solo from the balloon field in Clarence, New York.

The next morning at the very early pilots' briefing, Carroll informed us that the weather was a go to fly the falls. He stressed over and over that we had permission to overfly the falls but not to go down into the gorge. He said the FAA would be watching. Niagara Falls lies along the Niagara River, which forms a border between Canada and the United States, and consists of three main falls: the Horseshoe Falls (the largest falls, also known as the Canadian Falls), the American Falls, and the Bridal Veil Falls. Going below the lip of Horseshoe Falls was trouble; the FAA would shut us down. Also, Carroll informed us we would be flying from Canada down the river, over the falls, and landing in the USA. First, we had to go through Canadian customs. Then, we would meet at the park by the river to fly. After we flew over and landed back on the USA side, we would have to drive back to US customs and declare that we had arrived by balloon. We were all so excited!

About 25 hot air balloon teams headed for Canada, and we all met at the park on the Canadian side about an hour later. The weather forecast was good, and we all started inflating. Michelle and I were thrilled about what we thought would be a once-in-a-lifetime flight. We took off, and as Carroll had said, the wind carried us right down the river toward the falls. I kept the balloon basket about 10 feet off the water all the way down along the Niagara River, about one mile to the falls. Our hearts were racing as Michelle and I approached the Horseshoe Falls. We'd heard the roar of the falls as soon as we had started, and it just grew louder and louder as we flew closer and closer. Now, as we approached, it became a deafening roar, and the mist was rising above.

We crossed over Horseshoe Falls about 10 feet above the rim, and the entire basket and balloon shook from the reverberations. That feeling in a balloon was unprecedented for me. The falls fell out below us, and we maintained our altitude above the rim of the falls, flying through the rising mist, taking as many photos as we could while also just trying to take it all in! It was, of course, breathtaking and incredible; words cannot come close to describing the feeling and sights we were experiencing! Our speed remained constant as we flew at about 10 miles per hour down the river and across the gorge.

Before we knew it, we were over the gorge and flying over the good old USA toward the city of Buffalo. Carroll had told us to land as soon as possible, as our track might take us into congested areas with few landing spots. I started looking right away and saw an apartment complex ahead within minutes that I could tuck into with the little balloon. I landed between two apartment buildings in the parking lot. I contacted our crew before landing, and the shocked residents provided the address, which I relayed to them.

Surprisingly, they found us quickly despite going through customs. Michelle and I stood in the basket, leaving the balloon inflated until the crew arrived. We watched all the other balloons flying by, including the T-Rex Dinosaur special-shape balloon. The T-Rex pilot yelled down that he wished he was in a little balloon like ours so he could land there also! We quickly packed up and had a champagne toast in the parking lot with some residents who assisted us. Then we headed back to US customs to declare that Michelle and I had arrived by balloon. That evening we all tethered at the falls, according to my logbook. Funny, but I do not remember any of that!

~ ~ ~

At the pilot briefing the next morning, Carroll informed us that the weather was perfect to repeat the experience. However, despite his warnings, a few balloons had flown into the gorge on the first flight the day before, which made him very upset. I remember seeing others do it as we flew over and mentioning it to Michelle while flying over the gorge. Some idiots always must ruin everything, I said to her. Carroll was adamant that we had to follow the FAA rules if we wanted to make this an annual event, which he hoped to do after his years of work to put it all together.

Again, we all went off, and I repeated the same flight as the morning before. I brought Pat, our local crew member, with me this time, and everything turned out nearly identical. Some individuals flew down into the gorge again. Seeing this again made me really upset! Pat and I sailed over the rim of Horseshoe Falls, feeling the entire balloon shake, and on through the mist on our way to the same apartment complex landing in the parking lot 100 yards from where we had landed the morning before. Again, we watched all the other balloons fly over us as we waited for our crew to arrive.

There were no flights scheduled that evening. The next morning at the pilot briefing, Carroll was in tears. He fought through his emotion and his anger to tell us that thanks to a few jackasses who flew down into the gorge on both flights, and one who apparently flew under the Rainbow Bridge spanning the Niagara River to connect Canada and the United States, the FAA had pulled its waiver, and we could not fly the falls ever again! The weather was perfect. We could have done it an incredible three mornings in a row had it not been for these idiots! He instead had us do a Hare and Hound event from the Clarence, New York, event field.

This incredible event could have been ongoing and allowed hundreds of other pilots the thrill we experienced. To this day I am angry at those who ruined it.

On the 29th, we flew two additional flights from the event field to conclude an unforgettable one-off event. Thank you, Carroll, for putting it together and including us!

~ ~ ~

I had told our radio friend Ian Richards about our trip to fly the falls, and he said to contact him when we returned to talk about it on the radio. When we arrived back from Niagara, I called him, and he was doing a live remote from a bar just down the street from our little house in Burton. We had just driven home and were tired. Nevertheless, he urged me to come over for an interview about the flights.

Michelle and I drove the two miles to the bar and had a drink waiting for him to finish up a segment of his show. Ian then came over and asked me to follow him. He had his microphone in his hand and started right in, asking about our trip to Niagara Falls. It was very loud in the bar, so he walked into the men's room, where it was quieter. I was then a bit taken aback as he continued into a stall and motioned for me to join him. He then closed the stall door, all the while talking about the flights over Niagara Falls.

There we both were, crowded into this toilet stall, conducting a live radio interview! Then he asked how it felt and sounded as we flew over the falls. As he asked those questions, he flushed the toilet and stuck his microphone close to the flushing water and held it there for a few seconds. Then he said, "Did it sound like that, Craig?" He kept talking about how it sounded and felt, then flushed the toilet again. It was brilliant! I was laughing hard along with him. That was Ian. He had a brilliant way of getting his point across, with crazy and funny antics.

After the interview, I told Michelle what had gone down. The two of us just sat there laughing our heads off. We were both tired from the trip and had eaten little but were having such a great time watching and taking part in Ian's live radio remote that we stayed for a couple of hours and had a few drinks.

Michelle rarely drank much at all (I always joked that I had married my designated driver). She got very tipsy. We did not even make it the two miles home before I had to pull over. Michelle opened the passenger door and almost fell out of the car as she threw up all over the parking lot I had pulled into. I had to grab her and hold on to keep her from falling out!

~ ~ ~

In October, we once again headed for Albuquerque to fly rides at the Fiesta for the World Balloon Corporation. This time we took "Oh My God" in the little Toyota with a trailer as the chase vehicle. We rented a 15-passenger van in Albuquerque to transport the passengers. All went well again as the weather allowed all but one flight during the nine-day Fiesta that year, and we flew 71 passengers on eight flights.

One flight I landed on a road in a new housing development and radioed the crew, telling them to come around the road to get me. Unfortunately, they took a shortcut through a very large desert field instead of going around it on the roads. The Toyota and trailer made it. However, the van, with Michelle driving, got buried up to its axle in a wash only 100 yards from where I had landed on the paved road. Several other balloon teams came to help us, and they took our passengers back to the Fiesta Field for us while we worked to unstick the van.

After an hour of digging, pushing, and pulling, we successfully rescued the van without any visible damage.

~ ~ ~

A horrific and terrible experience happened after one of our flights when we did a double hop. The second landing was a brisk tip-over drag in the big old Raven balloon's nonpartitioned basket, with all nine of us ending up on top of each other in the tipped-over basket. We all crawled out laughing, and the crew arrived with the other eight passengers from the first flight. We brought out the cooler, and I began to tell the story about the traditional champagne toast and do the balloonist prayer. As I finished and opened the first bottle, a terrible sound suddenly caught our attention—an explosion that sounded like an M-80 firecracker going off very close. It startled all of us.

We all turned toward the sound to see a balloon basket falling and its envelope ascending without it from the high-voltage power lines. A

The Balloonatics

big plume of smoke billowed between them as the basket crashed to the ground with a terrifying thud only about half a mile away. Without the basket and its occupants, the envelope soared upward, flopping wildly like a toy balloon that had been blown up and let go. Smoke billowed out as it inverted, dumping its hot air as it fell back to earth. We all just stood there in shock, knowing what had just happened. We dedicated that toast to the people in that basket and prayed that somehow they might be okay, although I knew better.

It was a terrible ending to an otherwise wonderful morning. Our road back to the Fiesta Field took us right by the fallen basket, and we all looked on in horror as we passed only a few hundred feet away. The emergency crews were sealing off the area. Later, we learned that the pilot and his one passenger were killed on impact after the basket separated and fell over 100 feet to the ground.

That was not the only power line strike I ever saw at the Fiesta. I saw two others on previous occasions. The first one I saw was while setting up at the first Fiesta I flew in 1985, flying rides for Kinnie Gibson. A small balloon had flown in toward the field and hit some low power lines on the edge of the field, making a loud explosion on impact that turned our heads to see the aftermath, which I recall was not deadly.

The second one happened at another Fiesta. While I was in the air at about 500 feet, a balloon below me was attempting to land and hit wires with a loud pop and flying sparks. I had been looking down at them, and I remember saying just before they hit the lines that it looked too close for comfort. I do not think that one was fatal either. Overall, the Fiesta has had a very safe record, but when you have that many aircraft flying so many flights, accidents are bound to happen occasionally.

We didn't return to the desert to fly for Ron Frusher after Fiesta. We decided it wasn't financially practical anymore. This turned out to be the last Fiesta we ever attended as well. Things change. We decided to just stay home and concentrate on Michigan Balloon Corporation in Michigan.

~ ~ ~

When we returned to Michigan, the annual inspection for "Oh My God" was due. We took it to the local FAA-certified repair facility. The envelope failed the porosity test on several top panels, so we sold it as is, needing repair. We sold the envelope for $1,000 to a company flying in Napa Valley, California, and I don't remember who bought the basket later. It had served us well for the year or so we had it, having more than paid for itself flying many passengers. I just did not like the system, with the big open basket and eight passengers plus myself in it. We flew eight more paid passenger flights in Michigan after returning from Albuquerque that year, and then we bought a house in December in Holly.

We had been looking for a house closer to the Seven Lakes Vineyard in Fenton. One day, while driving around the area in Fenton and neighboring Holly, we looked at a few. On our way home, I saw a yard sign for another one, and we stopped to look at it. The owners were having an open house, so we got to walk through and walk the 4.25-acre property.

Both of us fell in love with the place. It was a large, three-bedroom farmhouse built in 1890, with 4.25 acres and a pond, and was only a few miles from the Vineyard. Additionally, there was a detached garage for two cars and a 16-by-60-foot outbuilding near the pond. The building was previously a chicken coop but was now utilized for storage. It was perfect! We did not know if we could afford it as self-employed owners of a new hot air balloon business, but we wanted it badly.

Our realtor, Mr. Sifferman, who had helped us buy our first little house in Burton, again got to work and made a miracle happen.

We moved into our new huge (to us anyway) farmhouse in January 1994, and it became the world headquarters for American Balloon Promotions, Inc., d/b/a Michigan Balloon Corporation.

1994

We sold our Burton house to the newlyweds Ron and Tari Pethick! They had met at Balloon Corporation of America when Tari's mom, Barb, started working there in the office around 1988. Soon Tari was crewing, and then she also started working there. She and Ron became the fifth couple to have met there and married and are to this day one of three couples still happily married, the others being Michelle and me, and Alan and Beth Clark.

Our new house had a straight two-track stone driveway down to a concrete pad in front of the garage. The first thing I needed to do was make a circle driveway so we could easily pull the balloon vehicles with trailers in and out. We had joined a trade association the year before, called Metro Trade, so I was really into bartering.

I found a local guy willing to trade for a balloon ride for four people from his farm for him putting in our circle driveway. His name was L.P. Mitchell. He was a great guy. His family was one of the first to settle in Holly, and they owned a large farm and property that he wanted to fly from with his father, who was a decorated military WWII fighter pilot. That spring, L.P. did a great job on our circle driveway. We flew him, two of his brothers, and his dad the next year from their farm. His dad told me after the flight that he had flown in most every aircraft known to man, but the balloon flight he had just taken was the best of all!

We settled into our new home and company headquarters, had a 500-gallon propane tank and pump installed next to the big willow tree by the new circle drive, and felt like we were in heaven! No more long drives to go fly and then refuel the balloons at the gas station. This was fantastic! And we still feel that way as I sit here today after 30 years in this beautiful old farmhouse.

~ ~ ~

We started the year 1994 with a big bang! I had been reading about a series of long jump flights that the Balloon Federation of America was promoting in its *Ballooning* magazine. This was a distance flight competition open to all. This gave me the idea of flying across the state of Michigan. I was not interested in all the details and paperwork needed to do a competition; I just wanted to do a long-distance flight. I called a few friends, and we decided to have a Trans-Michigan Balloon Race. We invited a bunch of pilots, and on February 26th, three balloons launched from the Grand Traverse Resort in the morning.

It was just a fun competition to see who could cross I-75 first, winner gets a case of beer. Interstate 75 runs north and south through Michigan, from Sault Ste. Marie in the Upper Peninsula, over the Mackinac Bridge, southeast near Saginaw Bay, south through Detroit, and on to Ohio and beyond. Depending on the upper wind forecast, we planned to launch from one of three locations. In January and February, we closely observed the weather for a favorable weekend forecast for our flight. The final weekend of February looked promising. The forecast showed the upper winds at 9,000–12,000 feet would come from the northwest that day, so we chose the Traverse City area to fly from. Since it was forecasted to be freezing, we packed up all the cold weather gear we had and drove the three-hour trip up to Traverse City on Friday the 25th.

The next morning, on the 26th, all looked great for the flight, although the surface temperature was minus 11 degrees Fahrenheit!

The Balloonatics

There was an inversion, which meant it was warmer up at 3,000 to 9,000 feet. It was bright and sunny with calm winds on the surface, so we flew. We put all our warm weather gear to the test and launched into a beautiful, clear, cold blue sky, quickly ascending to around 9,000 feet. The ground, covered with a foot of snow, made the view spectacular, and visibility was virtually unlimited!

Much to our delight, we found that it really was warmer up high, and we were actually quite comfortable with all the warm winter clothes we had on and the bright sunshine helping to solar-heat us up. Ron and I were flying in the Michigan Balloon, which was an AX-9 120,000-cubic-foot envelope. We had put in an extra 15-gallon propane fuel tank, so we had 60 gallons to start off with. Mark Sheppard and Larry were flying together in Mark's balloon, which was an identical Cameron balloon system. The third balloon was the Debut Automotive balloon flown by Mark VanBenschoten and Craig Bye, also the same Cameron balloon system.

About an hour into the flight, my feet were freezing. I figured I could warm them up by sitting on the seat Ron had made using two plastic milk crates duct-taped together with a pad on top. I sat on the seat and put my feet up on the top rail of the basket, then used the rotation vents to point my feet into the bright sun and solar heated my black boots! It worked well, and I did it a couple more times during the flight. I took some photos, but they do not do it justice. From 12,000 feet, we saw Lake Michigan, Lake Huron, and the Upper Peninsula as we crossed over Houghton and Higgins Lake.

Our track was taking us southeast toward the Saginaw Bay, and the object was to be the first to cross the I-75 freeway. All three balloons were flying within a mile of each other. As we got closer to the goal, we all inched higher to gain a little speed and beat the other guys. Ron and I ended up at 15,000 feet at one point and then quickly came back down below 12,500 as we had no supplemental oxygen to breathe and did not want to take any chances with that. We all crossed I-75 near

Pinconning, Michigan, all at about 12,000 feet going about 30 miles per hour.

We had been flying for four hours and now had to scream down fast to land before flying into Saginaw Bay! It is only about 10 miles from I-75 to the bay at that point, so down we came as fast as we could. Ron and I leveled out about 15 feet below ground and hit the cornfield with a gigantic crash! We rebounded about 10 feet in the air, crashed down again, and dragged across the frozen corn stubble rows, bouncing along with radios, our cooler, and other stuff flying out of the basket. We dragged about 200 feet to a stop near a big red barn. We crawled out and cheered, elated with our incredible flight but not too happy about our misjudged and unnecessarily rough landing!

We walked back, picking up all the stuff that had bounced out of the basket, and radioed Michelle that we were down. To our surprise, she was right there within minutes. We had flown 97 miles in four hours and 15 minutes and had a blast, so we began planning to do it again next year.

~ ~ ~

The 1994 flying season started out tough. The weather did not allow many flights that spring. Our next flight was April 22nd, with paying passengers. Then we flew only six times in May. June started off well as the weather finally turned for the better, and then disaster struck.

In mid-June, Seven Lakes Vineyard hosted a Wine, Food, and Music evening that Michelle and I attended with several crew members and our radio friends, Ian and Mary. It was a lovely evening, and the wine was flowing all too much, at least in our little camp. The small crowd of about 100 people was spread out on the grass around the tasting room on blankets, eating, drinking, and listening to music.

Ian's wife, Mary, and one of our female crew members who attended were two very fun and crazy gals. They were having a bit too much

The Balloonatics

fun, in fact, at this low-key family event. One of them decided later in the evening that it was time to show off her boobs, and the other one just had to follow suit and outdo the first one. I was having too much fun also by that time, and rather than try to stop this, I just laughed and enjoyed the show.

The next day, the Vineyard owner, Chris, called and asked me to come to the Vineyard for a meeting. He was very upset by my group's behavior and had gotten several complaints from others at the event. I apologized, of course, but he said he had no choice but to end our working relationship. So, just like that, we lost our beautiful Vineyard launch site.

I was devastated and felt terrible because I had done little to stop the debauchery of the night before. It was a very low point for us, and we are so lucky the internet and social media were not around back then. I told Michelle that the only good part was that we would now save the $100-per-balloon launch fee the Vineyard was charging us each time we flew, and we could now buy $5 champagne rather than the $16 bottles from the Vineyard. Not to mention all the extra wine we often ended up buying and drinking after many flights while partying late with some of our passenger groups.

~ ~ ~

We had to scramble to find another launch site and tell all our passengers who had bought a flight "from the Vineyard" that we no longer flew from there. All our literature and passenger info had to be changed. It was a terrible mess! Luckily, I remembered that the guy from Seven Lakes State Park, which was literally just across the dirt road from the Vineyard, had stopped by a few times and watched us fly. He had said we could come and fly from the state park anytime. I went right over there and met with him.

His name was Ed Herfurth. He leased and ran the park concession stand by the beach. Ed was quite a character and was delighted that I was interested in flying from the park. He worked as a painter at the Buick Motor Division plant in Flint; the concession stand was his side job. He loved the park and had a great bunch of friends and family who helped him run the concession stand. Ed was a short, portly guy with a big belly, longish white hair, and short-cropped white beard. His voice was gruff from years of smoking, but he was one of the nicest guys you could ever meet. With his help, we quickly worked out an arrangement with the state park to operate our ride business flying from a field next to Ed's concession stand.

All we had to do was add the park and the State of Michigan Department of Natural Resources as additionally insured on our business and hot air balloon insurance policies, and bam!, we were up and running in less than two weeks. It was incredible how quick and easy it was with Ed's help! Another big help was that other balloonists in Michigan had already established a balloon launch field out of a state park not far south of us.

Our arrangement was that the park would maintain and mow the field next to the concession stand and designate it as our balloon launch field. Our passengers would have to pay the state park entry fee unless they already had a yearly pass for the state parks. Seven Lakes State Park would benefit from the increased revenue from those extra entry fees paid by our passengers and spectators. It would also be an added draw for the park to bring in additional people. Ed's concession stand would benefit from additional customers, and we agreed to start an annual Seven Lakes State Park Balloon Race that would draw thousands of people and be the largest weekend income for the park every year. It was a win-win-win, and we saved a ton of money compared to our earlier arrangement.

The park allowed us to place a small storage unit on the launch field that was donated to us by a crew member (thanks, Randy!). We stored our inflation fans there, so we no longer had to strap them on the balloon trailers. (This is a big hassle and causes the most damage to them as the trailers bounce down the road, and sometimes they are not properly strapped down.) We rented a portable restroom for the early morning flights when the park was not yet officially open and the bathrooms by the concession stand were locked.

The park gave us a key to the entrance gate so we could enter and let our passengers in and out on those early morning flights. Showing up early in the morning occasionally caused a minor issue for us. Sometimes fishermen and their trucks and trailers carrying their boats were parked at the locked gate, waiting for the park to officially open. We had to refuse their entry, and they were unhappy with our special privilege!

~ ~ ~

Thus began a new era for Michigan Balloon Corporation, now flying from Seven Lakes State Park. It turned out to be quite the gem for us, thanks to Ed Herfurth! Flying from the park was beautiful. Our launch field was only 100 yards from Big Seven Lake, and the park is huge, encompassing about two square miles of woods, fields, and lakes. We revised all our advertising and brochures and were off and running with little more than a very embarrassing hiccup. In hindsight, it was a blessing, as we saved thousands of dollars on launch fees every year, not to mention the $16-per-bottle Vineyard champagne and all the extra wine we so often ended up buying and drinking.

The 1994 season shaped up to be a very good one. I flew 70 passenger flights and more than 350 paying passengers. Larry flew 20 flights and approximately 100 passengers, and Ron flew another 40 times and approximately 200 passengers. We also had a couple of other pilots that we subcontracted to fly their own balloons with our passengers on many busy weekends. Along with our Inflate-A-Tent and Cold Air Advertising Balloon rentals, we were very busy!

Operating out of our "new" big old farmhouse in Holly was such a joy! We were only 3.3 miles from Seven Lakes State Park, had our own refueling station in the driveway, and started another division of the company, our own balloon repair station. Our brother-in-law Scott Burdick had started a repair station after leaving his position as the production manager at Capt. Phogg's Thunder & Colt balloon manufacturing company. He no longer wanted to run it, as he had other plans for another business.

We worked out a deal to take it over for him and moved it into our detached two-car garage. Ron had learned to sew and complete many other balloon-related repair tasks when he worked for Capt. Phogg at the Thunder & Colt manufacturing facility with Scott. He got his repair man's certificate, and we now were in business as a balloon repair station. This was highly beneficial and added another income stream. And now we could do our own annual inspections and repairs on our balloon fleet as well.

We had good flying weather right through the fall color season in October, when we flew 18 flights, which is fantastic in Michigan! Then we flew two passenger flights in both November and December.

1995

The 1995 winter was a typical cold and windy Michigan winter, and we did not fly until March 3rd. We had been planning for the second annual Trans-Michigan Balloon race to take place the first weekend in February that promised good weather. February did not present any good weekends, but the first weekend in March did, so everyone who had signed on for the race drove to Ludington, Michigan. We had decided to use Ludington as the base for the now annual event. It is located on the west side of the state on the shores of Lake Michigan

The Balloonatics

and pretty much in the middle of the Lower Peninsula. This location would work well with most any wind direction we would ever have, as the upper winds are mostly out of the west.

By choosing the location ahead of time, we could promote the event and solicit local businesses for sponsorships, discounted deals on lodging and food, and similar benefits. We all arrived early and enjoyed some time together at the hotel pool and dinner at a local restaurant that was one of our sponsors. The morning didn't seem ideal for the flight, but the following one appeared perfect, so we spent the next day relaxing at the pool. A bunch of us went tobogganing at the state park, and there was a big jump at the bottom of the hill. We all tried to avoid it after the first person went over it and reported that it was not fun! Unfortunately, Michelle and her sister Karen hit it together on their first run, and they were both hurting and sore for a few days afterward.

The next morning, on March 2nd, we flew from the Ludington Airport. The upper winds were heading almost due east, which would again take us toward Saginaw Bay like last year, so we made some new rules. We did not want a repeat of last year, where we crossed I-75 at 12,000 feet and then had to scream down to land before crossing into the bay.

The new rules gave a maximum altitude of 3,000 feet when crossing over I-75, the finish line. Approximately 10 balloons flew, and we all again landed near Pinconning. Ron and I landed only a few miles away from where we had landed the year before, after a 126-mile flight in 3.5 hours! This time the landing was soft since we were able to come down slowly, level off at about 500 feet, and fly on for a bit before finding a landing site in a snow-covered field.

I had come up with a good idea for snow-covered field retrievals using two small five-foot-long toboggans tied together. I had first tried an old car hood; I waxed it and tied a rope to each front corner. That worked okay but was too big and heavy to carry around in the van or trailer. The toboggans were much easier to handle and worked great for smaller balloons, and we rarely, if ever, flew the big ones in the winter with snow on the ground. We returned to our home and "world headquarters" in Holly, excited to begin planning for an even bigger Trans-Michigan Race next year. All our Ludington sponsors were wonderful and wanted to sponsor it again.

~ ~ ~

Shortly after we returned from the Trans-Michigan Race, we got exciting news. Michelle was pregnant! We had been taking precautions to avoid having children for the first five years of our marriage since we wanted to travel and fly balloons. Now we had decided it was time to stay home and start a family. We were so excited!

~ ~ ~

We also had some exciting news on the business front. Larry had sold his interest in the Dockside Bar recently and had been working on selling another Buick Olympic Balloon contract to Buick Motor Division, ever since he heard Buick was going to once again be a major sponsor of the 1996 Summer Olympic Games in Atlanta. He had met and made friends with some of the decision makers in the Buick advertising and promotions department while on the first Buick Tour. We had flown many of them and some of their families, both from the Buick Headquarters in Flint and in the Simi Valley of California, during the 1984 Olympics. He landed the contract in the spring of 1995! The budget was tight, and our contract was not as lucrative as the first one had been, but we were very excited to have it and relive some of the glory years of 1983–84.

Buick bought us a new red GMC van, a matching red enclosed trailer, and a brand-new Cameron 105,000-cubic-foot red, white, and

The Balloonatics

blue Buick Olympic Balloon. We had the van and trailer logoed and done up with white and blue stripes to match the balloon, and we were ready to go "On the road again!" In July, we received the balloon, and on August 11, I had my first flight in it from Seven Lakes State Park, flying four paying passengers.

~ ~ ~

One day I received a call from the balloon company in Napa Valley that had bought our "Oh My God" balloon envelope. We'd sold it to them for $1,000 the year before as an envelope that had not passed its annual inspection and needed repair. They were very upset when they called and said they had been out inflating it, getting ready to fly passengers, when the FAA showed up and did what is called a ramp check. The FAA guy checked the paperwork and found that it was not the proper paperwork for the balloon. They had to cancel the flight and lost a sizeable chunk of money because of it. The registration numbers on the balloon did not match the numbers on the balloon's airworthiness certificate and registration paperwork!

Long story short, when we and the other guy both bought those two identical balloons on the same day from the balloon company in Phoenix more than two years before, we were each given the other's paperwork. The worst part was that no one noticed until the FAA showed up at that launch field in Napa over two years later! All that time, we all had been flying those balloons with the wrong paperwork. The Napa Valley company told me they had flown the balloon many times since they'd bought it from us. The two current owners of the two balloons were able to contact each other and switch paperwork to put everything in order shortly thereafter. Unbelievable!

~ ~ ~

For some unfathomable reason, we decided to move our office to downtown Holly. I think we thought it would seem more professional and that the downtown location would draw walk-in business. It turned out to be another short-lived and expensive move. We did not see enough, if any, additional business come of it and moved the office back to our home again after our one-year lease ended.

Our 1995 passenger ride season began as usual in April when we flew five times with several balloons. In May we flew eight times, and then in June we only had 10 flights with multiple balloons. This was a bad June, weather-wise, for us. On one memorable flight, I gave Bill another flight lesson and took my two small nephews along for the ride. We had hired Bill and his girlfriend, Nina, to be our full-time crew again for the season. Nina was also a college basketball player and about six feet, two inches tall. Between the two of them and all the fantastic volunteers who crewed for us for rides, we had a powerhouse crew!

My two nephews, Jeremiah and John, were ten and nine years old in 1995, and this was their first balloon ride. Their mother, my youngest sister, Beth, had dropped them off to spend a couple of days with us in Holly. On June 26th, we had only one balloon filled with paying passengers and wonderful weather. Ron flew the passengers, and I took Bill and Rick Day, another crew member, for a lesson, with Jeremiah and John as passenger/ballast.

I had Bill do a bunch of touch-and-goes, and the wind was blowing around 6–7 miles per hour on some of them. We bounced along a few times before coming to a stop and took off again. Jeremiah and John were having a blast. After the flight, we called Beth so they could tell her about it, and they told her they were "crash dummies" for Uncle Craig and Big Bill! Turned out they loved the flight but not so much all the "crash landings."

~ ~ ~

In July, the weather got better, and we flew 15 times. We also organized and ran the first Seven Lakes State Park Balloon Race. This was to become an annual event to raise money for the park and, later, some charities as well. My logbook shows I did a two-and-a-half-hour tether on July 21 and a three-hour tether on July 23 during the event where we offered tether rides for money and took up hundreds of passengers. The park charged all the cars a state park fee to enter, and they kept all those proceeds. This event would become their biggest grossing weekend by far every year.

One day in August, I was flying our Big Blooming Balloon with eight senior citizen passengers. We were flying over a big posh subdivision in Fenton with houses on large lots and wide-open roads to land on. I was flying very low and planned to land on the next subdivision road after going over one more house. As we approached the house, we saw a girl of about 14 or so on the diving board of the pool in the backyard. One of the male passengers in the balloon yelled down to her, "Show us your dive!" She responded by bending over and mooning us all! Some of the passengers burst out laughing, while others were a bit taken aback. I yelled out that we were going to land on the road in front of the house, whereupon she hightailed it into the house, never to be seen again!

~ ~ ~

We only flew 12 flights in Michigan that entire month of August; this was not typical. The only good thing about that August was that Larry and I hit the road again with our brand-new Buick Olympic Balloon.

Just like in 1984, Buick was a major sponsor of the 1996 Summer Olympic Games, held in Atlanta, Georgia. They were also a major sponsor of Little League Baseball, and a very large and important Little League tournament was being held in Fargo, North Dakota, at the Fargo Dome in August 1995. Buick wanted their new balloon to be there to promote both the Little League and Buick's sponsorship of the upcoming Summer Olympics.

When I heard of this first job for our new corporate balloon, I told Larry that we had to do this one together. Not only had neither of us ever been to North Dakota, but it was a chance to relive our old glory year of 1984. Ron would stay home and fly our paid rides, with Michelle running the office as usual. I bought a new Willie Nelson "greatest hits" cassette tape, and we were "On the Road Again."

~ ~ ~

Fargo is almost 1,000 miles from Holly, Michigan. Larry and I drove to Minneapolis, Minnesota, listening to that Willie Nelson tape and singing along. We stayed the night in Minneapolis and visited the Mall of America since we had never been there either. After exploring the massive mall, we enjoyed a satisfying dinner and a restful night's sleep before continuing our journey to Fargo the next day. We arrived in Fargo midmorning on Tuesday, and the job was to begin on Thursday, so we visited the local Buick dealership that had sponsored us.

We talked with the owners and managers and then checked into our hotel. Larry had just learned how to golf, and we had brought our clubs, so we set a tee time for the next afternoon at a local course. We had earlier called a local balloonist using the Balloon Federation of America's pilot roster. He had agreed to help us, so we called him, and he was free for dinner that evening. I wish I remembered his name as he was invaluable to the success of this trip!

Having a few extra hours before dinner, we found a little par-three golf course near the hotel and went there. I played the best golf of my life! I had not played at all in a couple of years but was hitting the ball like I never have before. I hit eight out of nine greens from the tee and ended up shooting a 3 over par 37. It would have been better if I had putted as well as I was hitting everything else.

The Balloonatics

At dinner that evening, the local attorney and balloonist told us that the only rule we had to strictly abide by in Fargo was not to fly outside the city into the farming country that surrounds the city. That idea was totally foreign to us, but he clarified that the farmers would not welcome us, and we would be very sorry if we flew out and landed outside of the city limits.

He said he had to plan his flights to always launch on the upwind edge of the city, fly over it and land on the downwind edge. Additionally, he provided us with the assurance that the city was balloon friendly and there were plenty of sites for launching and landing. He also offered to go along with us as ground crew on our first flight, which is always invaluable. We will forever be thankful to him and all the other balloonists who were always so welcoming and helpful to us on all our travels. We looked at a map of the city and the surrounding residential area and saw that it encompassed approximately a six-mile radius, so we had to be careful and hope for calm winds the next few days.

The next day, we got up early, drove all around Fargo, and went to the Fargo Dome, where the tournament was to be held. We got the tournament schedule and spoke with the people in charge there about our plans to tether and fly from the park. They showed us a spot where we could operate from in a practice field right next to the Dome. The Fargo Dome is located on the northeast side of the city. Free flights from there would have to be very short unless there was almost no wind, or it was blowing from the northeast.

We stopped back at the local Buick dealership that had sponsored us and met with the owner and general manager to make a plan. As usual, they envisioned us tethering all day, every day, in their parking lot. We had to educate them and convince them it would be more advantageous to them to garner more exposure by flying over the city, taking local press reporters and cameras along for the ride. Also, we could take some of them and their families along as well. They agreed to this plan as long as we did one or two tethers at the dealership since they had been advertising that the balloon would be there. The weather had been beautiful since our arrival, and the forecast promised the same for the next few days, which got us all very excited. We planned to arrive the next morning at the dealership and tether in the parking lot doing tether rides.

We went back to our hotel and started calling all the local press—newspaper, TV, and radio—inviting them to come out and see the balloon at the dealership the next morning and talk about going for a ride in the next few days. We had already sent out a press release to all of them prior to our arrival, and a few had already responded with interest. So this task was quick and successful, with most of the news outlets excited to come and see us in the morning.

Later that afternoon, Larry and I went to the country club, where we had a tee time at 5 p.m. Larry had acquired a ton of Buick Olympic Logoed attire and other swag, including Buick Olympic Golf Bags, balls, shirts, caps, and so on. We looked like walking Buick Olympic billboards when we walked into the clubhouse and onto the first tee!

They set us out by ourselves, and as we were warming up on the first tee, a foursome drove up in their two carts to play behind us. One guy in the foursome asked Larry what all this Buick Olympic garb was all about. Larry said without missing a beat, "We are part of the Buick Olympic Golf Team." The guy said he never heard of golf being in the Olympics. Larry said, "Oh yeah, first year. It's in a trial period. It was just decided by the Olympic Committee, and we are on the road to promote it."

They were duly impressed until Larry stepped up to the ball and totally whiffed at his first attempted drive! He laughed it off, saying, "Well, I guess I needed more warm-ups," and then tried again, this time just barely catching the ball with the toe of his driver and watching it dribble about 40 feet and roll under a pine tree to the right of the tee. The foursome roared out with laughter, saying, "Well, I guess we can kiss the gold medal goodbye this year!" I teed up next and thank God hit a good one, and off we went, all laughing like crazy, but we never said another word about it. Larry was not having a good day on the course, and we barely kept ahead of that foursome.

The next morning, we arrived to do the tether at the dealership. When we arrived and walked into the dealership, a big group of the salesmen, managers, owners, and other employees were there to greet us with a big cheer, laughter, and jeers of "Here comes the great Buick Olympic Golf Team!" Turned out that two of that foursome that played behind us the day before were salesmen at the dealership. They had told the story to all their coworkers, and everyone got a real good laugh out if it!

The weather was perfect, and we did a nice one-hour tether, taking lots of people up and down on the tether ropes, including about every TV, radio, and newspaper reporter in town. We were heroes now to the dealership folks, and they treated us as such for the rest of our wonderful time there. Again, I wish I had made more notes in my logbook of the names of the dealership and the people who helped us and treated us so well. Alas, as usual, I did not, and my memory does not recall the names but only great memories of the trip.

~ ~ ~

That evening, I flew from the field next to the Fargo Dome with some local press people and some folks from the dealership. We planned to do three short flights, landing and switching passengers two times. The weather was perfect for this as the winds were light and out of the northeast, which gave us the longest flight corridor possible from the Fargo Dome, approximately four miles, before we would come to the edge of the city and the unfriendly-to-balloons farmlands beyond.

I took off and flew low to avoid getting into any faster winds above. About a half mile into the flight, we flew over the Tharaldson

Park softball field on the campus of North Dakota State University. There were games going on in all the fields. We flew in from center field on one of them, heading directly down the center of the field toward second base and the pitcher's mound. I was flying at about 200 feet as we came toward the field and descended much lower and talked with the players on the field. We descended to about 50 feet as we flew down the center of center field. I noticed that the pitcher seemed to be perturbed by our uninvited disturbance of her game, and the play stopped as all turned to watch us fly in. The pitcher, who was a big gal, was just staring at me with what seemed like a growl on her face, slamming the ball into her glove over and over.

I descended lower to about 20 feet off the ground and maybe 50 feet behind second base. Then I yelled to the pitcher, "Hey, throw me the ball," and I stuck out my right hand from the basket. To my surprise, that pitcher reared back and threw an overhand bullet that smacked into my hand without me having to move it, and it hurt! Wow, what an arm, and what accuracy. I was amazed and glad that I caught it, but it really hurt! I yelled, "Holy smokes, what an arm you have" as I crossed over second base and saw a little smile come across her face. We were now only about 15 feet off the ground and slowly drifted directly over that pitcher's head. I simply dropped the ball directly into her glove as we passed over her. What are the odds? She had such a big grin on her face now, and everyone, including me, gave out a tremendous cheer at the amazing event that had just happened! I blasted the burners, and we slowly rose away from the field to the cheering crowd basking in a moment that is forever etched in my mind!

We flew on for a few more minutes, and I found a tight landing spot between some apartment buildings to do my first passenger switch. Then I took off again, doing the same in a subdivision about 15 minutes later. I made our final landing at the edge of town in a small scrub field just as the wind was picking up a bit. The Buick Olympic Balloon was all over the news that night!

On the last day, the 28th, I logged a 45-minute midday tether at the Fargo Dome. In the early evening, I logged a 30-minute tether followed by a one-hour free flight doing two hops, changing out passengers halfway through.

Larry and I left the next morning for home very happy campers after an incredibly successful Fargo Buick Olympic Ballooning and Golfing trip! It would be the last one we ever did together, and it was only fitting that it turned out so well.

~ ~ ~

Returning from our Fargo trip, we had good weather in September. I flew 17 passenger flights. On most of these flights, Ron and Larry flew our other two balloons. We also subcontracted with many other pilots to fly along with us in their balloons, taking our passengers, so we made up a bit for the poor start of the season. The first two weeks of October were good also, with nine flights again and multiple balloons taking passengers. Then the weather shut down on us, and we only managed a few flights for the rest of the year.

One flight that fall was one of the craziest and, in hindsight, one of the funniest ever! Two of my cousins booked a ride with their significant others. Kevin wanted to propose on the flight, and Kenny was going to be his best man, so Kenny and his wife went along for the ride. It was a nice fall evening flight, and we took off from Seven Lakes State Park, heading south. I remember flying low, and Kevin said he wanted to try flying the balloon, so I let him, and he did a superb job. Not long into the flight, Kenny started acting funny and asked me if I could land there or there or there, and I asked what was up. He said, "I really need to go to the bathroom!" His wife smacked him on the arm and snapped, "You really need to get that problem taken care of!" Turns out he really had to go! I started looking for a spot and soon came across some woods and was able to land between the woods and a small swampy area that was totally secluded. Kenny jumped out of the balloon as soon as I told him it was safe to do so and ran behind the first bush to do his duty. He took off his pants, in the pocket of which was the engagement ring Kevin had given to him for safekeeping. He squatted down to go. Immediately we heard him yelling, "Oh shit, ouch, oh shit, ouch!" He came running back to the basket buck naked while waving his pants around his head like a helicopter blade trying to keep the bees away from him! Turns out he had crapped on a ground bee nest! There was a swarm of bees stinging and following him as he ran toward us and jumped headfirst back into the basket.

I had reacted quickly and heated the balloon back up, blasting both burners as soon as I saw him running back to us. However, it takes a minute to get enough heat back in to take off. So, there we all were, swatting bees, with Kenny on the floor still swinging his pants around, trying to get them away. We finally took off quickly and left most of the bees behind. Some bees were still with us, and it took a few minutes to get rid of all of them. I think Kevin got stung a couple of times also.

Kenny, who had been stung so many times, was kind of out of it and unable to stand up for quite a while. Meanwhile, Kevin was panicking about the ring. He finally found it still in Kenny's pants pocket, which he then handed back to Kenny and said, "Here, put these back on, man!" After a bit, when we all had calmed down a little, Kevin proposed, and she said yes.

~ ~ ~

On October 26th, a beautiful, healthy baby girl blessed us! Katherine Marie Elliott decided not to wait until the 28th, which is my and my

The Balloonatics

mother's birthday. She wanted her own special day. We had planned carefully for this day. We had always paid for our own health insurance and had a plan in force with a company back then called Golden Rule (now UnitedHealthcare). Maternity coverage was very expensive. The plan covered complications of pregnancy but not the delivery. We researched and found an amazing pre-paid delivery program at St. Joseph Hospital in Flint that only cost $1,000, and we paid that small up-front cost gladly.

Michelle had been doing very well throughout the pregnancy with some minor issues and continued to run the office of our company right up to the end. On October 25, Ron and I flew passenger flights both in the morning and evening. As usual, we partied into the night afterward, probably even more than usual since the weather the next morning would not be flyable.

At around 1 a.m., Michelle woke me up and said her water had broken, and we had to go to the hospital. I told her she was okay and to go back to sleep. She kept shaking me, saying, "Craig, get up, we must go to the hospital! We are going to have a baby," and I kept saying, "No, go back to sleep." She finally yelled at me and shook me, and I finally came to my senses and said, "Oh my, I am sorry; let's go!"

I drove her to the hospital, having sobered up in a hurry, and they got her into a delivery room right away as she went into labor. The labor lasted over 18 hours! Nothing was working. She was in pain, especially toward the end. They kept pumping the painkiller into the epidural, but it was not helping. I could only sit there and hold her hand. It was scary.

Finally, they did an emergency C-section, and when they moved her out of that bed to take her to the surgery, they discovered why the epidural pain killer was not helping. The epidural needle had fallen out, and all the painkillers had been pumped into the mattress under her!

The emergency C-section was successful for Katherine but did not go well for Michelle. They gave her a spinal injection for pain, but it did little, and she screamed in pain throughout the procedure. Finally, after about 24 hours, we had a beautiful baby girl in our arms! Katherine's head was a bit elongated from trying to push through for all those hours (I called her conehead for a few days). Otherwise, she was in perfect shape and so beautiful, with a full head of two-inch-long blond hair! Michelle had a terrible spinal headache, as they called it, and they gave her lots of heavy pain pills and sent us home the next day.

We arrived home and had lots of help from our parents, thank goodness, as Michelle was in terrible shape and needed rest. Katherine was doing great and breastfeeding well, so all seemed like it was going to be okay. That night Michelle woke me asking for a glass of water. On my way back up the stairs bringing it for her, I heard her choking and ran to the bed to find her on her back choking in vomit. I turned her on her side and smacked her on her back several times to get her breathing. That helped, but she was still out of it.

Her eyes were rolled up in her head, and she was twitching. I called 911 and kept her on her side, moving her back and forth and trying to make sure she was breathing. I called her parents, who lived only 10 miles away. They came right over and got there just as the ambulance arrived to take us to the hospital. Michelle's parents stayed at our house with Katherine, who had been and was still asleep all the while.

Michelle had suffered a seizure, and they put her into intensive care; she was alive but unresponsive. Our families rallied around us and came to help me take care of Katherine. Amazingly, my oldest sister, our sister-in-law, and Michelle's cousin had all also recently given birth to daughters and were breastfeeding. They all came to our house and took turns breastfeeding and pumping breast milk to be refrigerated and even frozen to be fed to Katherine. Michelle and I had read all about how important to a newborn's health breastfeeding was, so this was a godsend for our baby girl, and we are forever grateful. My mom came and stayed with us, and Michelle's parents were over every day while Michelle remained in the intensive care unit.

Michelle finally improved after several very scary days. In the hospital, she suffered one more seizure, but after two weeks, she was released home. Finally, she could again hold and start nursing our beautiful baby. She was put on anti-seizure medication and saw a specialist for several months thereafter and slowly recovered. She does not remember most of it to this day.

Our Golden Rule health insurance covered the entire hospital bill of almost $50,000 since it was all caused by complications of pregnancy. We never had to dispute anything with them. They were great! There were several thousand dollars' worth of other bills, such as the ambulance, however, that were not covered. My parents paid those for us, so we got through it all financially unscathed, thank God!

Katherine thrived with all the help we had from our families, and she brought such joy to our house. Being a parent seemed to come naturally to us both, and we soon settled into the constant duties of rearing a newborn baby with joy in our hearts. We were also very lucky in that Katherine turned out to be a delightful baby and easy to take care of, with no genuine issues—that I can recall, anyway. Of course, you will have to ask Michelle about that! As usual, she did all the work; I just had fun!

1996

In 1996, our flights began with a balloon wedding in Bay City on Valentine's Day. Our plan was to fly away, but the weather had other plans. With breezy and snowy conditions, we were able to pull off a cold, windy, snowy tethered balloon wedding.

Just four days later, we headed off to Ludington again for our annual Trans-Michigan Balloon Race. This year Larry had secured Buick's sponsorship, so we named it the Buick Olympic Trans-Michigan Balloon Race. We had a nice budget and could offer all the pilots and crew much more than in the past, like free hotel rooms, more food, and show-up money.

The weather turned out great on Sunday morning, and all the pilots had a fantastic flight, with calm surface winds for takeoff and landing later in the morning after they flew over Lansing, with pilot Andy Baird's GPS registering 72 miles per hour at 9,000 feet. We had a car up for grabs with a key grab pole set up in Flint, a short distance of only 153 miles away. One pilot actually got within 20 miles of it! All went well, except that my drinking once again got me in trouble.

My mom and dad came to the event and stayed with all of us at the hotel. Dad and I, along with a few other partiers, closed the hotel bar down the first evening. My dad sometimes had the same drinking issue that I have, in that we liked it too much and rarely knew when to say when. I again was the Balloon Meister for the event and had declared a mandatory 6 a.m. pilot briefing for the next morning, even though the weather did not look good at all.

As the evening progressed, I knew we would not fly the next morning from all the weather reports we kept checking, but the following morning, Sunday, was looking great. My dad and I got into too many Maker's Mark toasts, and the next morning I could not move. Michelle tried and tried to get me up for my stupid "mandatory" pilots' briefing, and Larry and several others did so as well, banging on our hotel door to no avail. I was so out of it that I could not get out of bed.

Very sad and embarrassing indeed. Larry did the briefing for me and sent everyone back to bed. That afternoon when I finally got up and around, I endured endless but much deserved ribbing and actual scorn from the other pilots and crew. That Saturday evening, I did not drink and went to bed early!

~ ~ ~

The Balloonatics

On May 4th, Ron and I took our friend and local radio legend, Ian Richards, for a fun flight in Ron's new balloon, a Cameron C-80. He had sold his smaller balloon and bought this one, which was perfect for private charter flights (two passengers and a pilot). Ron needed a bi-annual flight review, and we invited Ian along for the ride.

~ ~ ~

On June 14th I made the maiden flight in our brand-new 10- to 12-passenger American Dream balloon. We named it that because we were living it (or so we thought)! It was a red, white, and blue Cameron A-210 with a 210,000-cubic-foot envelope and huge T-partitioned basket. Ron was going to be gone a lot, piloting the new Buick Olympic Balloon Tour, and our ride business was continuing to grow to where we needed more passenger capacity. We went to our bank and secured a loan for the purchase. The first flight was a publicity flight with a

Part of our Michigan Balloon Corporation fleet.

bunch of local media on board to generate free press. With the new American Dream Balloon along with Big Blooming Balloon, the Michigan Balloon, the Buick Olympic Balloon, and Ron's balloon, we could put up five at once and fly 30 passengers each flight, if we could find five pilots that day.

I flew American Dream 52 times that year. Ron and Larry also flew her about 10 times. On my 52 flights, I carried 539 passengers, with an average of 10.36 passengers per flight. She was a real workhorse and joy to fly, with triple burners and the Smart Vent quick deflation system.

~ ~ ~

One flight I remember that is noted in my logbook was an offsite flight from Ubly, Michigan. Ubly is in the thumb of Michigan, in farm country just west of Port Huron. We flew from the farm of a newly retired farmer and seven of his friends, also all farmers in the area. They were all sizeable men—not fat, just big, all well over six feet tall and 250 to 350 pounds. All were in their 70s and 80s but were in great physical condition. They were wonderful people.

We arrived at the farm before sunrise on August 4th to a heavy fog, too foggy to fly in, so we all went out to breakfast, hoping it would burn off soon. It burned off after two hours, and since the forecast was for light winds all day, I decided to go for it. We launched almost three hours after sunrise. We took off from the farmer's cut hayfield, and I asked him if we would have more cut hayfields to the north where the winds were going to take us. They all said yes.

We had a great flight, and about 45 minutes into it I again asked them where all those cut hayfields were. All we had seen were crops in every direction interspersed with woodlands. They had been having a great time looking at all the farms from a new perspective and just said, "Looks like no one else planted hay this year?"

The Balloonatics

The winds were picking up a bit, and I told them we had to land soon, but I saw nothing ahead except crops, and we may have to land in one. After about 10 more minutes, I saw a few good-looking fields to land in with different crops in them. I asked them which one would be the best option to cause the least damage, as we were going to drag through the field for about 100 feet in the now 10–12 miles per hour winds and would then have to drive the van and trailer out to pack the balloon up. They all pointed to a brown one and said to take that one; it was barley.

I landed, and we dragged through the barley, tipping over while coming to a stop close to the road. They all loved the flight and especially the windy drag and tip-over landing! We packed up and drove out of the field and went to the farm that owned it. My passengers knew the farmer, and I wanted to offer to pay for any crop damage. We drove all around the farm but could find no one, so they told me they would contact him. I asked how much they thought I had damaged and what I should compensate him. They all thought for a minute, and one of them said, "Oh, probably just a six-pack—we'll take care of it!"

~ ~ ~

On August 26th I flew "Big Boy." An advertising company contacted us and inquired about using one of our balloons in a TV commercial for one of its clients. I had negotiated a deal with the company charging an hourly rate and explained what we could and could not do. We signed a contract and found out the client was the Big Boy restaurant chain, and I was going to be flying with a Big Boy statue in the basket. They wanted to film it so it looked like Big Boy was flying the balloon. I had to duck down in the basket and try not to be seen.

Brian, my former neighbor and good childhood friend, turned out to be the delivery driver who brought Big Boy to our house in a truck. His family lived next door to us when my family lived in Utica back when I was in the 5th–7th grade. Brian and his younger brother Dean and I used to have lots of fun together back in the day. I remember drinking my first beer with them in the underground fort we dug in the field between our houses after taking three beers from my dad's garage refrigerator. We had not seen each other since my family moved to Okemos after 7th grade. Small world, for sure! The filming went great and took over three hours, but they only used about five seconds of it in the TV commercial. You can see it on the website.

~ ~ ~

On September 2nd, I took Katherine up for her first balloon ride. She was just over 10 months old. Buick had sponsored us to fly over the Straits of Mackinac and the Mackinac Bridge with both the Buick Olympic Balloon and our Michigan Balloon during the annual Mackinac Bridge Walk. This is a huge event every Labor Day. If you look at a map, you will see the difficulty of completing such a flight in a hot air balloon. The Mackinac Bridge connects the Upper and Lower Peninsulas of Michigan by traversing the straits that connect two of the Great Lakes, Michigan and Huron. The bridge is nearly five miles long, which means it crosses a lot of water, and the lake-effect winds can be significant.

We had a contingent plan in place that was used because the winds were nonexistent that day. It was one of the most perfect days ever, especially up there, where it is usually windy. It was absolutely perfect, not a cloud in the sky, temperatures in the 70s, and zero wind! Our contingent plan was to tether the balloons, one on each side of the bridge, at the start of the walk in St. Ignace, in the Upper Peninsula. I had the Michigan Balloon tethered with 150-foot tether ropes going straight up and straight down. I would go up and get the ropes tight and just sit there admiring the incredible view. We were not taking riders, so it got boring except for the view.

The Balloonatics

After an hour, Michelle went to check on Larry and the Buick balloon on the other side of the bridge. She left Katherine with Cindy, one of our very trusted crew members, who often babysat for Katherine and helped us organize many events. I came down and decided to take Katherine up with me and asked Cindy to bring her to me. Cindy asked if I was sure about this, and I said, "Yes, please bring her to me," so she did.

Katherine was not even afraid of the loud burners as I lifted off, holding her tight and making sure I kept her ears as covered as I could. She had been around the balloons since birth (heck, since inception). Michelle and Cindy always took her out to the launch site at Seven Lakes to check in our passengers and watch the balloons take off.

We slowly rose up to 150 feet, and I showed Katherine the sights. I loved it, and Katherine seemed to as well. She had a smile on her tiny face! We stayed up there for about 10 minutes, and whenever I had to use the loud burners, Katherine would just close her eyes. I did my best to shield her ears from the noise, and it never seemed to bother her. As we were up there, Michelle returned from the Buick balloon and asked Cindy, "Where is Katherine?" Cindy just pointed up at the balloon. I heard Michelle was not thrilled about that at first, but when I brought her down and handed her back to Michelle on the ground, all was well and beautiful. That was a very special moment for me.

1997

The 1997 season began with the Trans-Michigan Balloon Race from Ludington, and Buick was our major sponsor again. Word of the event had spread, and we had a big turnout of over 20 balloons that year. Three teams from Cameron Balloons attended—Andy Baird, Mike Howard, and Bruce and Tucker Comstock.

Bruce and Tucker brought a new experimental balloon they had just built, a small ultralight designed for two passengers plus pilot. The envelope had Velcro and little metal clips holding it together at the equator, allowing it to be separated into two pieces. Tucker planned to use it at her adventure travel business in Costa Rica. They built it with the intention of allowing three people to fly in it and then backpack the entire system out of the remote area they were likely to land in.

Also, our radio friend Ian Richards came to fly with Larry and do a live radio show during the flight. The weather did not look good, with windy and snowy conditions, as we all arrived on Friday. I did NOT call for a mandatory pilot briefing on Saturday morning! We all slept in, and many of us needed it since we stayed up late drinking and partying as usual. Some of us went to a restaurant that night that served 75 different beers from around the world. You could get a plaque on the wall if you drank every one of them. Most people took quite a while to place their plaque on the wall. I asked the owner if we could do it as a group, so the Trans-Michigan pilots and crew group of about 20 earned our plaque that night.

Several of us ended up in the hotel hallway later that night playing hockey with a tennis ball. Then Ian brought up two luggage carts, and we had "chariot races" up and down the hallway, taking turns riding and pushing the luggage carts. Many people on that floor did not find it amusing, and eventually hotel security had to come and send us to our rooms.

Saturday was a blowout, and most of the balloonists stayed in the hotel, lounging and playing in the large indoor pool area. Sunday morning looked better, and we tried not to party so much Saturday evening. Sunday was flyable although windy and overcast, so we all went out to Ludington Airport, and most pilots gave it a gallant effort in the windy, icy conditions. It was windy enough for Mike Howard to simply open the mouth of his balloon and never even turn on his fan to inflate and take off. He flew solo and had a propane heater in the

The Balloonatics

basket to keep him toasty during what would prove to be a long flight.

One Balloon Works balloon suffered broken uprights trying to take off in the wind. Mark Sheppard dragged his van and trailer, to which his balloon was tied off, 200 feet across the icy tarmac from which we were launching before aborting and staying on the ground. I was planning to fly 12 passengers in the American Dream balloon and decided not to even try. Larry did a nice windy inflation and launch of the Buick Olympic Balloon. I was helping and noticed that he was also dragging the Buick van and trailer on the icy asphalt. I yelled to everyone to get out of the way before he launched with Ian flying along with him.

Bruce and Tucker then inflated. I helped them and was dragged along, holding on to their little aluminum and fabric gondola, ripping a hole in the knee of my pants as they burned and burned with their little burner to get off the ground. I dragged along about 50 feet until Bruce said to let go just before they came to the end of the tarmac and a 10-foot-tall snowbank, which they cleared by about one foot before sailing away into the gray overcast sky. Bruce wrote an account of this flight, including their harrowing landing, in his brilliant book *A Life in the Air*, which I highly recommend.

About half of the balloons ended up flying that windy frosty morning, and I heard some marvelous stories afterward of their cold flights and landings in the snow. With the overcast, the pilots never could take advantage of the sun's warmth. Only Mike Howard, with his onboard heater, was at all comfortable during the flying that cold winter day. All but Andy Baird and Mike Howard landed after about an hour of flight. Andy and Mike both stuck it out and crossed I-75 after about seven hours of flight time, with Mike declaring he was the winner.

Here is part of the story that I never heard until I reached out to Mike and Andy as I was writing this book. Mike wrote:

Craig Elliott

Back in 1997, I was working for Cameron Balloons US. Along with Andrew Baird, Lorne Whittles, Steve Davis, and Tucker and Bruce Comstock, we were very kindly invited to take part in the Trans-Michigan Balloon Race by Craig Elliott. The forecast for Saturday morning was not ideal, but Sunday looked a little better. When Sunday morning came around, if the truth be told, the conditions weren't much better, with strong winds at the takeoff site and low clouds at around 1,000 feet, with tops forecast to be between 2,000 and 3,000 feet. Personally, I would have been happy to cancel and go home, but the trouble was, whenever Andy, Lorne, Steve, and I found ourselves standing on a launch field together, one of us would back the others into a corner and we would all end up flying. Because it was his birthday the day before and we had given him the bumps, I think this time it was Andy, out for revenge, who insisted we should fly.

To have any chance of flying across the state of Michigan, you required six to seven hours in the air. So, before we started the inflations, we thought it prudent to visit the toilets in the FBO at the airport. As I stood there in the freezing cold trying to encourage myself to pee, Steve was banging on the door telling me to hurry up. To which I responded, "Steve, do you know how hard it is to get three inches of skin out of six inches of clothing?" Apparently, Steve almost wet himself with laughter.

I watched Andy take off, and then my actual launch was fairly standard, for one where it was so windy you didn't need a fan and just held the balloon mouth open. Once there was enough cold air in the balloon, I turned on the burners, and with everything already loaded in the basket, I found myself airborne very quickly and following Andy across the great state of Michigan.

The Balloonatics

For the first hour of the flight, the balloons that managed to launch stayed in the very cold temperatures below the cloud base. Fortunately, I had been given a hunter's heater system, which required me to sit inside the upright sleeping bag contraption with an internal gas stove heater at my feet. I couldn't have been more toasty and warm. However, the radio was awash with pilots commenting how cold they were and how they were looking for landing sites.

After two hours into the flight, there were only two of us still in the air, Andy and myself. By now we had both found holes in the clouds and climbed above the tops, where the temperatures had significantly increased, and the sunshine made it feel warmer. The cloud skimming was something I will never forget.

Three hours into the flight, the clouds had dissipated. Below and ahead of us was a beautiful winter scene of farmland, woods, and a few small settlements. At this point, Andy and I had managed to stay together and, as the only two balloons still airborne, took the opportunity to chat about all nature of random topics to kill the boredom.

About four hours into the flight, the previous night's dinner was beginning to make rumbling noises in my stomach. At the time, I had been comfortable I would be able to hold it until landing. I was wrong. Very quickly I realized I had two choices. Throw away the competition race, land, and use the nearest facilities, or something else! Given the fact it was only Andy and I now racing, and he was the reason we were flying that day, I chose the "something else" option.

Looking around the basket, I searched for anything that I could fashion into some type of bucket. Surprisingly, there really wasn't anything other than my new pilot bag, and I just couldn't bring myself to soil it.

Looking at my outside surroundings, I was over a very large, wooded area that seemed to run for miles and miles. It was at this point that a lightbulb moment came to me.

Making sure Andy was far enough away so he couldn't see me in the basket, I began to undo my trousers. My plan was simple: stick my butt over the edge of the basket and poop. Unfortunately, the execution was not quite so simple. Very quickly I realized I needed to get my now cold and naked butt a long way over the edge so that the release wouldn't soil the side of the new Cameron basket with its multicolored weave and leather rope handles, which we were hoping to sell to a customer one day.

As I sat on the rim of the basket up to my knees, with my meat & two veg dangling well over the side in the freezing cold, gripping the burner frame for dear life, two thoughts came to mind. The first, which made me giggle, was that if this lands on a hunter's head, he's going to have a hard time figuring out what kind of flying animal had just shat on him. The second, which was a little more of a concern, was that if my hand slips and I tumble out backways, sometime in the spring when the snow melts and the freeze begins to thaw, hunters will come across the body of a man in winter clothing whose cause of death had clearly been a fall from a great height. But figuring out why his trousers were around his ankles would have been the head-scratching question. A conspiratory theorist would love this!

Having done my business and feeling rather pleased with myself that I hadn't fallen out of the basket, I wanted to share my experience with someone. Given the fact Andy was the only person I was in radio contact with, I decided to offload to him.

Me, on the radio: "Andy from Mike."

Andy: "Go ahead."

Me: "Have I got a story for you when we land."

The Balloonatics

Immediately Andy came back with: "Is it a number 1 or a number 2 story?"

Completely shocked and thinking he had binoculars in his basket, I replied: "A number 2 story, but how the hell did you know?"

To which he simply replied: "Because I was doing the same thing."

Me: "How did it feel releasing yourself over the basket?"

Andy: "I didn't. I did mine in a plastic bag."

Apparently, he used the "backwoods camping technique," which usually involves leaning up against a tree, but in his case, he used one of the tanks. His biggest concern was not being able to reach the burners while doing his business. Brave man, I thought. Hats off to him.

In the end, I think I beat Andy to the finish line by less than three minutes, and to this day I put it down to the extra weight he was carrying in the plastic bag in his basket!

~ ~ ~

We spent the rest of 1997 flying passenger rides at the park. One evening Ron flew our eight-passenger balloon with a group of older ladies. When they were about 500 feet in the air, Ron started pointing out sights. While turning around quickly with his arm extended, he accidentally knocked the wig off one of his passengers, a cancer patient who was bald. He was aghast as he saw it fly off her head and sail overboard, looking like a dead bird falling to the ground. Ron turned ten shades of red and apologized profusely. She laughed and said, "No problem. I didn't like that wig, anyway!"

We organized another successful Seven Lakes State Park Balloon Race in July. We had a very successful passenger flying year with wonderful weather. I logged 89 flights, most in the American Dream balloon, and flew over 800 passengers myself. Ron flew alongside me on most of those flights, flying approximately 400 passengers as well in the Big Blooming and Michigan Balloons. We also had several other subcontracted pilots flying for us on many weekends, and they flew approximately 100 more passengers for us that season. Michigan Balloon Corporation was doing very well with the passenger ride sales and Cold Air Advertising and Inflate-A-Tent rentals.

1998

The 1998 season began with a flight from the Cameron Balloon Factory on February 7th. We called it the Trans-Michigan Balloon Race, and several other balloons joined us for a winter flight. Buick did not renew their sponsorship for the Trans-Michigan Race, and the weather never looked good to do the flight. We had other commitments after mid-February, so this was what we did in place of it. I flew with Ron and our friend Bernie, who was taking flying lessons.

I remember this flight only because of the error I made when we flew down into a huge gravel pit and I flew us right up as close as I could to the 100-foot vertical rock wall at the end of it. Then I hit both burners and rocketed up over the wall, or so I thought. I ended up hitting the wall about 20 feet below the rim, and we dragged the basket up the last 10 feet before coming out swinging like a pendulum! Not very impressive, but thankfully, I had caused no damage or injury except to my pride.

On February 14th we did a wedding flight in the Michigan Balloon. Two more flights were flown before Michelle, Katherine, and I flew to Palm Springs, California, on February 28th. Our friends Clotaire and Sue Castanier had hired us to come out and run their balloon ride business for two weeks while they attended a wedding in Tahiti. We

The Balloonatics

stayed at their house, and Michelle did her thing for them, managing their office, selling rides, and so on, and I flew the rides.

Clotaire had a classy operation. He kept his eight-passenger balloon and pickup truck housed in a hangar at the airport in Indio, California. His two crew guys would bring it out to the launch field and get the balloon ready for inflation. Clotaire would drive his van to the various resorts and pick up the passengers. He had a tip jar on the console in the van's front between the two front seats.

When he picked the passengers up, he would tell them he was their chauffeur. As he drove to the launch site, he would call his crew on the radio to tell them to start the fans to fill the balloon when he was 10 minutes away. When he arrived at the launch site, he would tell his passengers that now he was going to be their pilot.

Mid-flight, he would take out a little table he had made, set it on the partition wall inside the basket, and serve the passengers champagne and cookies in flight, saying, "Now I am your server." After landing, the crew arrived and packed up the balloon while Clotaire would take the passengers back in the van, saying, "And now I am your chauffeur again." The tip jar always filled up!

We enjoyed good flying weather and were incredibly blessed by the fact that a week before our arrival, a big rain had drenched the desert. All the dormant desert flowers that only bloom once in a great while were all abloom, and the desert floor was covered in color.

Everything went well. We had a wonderful time together exploring the desert again, this time with little Katherine. I flew six flights, taking up 33 passengers. I made one big mistake one morning and left two passengers waiting for me at the Marriott Resort. Turns out there were two different Marriott Resorts, and I went to the wrong one to pick them up. After the flight I realized my mistake.

When I got back to the house, Michelle told me I had to call the passengers and the resort concierge, as they were understandably upset. I called and apologized over and over. Amazingly the passengers were from Michigan and only lived a 30-minute drive away from where we flew at Seven Lakes State Park. I offered to fly them for free in Michigan, and that helped to smooth over the issue. We flew them a few months later in Michigan, and all was good.

We returned at the end of March and soon announced the great news that Michelle was pregnant again, and we were excited to welcome a new addition to our family! Then I only flew two flights in the next two months because of this.

The Beginning of the End

Starting around 1996, I had begun seeing articles in the BFA's *Ballooning* magazine and *Balloon Life* magazine about a new system for tethered helium balloon rides. There was a company out of France that had built and run one in Paris, and it was making them a lot of money. They claimed it would operate in winds of up to 25 miles per hour and take up to 30 passengers at a time to an altitude of 500 feet on a one-inch-thick steel cable tether operated by a large electric winch. My dad always told me to "stick to my knitting," meaning stay on course with what is working. But I was always looking for the next great thing, and this newfangled tethered helium balloon sounded like a winner to me.

I began to research this system and got more and more interested until one day in 1997 when I saw an article in *Ballooning* magazine. Sir Richard Branson's Virgin Group had begun a division called Virgin Aerostations. Their mission was to set up many of these tethered helium balloons across the world, and they were looking for partners!

Well, that was all I needed to get me very excited, what with my earlier experience flying the hot air balloon for Virgin Atlantic and first meeting Sir Richard in Oswestry at the Thunder & Colt balloon factory. I wrote a letter to Sir Richard expressing my interest. I was pleasantly surprised when his office responded quickly, and they connected me with a chap named Hugh Band. Hugh oversaw Virgin

Aerostations, and we soon were in conversations about setting up the first operation in the USA.

So right when our Hot Air Balloon Ride operation was really taking off and growing, I convinced Larry and Michelle that we should take a big gamble, scale it way back, and focus on forging a partnership with Virgin Aerostations as their USA operator of tethered helium balloons. We sold the American Dream balloon, thus reducing our hot air ride passenger capacity, and began searching for a location to put our first Virgin Aerostation USA.

We formed a partnership with Virgin Group's Virgin Aerostations and chose the French company Aerophile to build the system, as they had built the few operating systems in the world at that time. The total cost of the system, including site prep, shipping, and so on, was estimated at about $1.2 million. Larry and I both re-mortgaged our homes and each put in $50,000. Virgin Aerostations put up the rest.

I traveled to the Grand Canyon and met with the head ranger there about setting up on the ridge of the Canyon, did the same at Niagara Falls, and tried but got no interest at Disney in both California and Florida. We looked at a bunch of sites and somehow ended up in Birch Run, Michigan! I wanted, tried, and almost had secured a site in Frankenmuth, Michigan, which is a big tourist destination with tons of walking traffic all spring, summer, and fall. When that fell through, our friend Bob Conlee offered us his site at the intersection of I-75 and Birch Run Road.

This exit is the main exit to get to Frankenmuth and is only 10 miles away from that city. It is also the exit for one of the largest outlet malls in the country, Birch Run Premium Outlets. Turns out this was the second-busiest exit on the entire stretch of I-75. It seemed like a suitable spot, and we were really chomping at the bit to get our first one up and running, so we went for it.

We had everything all set, or so I thought, when we ran into our first snag. The Village of Birch Run's planning commission turned

The Balloonatics

out to be a big hassle. It took months and many meetings to get their approval, which caused a delay in starting the site work.

These systems required a lot more site preparation than we had realized, and the entire project ended up coming in at over $1.2 million! Many snags and several months later, we were ready. The system had been shipped and was in storage in Flint. Teams from the German balloon envelope manufacturer, Wormer, and the French manufacturer of the rest of the system, Aerophile, along with Hugh Band and his team from Virgin Aerostations, flew in. We had put out notice in all the press and to all the local balloonists that we needed help to inflate the giant 200,000-cubic-foot helium balloon and had a large group ready to lend a hand.

On May 15th, 1998, on a spectacular calm day, we began inflating the envelope. We had two semi-trailers full of helium on site and spread a huge tarp on the parking lot next to the balloon site behind Bob Conlee's Mobil Gas Station/Travel Center. Ron had sewn together more than 200 sandbags, and we had a crew filling them with sand for the inflation of the netted envelope. It took all day with over 30 helpers as the envelope slowly rose off the tarmac in its net. We ran around yelling "down one diamond" to the crew surrounding the balloon, telling them to move the sandbags lower on the net to let the envelope continue to rise.

By nightfall it was fully inflated, hanging by all those sandbags in the parking lot. Now came the tricky part. We had to move it over 100 yards and attach it to the load ring. The load ring was attached to a one-inch steel cable that was attached to the huge winch below in a 10-foot-by-25-foot basement we had built. Until that was completed, the balloon would be held only by the hanging sandbags and 30 or so crew members. The danger was that a gust of wind could take it all away!

The balloon was massive and majestic standing in the night, lit up only by the parking lot lights and vehicle headlights from all the spectators who had been gathering all day. This was such a thrilling experience. I remember it vividly as we all worked together, walking the huge, colorful envelope over to its landing pad. In still perfectly calm winds, we attached it to its load ring. What an immense relief when, after three more tiring hours attaching the gondola, it was complete! Twenty-one hours after we had begun early that morning, we could now relax and send everyone home as the balloon was secure and ready to do some test flights in the morning.

~ ~ ~

The next day was a whirlwind of testing out the new equipment and learning how to operate the balloon. First, we conducted a series of unmanned ascents with the balloon, as we could operate it from both the ground and the gondola. Then it was time to go up.

Flying in a hot air balloon is completely different and a million times more fun than tethering the same balloon to the ground with ropes. When a balloon is tethered, any wind will try to blow it away, and the ropes—or in this case, the single one-inch steel cable—will keep it from blowing away. If you are in the basket or gondola of a balloon while it is tethered and windy, it can get exciting.

Going up in this huge, tethered helium balloon with only one cable holding it down meant it not only would be blown around by the wind, but if there was very much wind, it would pendulum back and forth in said wind. If it was relatively calm, it went straight up and straight down. The envelope had tons of lift. It was held down by the cable and then let up by the winch and brought back down again by said winch and cable.

Lift could be adjusted by adjusting the ballast bag, which was a bag inside the envelope that could be pumped full of air, thus making the envelope heavier, or the air could be pumped out, making the envelope lighter. This also would pressurize the envelope, making the wind move around it and not blow it around as much.

The Balloonatics

Our Virgin Aerostations tethered helium balloon.

The "pilot" in the gondola controlled all of this, and there were duplicate controls at a command station on the ground. Incidentally, there is a reason I put quotation marks around the word "pilot." Another hoop we had to jump through during the planning and approval process was determining whether the system was going to be classified as an aircraft and thus require FAA approval and oversight. As it turned out, the FAA wanted nothing to do with it. They decided that since it did not travel anywhere except up and down 500 feet, it was not an aircraft. The State of Michigan therefore classified it as a "carnival ride." The Michigan State Carnival Ride Department inspected it, and we were now all "carnies."

~ ~ ~

The first day of learning how to operate it was very exciting. We had the crew from Germany, France, and England on board with us all day to teach us how to operate it. That evening we all went out to dinner again as we had been doing for the last week together, and we celebrated.

Later that evening, around 10 p.m., it was just Hugh Band and I drinking at the bar, and Hugh looked at me and said, "Let's take her for a night flight." We had been talking about how we were going to market the rides and how it would be cool to go up at night and see all the lights for 20 or 30 miles around. I asked Hugh if he was sure, and he said "Yes, let's go for it, and you can see for yourself how cool a night flight is." I said okay, and we toasted to it!

So Hugh and I finished our beer, and off we went to "fly" the new tethered balloon! It was around 11 p.m. and perfectly calm on the ground, with not a cloud in the sky. The stars were shining brightly. The massive balloon was standing there, over 100 feet tall and looking incredible.

Hugh and I went around the outer perimeter of the site and unhooked all 24 of the 1.5-inch outer tie-down ropes. These ropes were attached at the equator of the balloon net. At the ground, each rope connected to a hand-operated come-along winch, each of which was connected to an enormous concrete block that weighed two tons and was sunk in the ground.

After we unhooked the balloon, we attached all the rope ends to the gondola. I got in the huge, round aluminum gondola as Hugh stood by the secondary/backup ground control panel. I pushed the up button in the gondola's main control panel and rose as the giant, below-ground winch unwound the one-inch thick, 500-foot-long steel cable.

I felt my heart racing as the balloon ascended. Years of work planning, negotiating, and overcoming setbacks had led to this moment, and I was realizing my dream. I floated up gently in our new 100-foot-tall, tethered, helium-filled balloon—one of only a few like it in the entire world! It was an extremely proud moment.

The Balloonatics

As I rose into the night looking down at the twinkling lights below, I envisioned selling night flights to groups, party flights with food and drinks, wedding flights, and more. I radioed down to Hugh telling him how fantastic it was. I ascended to 100 feet, still moving straight up. At 150 feet, a remarkable scene unfolded—the dazzling lights of Frankenmuth in the distance. This was awesome!

I continued a gradual ascent to 200 feet, then 250 feet, mesmerized by the view, until—WHAM!—the balloon entered a fast-moving wind shear. The gondola, suspended some 50 feet below the bottom of the balloon, was instantly pulled sideways at an incredible angle. I was thrown against the side as the floor tilted at a 30-degree angle. Struggling to reach the controls on the other side of the gondola, I radioed Hugh that I was coming down. Before I was able to reverse course, the gondola entered the wind shear. The strong wind that had so violently interrupted my peaceful and triumphant first night ride buffeted me! Swinging back and forth like a pendulum, the entire system was tilted at an angle of 30 to 40 degrees. I hung on for dear life, praying the system would hold together in this craziness.

The winch moves slowly. It took forever it seemed to start coming down as I swung back and forth at a very uncomfortable angle. The one-inch cable, the only thing holding me to Mother Earth, was grinding on the bottom inside frame of the circular aluminum gondola because of the extreme angle we were being blown about by the wind. Finally, as we descended below the wind shear back into the calm winds, the balloon swung back the other way and continued to swing back and forth like a pendulum. I continued to descend slowly, with the violent swinging motion gradually subsiding but continuing all the way to the ground.

Getting out of the gondola, I wanted to kiss the ground! The enormous balloon above me continued to swing back and forth for a very long time before calming down and once again standing still in the still air on the ground. I did not know what to think at that point. Hugh and I went around the balloon for the next hour hooking back up and tightening all 24 of the tie-down ropes. I began to have some doubts about this new contraption. We went back to the bar, as I really needed a drink at that point. We just made it back for last call and talked about what had just happened and what we were going to do going forward.

The next day, the weather was perfect for more test flying, and I let Larry go for it. He and Ron took turns, and all went well with the nighttime wind shear now gone. The balloon went mostly straight up and down, and my thoughts returned to positive images of throngs of people lining up for rides. We did a lot of testing and training on the system, and we had it inspected and given a seal of approval by the State of Michigan carnival folks before we started offering rides to the public.

~ ~ ~

A few days later, reality set in again when we had to storm moor the balloon for the first time. This was a very labor-intensive process we had not expected or been warned how difficult it was. If storms were expected to have winds above 40 miles per hour, the balloon had to be put into storm tie-down position. This entailed positioning and clamping down a bunch of large, heavy, inflatable cushions on top of the tall circular gondola.

There were twenty-four 1/4-inch steel cables attached to the envelope net at the equator that had to be inserted into 24 ground winches. Then, using the 24 electric winches that were secured to the ground by large concrete pads, the huge balloon envelope was pulled down and squashed tight on top of the inflatable cushions.

Since the winches were not synchronized, we had to perform this operation slowly and carefully, ensuring an even descent to avoid one side coming down too fast and not aligning with the inflatable

The Balloonatics

cushions. Additionally, we needed to maintain equal tension on all 24 storm-mooring cables. Also, all 24 of the outside tie-down ropes that are used to tie the balloon down during non-stormy conditions had to be tightened equally using the 24 hand-operated come-alongs.

All of this could be done in under an hour if you had 10–12 able-bodied people who knew what they were doing. We did not have 10–12 people and only had one guy still there from the balloon manufacturer to show us how to do it. It took us several hours that first time with about 8 people doing some very physically demanding work to get it storm moored.

We had rented an apartment in Birch Run for Larry and me to stay in when we were in charge of the balloon. The first week was my turn. With the balloon storm moored, I went out to dinner with Bob Conlee and some others. We ended up, of course, at the bar, and I, of course, stayed too long. I crashed out in the apartment at around 1 a.m.

There were storm warnings out for later that morning. We had hired a security company to guard the site after hours, and later that night, a tremendous storm rolled in, packing winds of 70+ miles per hour. The security guard tried to call me, but I never heard the phone. At around 4:30 a.m. the guard was finally able to wake me by driving over and pounding on the apartment door.

I drove over to the site in a driving rain, wind, and lightning to see the balloon being thrashed about violently by the winds and knew right away something was wrong. The side of the balloon was caving in, and the entire thing was bouncing up and down on the inflatable cushions on top of the gondola. It was thrashing around so much I just could not believe it.

I immediately thought, *Why is this happening?* It was supposed to be pressurized to withstand this kind of wind. It even had a backup generator to power the internal pressurization fan inside the envelope in case the power went out. The power had not gone out. I ran up to investigate.

To my horror, I could see that the power cord connecting the pressurization fan with an industrial locking plug when it was storm moored had somehow come unplugged. The balloon was not pressurized and so was being battered by the 70-mile-per-hour winds with gusts even higher. It was impossible for me to plug the fan back in without risking serious injury or even death because the entire thing was bouncing around so violently. The big steel load ring and all the ropes and cables were being thrashed about with the plug hanging in the middle of it all.

I ran back to shelter on the side of the Conlee Building and sat in the car watching what I figured was the end of the balloon. There was nothing I could do, and I felt so helpless and distraught. My neighbor and good friend Bernie, who was now training with us to be one of the "pilots" for this balloon, had driven up from Holly to see what was happening. He joined me in the car and tried to console me as I sat there almost crying, figuring it was going to be all over before it even started.

We watched in horror for about 20 minutes as the system was battered. I could not believe it was still there, intact, when the winds finally subsided. Bernie and I ran up as soon as we figured it was safe and plugged the fan plug back in, and soon all was okay.

The next morning the weather was beautiful again, after thoroughly inspecting the system, we put it back up in the operating position. To our astonishment, we found no damage whatsoever! That thing was built like a tank! We then fixed the problem by lengthening the power cord for the pressurization fan and installed a more secure locking mechanism on the connection plug. Furthermore, we opted to duct tape the plug connection from then on as well.

We hired and trained a crew of ground personnel who would sell tickets and escort passengers to the waiting area. A crew of "pilots," including myself, Larry, Ron, Bernie, and a gal named Sue, were trained to operate the balloon. The state carnival inspector came out to

The Balloonatics

inspect our operation one more time and gave us the carnival operators permit. We were now in business as a carnival ride (a fact we did not advertise).

~ ~ ~

Through many promotions, we garnered an abundance of free press articles and took part in various radio and TV interviews to introduce the new attraction. We also placed ads in all the same places where we advertised our Hot Air Balloon Ride business. The city of Birch Run again made our lives difficult by not allowing us to put any banners or permanent advertising on the balloon, citing the city's local sign ordinance.

This was another of the many setbacks we had never expected. We fought with them for one year before they allowed us in our second year of operation to put three large banners on the balloon that simply said "RIDES." We had planned to do this from the start and sell sponsorships as well. Billboards along I-75, which ran 450 feet west of the site, were going for over $1,500 per month, so we could have sold space on the balloon as a flying billboard.

Also, much to our dismay, we found out that most people driving by did not know that they could stop and take a ride. They thought it was just a balloon flying by. Anyway, our highly anticipated grand opening came with much fanfare and press coverage, but the throngs of riders never appeared.

We ran the balloon up and down every day the weather allowed and quickly learned that the operating parameters were not quite what we expected. Instead of up to 30 passengers, we could only take about 20 in calm conditions. Instead of wind speeds up to 25 or 30 miles per hour, we found around 20 to be the max, and even then the ride was more like a very exciting thrill ride at an amusement park than a balloon ride.

At 15 to 20 miles per hour, the balloon would be blown back and forth on the tether cable like a pendulum, and most people found it frightening. I did not like it at all unless the winds were pretty calm. It was nothing like flying serenely in a hot air balloon!

Several times when I flew passengers with the wind blowing the balloon back and forth at an angle of almost 45 degrees, the gondola would also tilt back and forth, and the passengers would scream like you hear on a roller coaster ride—only they were not having fun! The wind would blow us way over downwind, then swing us back upwind, and blow us back again. It would get worse and worse each time until we finally had enough and went back down, all the while swinging back and forth like that.

One day Andy Baird from Cameron Balloons and his wife showed up on their way down from up north and took a ride. I was running the balloon that day, and it had been getting windy. I was considering shutting down soon but had a few people lined up when Andy showed up.

We loaded Andy and his wife along with about eight others onboard. The first 200 feet up were fairly calm, but then we got hit with the wind. We swung back and forth more and more as we rose. I saw Andy and his wife crouching down and holding on tightly to the side of the gondola as their eyes got bigger and bigger the more we swung back and forth. They were not having fun. I ended the ride short and pushed the down button. Everyone rushed off as soon as I opened the gondola door!

~ ~ ~

One time I was running the balloon on a hot summer day, and all was going well, with a trickle of riders coming and going. We were at the end of the cable with about 10 people on board at 500 feet straight above the site as the winds were calm. I was looking about, pointing out some sights to the passengers, and saw a dust devil forming across

The Balloonatics

Birch Run Road in a big parking lot. Immediately, I pressed the down button. I said to myself, *This is not good. Please go the other way, you little devil.* It had other ideas.

That thing quickly formed into a monster and began moving toward us! I could not believe how fast it grew. As we slowly descended from 500 to about 450 feet, it overtook us. Suddenly, dust and small debris started swirling around in the gondola, and then the balloon got caught in the swirl. The fast circular swing whisked us away, rotating quickly and increasing the angle of the balloon and gondola with each rotation.

The angle was so steep that we were almost swinging over I-75, the hotel next to us, and Birch Run Road, all of which were about 400 feet away from the landing pad. I was yelling over the wind to everyone to stay calm while they screamed in horror as we swung in fast circles around and around over the site, gondola tilting round and round as well. As the winch dragged us down, our circular speed increased as the cable got shorter and shorter until finally the devil moved on over I-75 and released us from its fury.

We continued to circle around and around all the way down to the landing platform. We all looked like we had just been through a dry hurricane or a sandstorm when we finally touched down, still circling around and around in ever tighter circles. The passengers could not wait to exit and run to their cars after that one! The giant balloon above the gondola kept going around in circles for the next 10 minutes as the gondola sat rocking below on the landing pad.

~   ~   ~

We tried everything to get press coverage and advertise the tether rides, but our numbers never even got close to what we needed to break even. We did one promotion with the local radio celebrity Johnny Burke and his sidekick. I had flown Johnny a couple of times in our hot air balloons. He had been promoting the tether rides for us, and when I called to invite them to come and do a live remote from the site, he came up with an idea.

They came out to do the live remote and had a young couple with them. The gig was to take up the young couple, and the guy was going to propose to the young lady in the balloon at 500 feet in the air. He would then, in his nervousness, pretend to drop the ring from the balloon. This would all be done live on air. Then Johnny and his sidekick would encourage all the listeners in the area to come and help us scour the site for the "lost" ring. We had fun, as a bunch of good-hearted people fell for the gig and came out to search. After a bit, someone "found" the ring, and we went back up to complete the proposal.

That promotion went well, but most were not as successful. We bought billboards on I-75; we upped our advertising budget. I constantly sent out more and more press releases. We did all we could to increase traffic, but to no avail. I remember—and it haunts me to this day—something I said during one of the many Birch Run City Planning Commission meetings when we were proposing the site and trying to get their approval. They asked why we thought it would be successful, and I had confidently quoted a line from the movie *Field of Dreams*: "If we build it they will come," which got a chuckle from all the meeting attendees.

Unfortunately, that never happened. We learned the hard way that all those millions of cars driving by every year had three destinations and no time to stop for us. They were either going up north, going to Frankenmuth, or going to the Birch Run Outlet Mall on the other side of I-75.

It soon became drudgery to operate that balloon and keep it safe by storm mooring it every time bad weather was forecasted, which is quite often during Michigan summers. Making that storm mooring decision and then trying to scrounge up as many people as we could to come help was agonizing and began to wear on all of us.

We just could not believe that we had so few customers and were

The Balloonatics

bleeding money from the get-go. We saw the folly in our expectations, and it was extremely upsetting. I decided we should host a hot air balloon event in the field on the other side of the hotel next to our site. This would surely help bring awareness and customers to take a ride.

~ ~ ~

Michelle and I went to work on this project and in two months pulled off an event with 20 hot air balloons flying two flights, but no one came! We had a beer tent and entertainment, food vendors, and hot air balloons, but no visitors! We had parking for hundreds of cars right next to the balloon launch field, with parking attendants on site to collect $10 per car. We took in less than $400 in parking fees. The four or five food and souvenir vendors that we had sold a space to all revolted and demanded their vendor fees returned to them. It was a total disaster except for the memories before and after.

The day before the event, after we had everything set up, including the beer tent, we all began unwinding and partaking in the beer. A couple of our friends and pilots who were helping had brought their golf clubs. We decided to have a driving contest on the balloon launch field. When Ron and another pilot went out to retrieve the balls, Larry said to another pilot, Sean, "I bet you $10 you cannot hit Ron."

Ron was about 220 yards out there, and Sean yelled, "Look out, Ron!" and hit one at him. It missed by a long shot, and Ron taunted Sean, saying, "You can't hit me!" and dancing about. Sean teed another one up and smacked a line drive while Ron was prancing out there, saying, "Nah nah nah nah nah nah," as the ball curved at him. I remember it all in slow motion as that ball made a beeline right at him as he slowly realized it. His "nah nah" taunting suddenly turned into "oh no" terror as he tried to move but was too late. The ball smacked him just below his left collarbone with a sickening thud that we heard some 220 yards away!

We all froze in our tracks as Ron fell backward and lay there holding his chest, groaning in pain. As soon as we realized he was not dead, we all burst into devious laughter. We could not believe what had just happened! Poor Ron did not find it funny at all. He had a golf ball–sized welt, complete with divots, on the left side of his chest between his left breast and collarbone for the next week.

After the event, having closed the beer tent by ourselves since no one else showed up, several of the pilots decided, in their fine mental state, that they wanted the Pepsi cooler belonging to the vendor I had hired to supply the beer tent. They loaded it up in one of their trucks and put it in one of their garages, where they thought it belonged and looked good.

That did not sit well with the beer tent vendor, and he presented me with a bill for $1,200. In the end, we worked everything out, and the guys sheepishly returned the cooler to its rightful owner. He took it all in stride with a touch of disgust. It was a fitting end to the financial disaster the event turned out to be.

~ ~ ~

In hindsight, I realized I had rushed the event without doing enough pre-planning and promotion. Also, it took place on the same weekend as several other long-standing events around the area that I was not aware of. After that weekend, I was pretty much totally demoralized. Not only was the Birch Run project a total disaster, but I had let Michigan Balloon Corporation and its profitable Hot Air Balloon Ride, Cold Air Advertising Balloon, and Inflate-A-Tent business slide.

We were struggling financially. Birch Run was bleeding more money every day. Then real disaster and heartbreak struck. Michelle went in for a scheduled routine prenatal appointment for an ultrasound and was told the baby had died. I remember trying to be strong when I was around Michelle. But I totally lost it a couple of days later when I

The Balloonatics

told my friend Bernie while we were getting ready to operate the Birch Run Balloon for the day. I cried my eyes out.

In an effort to keep the Birch Run operation afloat, we cut staff and did whatever we could. Despite finally getting approval for the next season to put three "Rides" banners on the balloon, which we hoped would help, the first year ended in terrible defeat. At first, our plan was to keep the balloon up year-round, but we soon recognized the sheer folly of that idea. Consequently, we opted to take it down after the fall color season and store it for the winter.

In late October, we assembled a bunch of ballooning friends and deflated the massive balloon and its 200,000 cubic feet of helium (worth approximately $20,000 at the time). We had a storage facility lined up in Flint and thought we would just deflate and pack it up in a big moving truck and put it in storage for the winter. As usual, it did not turn out so simple.

It was a chilly morning when we deflated the balloon, and water condensed on the inside of the balloon. We discovered several gallons of water inside the envelope as we were packing it up. We could not store it wet like that, so when we brought it to the storage facility, we had to dry it out inside. This turned out to be much harder than we ever thought it would be—like everything else with this project.

We spent the next week crawling inside the pitch-black envelope through the only opening at the top, where the helium valve is located, which was only two feet in diameter, bringing in fans, lights, and mops and buckets. In the storage facility, we laid down tarps and spread out the 1,200-pound balloon. We could only partially inflate it because of the 20-foot ceiling in the building.

The second day I had the task of going to the Home Depot store to buy more lights, fans, mops, and other supplies. On the way out, I was hungry and bought two hot dogs from the vendor at the store's exit. On the short drive back while scarfing down the hot dogs, I bit into one and—crack!—broke a tooth on a piece of bone or something in the hot dog. Wow, did that hurt! I was in pain for the next two days until I could get to a dentist to pull the tooth and put in a bridge. Talk about adding insult to injury or visa versa! I was ready to blow that balloon up with dynamite! The process of drying it out and putting it to rest for the winter took us a whole week, which demoralized me even more.

~ ~ ~

That summer of 1998, while concentrating on the disaster in Birch Run, I flew only 59 hot air balloon flights and only 282 passengers! That was dismal compared to the previous year's 89 flights and over 800 passengers. The Seven Lakes State Park Balloon Race was again a colossal success, thank goodness. That and the trip to California were about the only positive happenings the entire year. That fall and early winter was a tough time, filled with financial worries. After a couple of months, with the Birch Run operation finished for the year and the stress of operating it every day waning, we had hope again of making a go of it the next year, and planning began for that last effort.

We also had another go with the Trans-Michigan Balloon Race, this time from Holland, and partnered up with a local pilot from there, Mark VanDis. We spent a lot of time in November and December planning for that event, which we scheduled for the first good weather weekend in February.

1999

In January 1999, we had some fantastic news when we learned Michelle was pregnant again! Losing the Angel Baby the year before had been hard on us all. We really wanted to have another child and little brother or sister for Katherine. Katherine would be four in October, so we did not want to wait too long. Michelle and I were not getting any younger, either.

That winter we rebuilt the Big Blooming Balloon envelope. She had flown over 600 wonderful flights and tons of passengers, and the top two-thirds needed replacement. Ron and I worked through the winter removing all the old fabric and cutting all the panels of new fabric. All the flowers were now gone, and only half of a few stems remained to be seen in the old bottom third. Ron renamed it "Stems."

The first hot air balloon flight I logged in 1999 was February 14th, a Valentine's Day flight for the Trans-Michigan Balloon Race. I remember nothing about that flight and am perplexed about that logbook entry. What I remember about that event was that the weather did not cooperate, and we scrubbed the first morning's scheduled flight. The second morning I wanted to scrub as well, but several of the pilots protested and said they wanted to go out to the airport and try to at least fly a short flight. I agreed to this and was glad I did because there was a small crowd gathered in the snow at sunrise at the airport waiting to see some balloons fly. It was snowing and was breezy, but several balloons took off for a short flight, with most electing to stay on the ground. I stayed on the ground that morning.

Since we had put it away in storage, Larry, Hugh Band, and I spent a lot of time talking on the phone about how to promote and make the Birch Run Balloon a success. We had gotten approval for the "Rides" banners on the balloon and thought that would help. Along with all the new advertising and promotions we were planning, we had big hopes of at least breaking even in our second year of operation.

We made lots of changes and every cost-cutting move we could without jeopardizing safety or security. One big change that I was at first upset about but later realized was an enormous relief was that I was demoted from being a manager and would now be a "pilot" only. Turns out some employees complained I was difficult to work for and was too "authoritarian" in my managerial style. I understand this now. I was under a lot of stress and am normally not very patient anyway.

Larry took over most of the duties of running the operation. Additionally, we promoted an employee who had proven herself as a hard worker in the first year to assistant manager. This relieved me of lots of stress and freed me up to concentrate more on Michigan Balloon Corporation and its ride program.

My next logged flight and the start of the 1999 season was on April 24th. I flew 73 flights and 484 passengers, with the final hot air flight taking place on October 11th. That must have been an early winter or just a very windy, rainy October. Nothing stands out in my logbook for that season, but one thing sure stands out in my memory.

Our Birch Run Tethered Balloon operation once again was a big disappointment financially. We spent another $20,000 on helium, plus all the other expenses of taking the envelope out of storage, re-inflating it, testing, and recertification by the state "carny" division. It continued to bleed cash from the day we started it back up and running. In June, we decided to put the equipment up for sale and close it down for good that fall. The Virgin Group found a buyer, and we were all set to end our misery that fall.

~ ~ ~

On the third weekend of July, as usual, we had the Seven Lakes State Park Balloon Race scheduled. That weekend had proved to be a fantastic choice as we flew at least one flight every year, and most years we had perfect weather and flew every flight! The event had proven to be an enormous success and a great money maker for the park, as well as a great promotion for MBC and our ride program.

This year the weather forecast was perfect again, although it was going to be hot and humid. The Saturday morning of the event, the weather was beautiful, but it was quickly warming up to the humid,

The Balloonatics

90-degree-plus forecast. Ron and I, along with many wonderful crew members and other volunteers, spent several hours on final preparations setting up Cold Air Advertising Balloons and our Inflate-A-Tents at the park.

We had just finished setting everything up and were sitting down for a break around 11 a.m. when I got a call from Larry. He nonchalantly asked me if I had everything up and ready down there, and I said yes, we had just finished! He then, in his typical laid-back fashion, said, "Well, you better take it all down." I asked what he meant, and he said, "You will get 70-plus-miles-per-hour winds and a thunderstorm racing through there in about 20 minutes, and by the way, the Birch Run Balloon is destroyed."

My heart sank, and I had to catch my breath as I yelled, "What do you mean?" Larry had been up in Birch Run operating the balloon and taking a few riders up and down since 9 a.m. He quickly told me that a thunderstorm had popped up out of nowhere just north of Birch Run around 10 a.m., and there had been no time to storm moor the system. He said, "We will talk about that later, but it is done, and you need to get everything down and secure there and fast or it will also be destroyed." I said okay and hung up. I experienced devastation for nearly a minute, but then a wave of relief swept over me, and I became overjoyed that Birch Run was finished!

I ran around and informed everyone what was about to happen, and everyone jumped into action. We got everything down and secured just in time for those 70-miles-per-hour winds and rain to blow through and out. The temperature dropped by 20 degrees. In 45 minutes, the sun came back out, and it became calm and hot and humid again. We flew that evening and every flight of the event that weekend.

Here is Larry's account of the Birch Run balloon destruction:

> It was one of those typical mid-July days in Michigan—hot and humid, with increasing thermal activity (rising and falling

columns of air associated with midday heating of the earth's surface), combined with an approaching cold front located to the northeast moving slightly south, mostly east. A double whammy of convective activity. It just needed enough moisture in the air to give it some fuel.

This combination is a known precipitator of thunderstorms. It was our job as operators-in-charge ("pilot-in-command" isn't quite the correct title here) to understand how the weather functions and make informed decisions about when to take the balloon from "standard mooring mode" to "storm mooring mode."

Unlike a hot air balloon, this gas (helium) balloon was always at maximum lift. A winch system allowed the balloon to rise and be pulled back down via a cable attached to a very large underground winch. While the balloon was held to the launch platform with downward pull, the envelope itself needed to be stabilized for horizontal oscillation with the standard mooring mode when not in flight mode. This involved a mooring line system using 24 one-inch ropes tied to the balloon equator, and at the other end, 24 equidistant concrete blocks anchored in the ground around the circumference of the envelope. In most circumstances, this system was sufficient and could be completed by one to two people. Storm mooring mode was a different beast altogether.

The challenge with the balloon during a storm with high winds is the mass and velocity. The balloon envelope has a lot of mass, which, when stable (in light winds), is relatively inert and can be controlled with the 24 mooring lines. However, when high winds are present, the balloon begins to gain a lot of horizontal and vertical velocity. From physics, we know that an object's momentum is its mass times its velocity. In this case, the resulting momentum adds a lot to the energy equation and can be very destructive. So, to minimize this, the idea is to pull the envelope down to the gondola so there is no space for the velocity to build up. To do that, there were 12 electric winches installed just outside the landing platform located below the circumference of the envelope equator. Twelve quarter-inch wire strands were attached to the envelope, which could be connected to the winches. When activated, those winches pulled the balloon down to the gondola. Great idea, but it had to be done carefully, in light winds, and it required at least four, and preferably six, people.

Since there was usually only one to two people on site, it took time to get people (usually volunteers) to the site to help. This required a decision to be made at least one and a half hours before a storm. With the help of our real-time weather tracking video feed, we could see approaching storms in plenty of time to call in the resources we needed to prepare the system for the storm. For one and a half summers, this wasn't a problem.

On the auspicious day in July to which Craig refers, I was the operator-in-charge for the day. I had suspended flight operations due to convective activity, but it was minor, and there was no imminent local storm activity near us, although I was watching a line of development about 150 miles north and west of our location, tracking east with a very slight southward component, showing it would not be a threat to us as it would track well north. Not a threat to us, so no worries—the balloon was in standard mooring mode.

I went off to do my system checks and grab a bite to eat. When I came back an hour later, weather conditions appeared to be the same in the area, so I wasn't too concerned when I flipped on the monitor to get a broader picture of any recent developments. The line of storms I had been watching to the northwest had continued to track mostly due west as predicted. To my chagrin, however, what I failed to predict is the buildup that continued south as it advanced east. It was now a monster stretching from about Alpena to Owosso—nearly 200 miles. At the speed it was traveling, it would take about 20 minutes to get to us, and the computer monitoring system was showing wind speeds of more than 70 miles per hour—not good.

With a 20-minute window, I didn't have time to get people on site to pull it down into storm mooring mode. The balloon would have to ride out the storm in standard mooring mode. It didn't fare so well.

Once the winds struck, the envelope immediately started bobbing up and down violently. As it was pressed down to the ground, the mooring lines designed to inhibit its horizontal movement became loose, allowing more horizontal movement. The resulting horizontal and vertical momentum from the maturing process became too much for the mooring lines to withstand the resulting energy. Watching from the safety of the building, I could hear the "ping" of the snapping lines. Knowing the winds would soon subside, I was prepared to let all the lines snap, confident the one-inch steel winch cable would hold. But just as I made that decision, I saw the load ring snap in two.

The envelope of the balloon is encased in a rope mesh that has load cables attached to the mesh and runs down to a load ring. That load ring is then coupled to the gondola with its own cable system. Therefore, the lift from the envelope is transferred to the mesh, which is then transferred to the cable system. The last element in the equation is a one-inch steel winch cable attached to the wire mesh on one end and a powerful winch system in an underground bunker below the landing platform. Activating this winch allows ascents and descents. Both the load ring and the winch system are critical to keeping the balloon from becoming an uncontrollable airborne threat to aviation and the public on the ground.

The Balloonatics

The load ring breaking sent alarm bells ringing. I had to ensure that the vessel didn't go airborne. With winds of 70 miles per hour, skin-piercing horizontal rain, a one-inch rope flying and snapping, the balloon oscillating violently, the gondola being thrown and pitched uncontrollably, and a very concerned assistant manager screaming at us to get back inside, I rushed out to the platform with Devon, the son of the landowner, climbed into the gondola, grabbed the rip cord, and deployed the rapid deflation device as fast as we could. It required both of us to rip the deflation port free. Tearing out that deflation device is permanent until repaired at the factory in France—a very expensive proposition. In the process of deflating, the envelope was thrashed around on the electrical transformer, further damaging the envelope and increasing the cost of repairs exponentially. Within seconds, both the danger, and the project, were gone.

Our agreement with Virgin Aerostations stipulated that we were responsible for paying back their investment in the operation. So, my initial relief at the end of it all was not long lived. Not only had they invested the initial $1.2 million, but they had also paid for almost all the other many ongoing operating expenses during its short, cash-bleeding existence. The insurance policy they had in place on the system paid them a nice sum, but it was at best half of the total they had invested.

As we dismantled and shipped everything off, there was much more expense involved as well. We also had to restore our friend Bob Conlee's site back as close as possible to its original condition. Larry and I envisioned ourselves now bound to a life of debt that we may never have been able to repay!

In the end, we were extremely blessed with the manner in which all parties involved resolved to dismiss us from that terrible burden. We are forever grateful to Sir Richard Branson, Hugh Band, and Virgin

Aerostations for writing off the entire folly and not coming after us for repayment.

We built it, but they did not come. This was both one of the biggest achievements and biggest failures for us "Balloonatics." It taught us a lot and had glorious moments. At the same time, it was by far the worst and most stressful two years of our Balloonatic lives!

~ ~ ~

On September 20th, a new baby girl blessed Michelle, Katherine, and me! Madeline Suzanne Elliott, just like her big sister, was delivered by C-section. However, this time it was a scheduled C-section, and everything went perfectly. Madeline was healthy, just as Katherine had been, and we settled in that fall and winter all together to take care of her. Katherine was a fantastic big sister and loved helping take care of Madeline, and this time Michelle was in and out of the hospital and healthy also!

After Madeline was born, my dad told me I needed to find a "real job," and I concurred. My life as a full-time Balloonatic had been fantastic, and it was again now that Birch Run was over with. I could now concentrate on MBC. However, trying to make a living ballooning full time in Michigan weather is very tough. I now had a family of four to support and realized I needed to at least supplement my meager Balloonatic income with something else. Larry was happy to get back to his family, other business, and home up north. Ron and Tari were also thinking of starting a family, and he was realizing that he needed a "real job" as well.

My dad was so excited that I was going to get a "real job" that he took me to the Men's Wearhouse clothing store and bought me three nice suits and a $200 pair of dress shoes! With his impeccable style and success in public education, he was always a snappy dresser.

While he was in college, he sold men's clothes at a shop in Centerline,

The Balloonatics

Michigan, where he grew up. He worked nights at a men's clothing shop to support my mom and me. One night, while getting ready to close the shop, he and another employee were robbed at gunpoint, tied up, and locked in the closet.

I lucked out and found a good sales job right away selling cellular phones for a company called Airtouch Cellular. They were the big cellular company in Michigan in 1999. I knew nothing about cell phones, but they were just becoming popular, and everyone wanted one. The industry was changing rapidly, and this job had great potential.

They hired me with a nice base salary, good full benefits, including excellent health insurance, and commissions that would grow as my book of business grew. I was part of a small team in Flint selling business accounts to small and midsize businesses. In addition to our salary, we received a 10 percent commission on the monthly bill from every account we sold. Several of the salespeople who had been there for two years since the team started were making six figures!

I was excited. The job was flexible. We worked out in the field, so I could still fly balloon rides in the morning and evening when the weather was good, and sell phones during the middle of the day. As long as I hit my monthly sales quota, I was golden. Since I started in the winter, flying balloons did not interfere with this job much. That spring and summer, it got tougher, and I had to work long hours when the weather was flyable. I always hit my sales quota, although for a few months in the summer, it was nip and tuck, and I almost did not make it.

At the end of December after Christmas, Michelle, Katherine, baby Madeline, and I went to my aunt Trisha and uncle Les's house for a big New Year's bash. Everyone had received warnings about the chaos that would ensue from the year 2000, Y2K, with computers crashing and not being able to handle the millennial change.

Airtouch had been sending us all kinds of warnings and telling us what to do if this or that happened. It was all for naught, and in the end the world kept on spinning on New Year's Day 2000. I took Prince's advice, though, and partied like it was 1999 New Year's Eve, much to Michelle's dismay and disapproval.

A New Century

2000

The balloon ride season started with the first logged flight on April 29th, 2000. I have no actual notes in my logbook all season and flew 58 total flights, taking 417 passengers, with the last flight of the season logged on November 11th, 2000. I had a great fall season in Michigan, flying 10 flights in October and five in November. That's a significant improvement compared to the year before!

Sometime that fall, my manager at Airtouch called all the team together for a meeting and told us of a possible upcoming merger with a company called Verizon. Verizon was a larger cellular company that was expanding, buying up all the smaller ones it could. The manager mentioned upcoming changes and the potential for improved circumstances, including stock options from Verizon, which would greatly benefit us in the long run.

That did not happen. Late fall of 2000, Verizon bought out Airtouch and went about cost cutting, and we all got the ax, including our manager. I remember him calling us into his office one by one and crying as he told us the bad news. The good news was that we got a nice severance package of six months' salary and continued benefits, which was a huge relief. I had six months to find new health insurance for the family and decide what to do.

2001

I started looking for a new job but couldn't find any that matched the flexibility and quality of the one I had recently lost. We still had MBC to run, and I still had to fly passenger rides a lot in spring, summer, and fall. The generous severance package I received from Airtouch Cellular helped me avoid having to jump into the first thing that came along, but nothing was looking good.

The winter passed into spring, and I still had found nothing. I had to get health insurance for the family and was used to buying my own as I always had to in the past, so I began shopping for that. The guy who sold us a family health insurance plan suggested I get my insurance license and join his team.

Selling insurance did not sound interesting to me, but after hearing him out, I thought it might be a perfect fit. It was 100 percent commission sales. I was working for myself. The flexibility and lucrative commissions were excellent. He showed me how he was making good money helping people find affordable insurance like he had just done for us.

I talked it over with Michelle later and went for it. I was always good at passing tests, and the insurance license test was easy for me. Within a couple of months, I was selling health insurance, and the spring balloon ride season was in full swing as well.

The first flight of 2001 was on March 3rd. I flew 55 flights and 321 passengers, with the last flight of the season on November 17th. There is only one note in my logbook worth mentioning, and that is on May 17th. I brought our Michigan Balloon to Katherine's elementary school and did a complimentary school program and tethered, taking up several teachers and the principal. Making Katherine proud of her Balloonatic daddy was truly special to me.

The insurance sales went well my first year, and Michelle and I thought about our family's future and if the ballooning business was in its best interest. Juggling two young daughters and the responsibilities of the MBC office made life challenging for Michelle. During the balloon season when Katherine was little, we placed her in day care, but Michelle no longer wanted to continue doing that. Although Katherine was a great help in entertaining Madeline, we desired to be more present for our children, but the balloon business demanded a significant amount of our time.

The phones constantly rang as Michelle managed two little girls while I was out selling insurance. The office was in the house, and it was getting hectic. We began considering selling the business, but who would buy it? There are few hot air balloon pilots in the world, and even fewer are interested in running a balloon ride business.

2002

In 2002, the first logged flight was on New Year's Day! Ron and I took out the old Michelob Light balloon for a winter fun flight. (Ron had acquired the balloon, so it was no longer owned by Ryan Distributing and no longer under the strict "no fly on New Year's Day" rule.) I flew a lesson on January 28th, and the ride season got underway in April. I flew 60 flights that year, flying 380 passengers. The Seven Lakes State Park Balloon Race went well once again, and the highlight of the year came at the local Groveland Oaks County Park Balloon Race.

The Groveland Oaks event was run by the Southeast Michigan Balloon Association, and I won first place flying a four-passenger balloon full of passengers each flight, but that was not the highlight. The highlight was when I took all three of my girls on a family flight, with Madeline experiencing her first balloon ride.

Another highlight of the event was having the late, great Ted Gauthier—a fire marshal, registered nurse, hot air balloon pilot, and fixed-wing pilot who passed away many years later—compliment me on my flying after the first flight. I had flown over him at about 100 feet above the ground, heading for the target, while he was just 10 feet off the ground trying to get a bit more northerly direction. I finished in first place, with him coming in second on that task. Later, at the park, he praised my flying skills, admiring how I skillfully navigated between two lower wind directions to fly directly over him toward the target. Coming from Ted, that was a great compliment!

One evening I remember from that year came after a flight from Seven Lakes State Park. Ron, some of our crew members, and I were finishing the champagne and drinking beer in the parking lot at the park. The park is very large and, lacking night lighting, very dark. Ron noticed a large plane flying unusually low and coming straight for us on its way to the Flint Bishop Airport located 15 miles north of the park. Passenger jets flew over us frequently, coming from Detroit Metro Airport, but this one was extremely low, maybe only 500–600 feet above the ground. Ron said, "Hey watch this," and jumped into the basket of our big balloon, which was on a flatbed trailer. He quickly lit the pilot lights and waited until the jet was about an eighth of a mile away, coming straight for us. Then he turned on both burners using the whisper valves that feed liquid propane into the burners, creating a huge yellow fire ball 20 feet tall. The entire parking lot lit up like it was daytime, and that huge jet immediately made an evasive maneuver, banking and veering sharply left. I can only imagine what the pilot thought! I was worried we might get a call from the FAA.

2003 and Beyond

The 2003 season began with the first logged flight on April 24th. I flew 49 flights with 295 passengers that year. Apart from the number of passengers, I have no other entries in my logbook for those flights. This was the last season for us with Michigan Balloon Corporation.

Larry had flown little in the past few years while living up north, running businesses, and raising his two girls with Gretchen. Ron had taken a job in sales because he and Tari had decided to start a family, and she probably had told him to get a "real" job. We all could see the writing on the wall.

In recent years, I had started communicating civilly with and making progress in building a better working relationship with our competition, Eric, at Balloon Quest. I realized Eric was an honest and very hard-working guy who loved flying balloons and, like me, made it his profession. He had found his opportunity through Capt. Phogg, just like I had.

I had to admit that I was wrong to have acted so unprofessionally and to hold such animosity toward him. Larry and I approached Eric with the idea of buying MBC. It just made sense to combine the two businesses. I could then still fly and make money flying. Balloon Quest would benefit by not having MBC as a competitor. They would have another pilot, me, and our balloons to handle the increase in business they would gain by not having us as competition. Michelle could devote all her time to our girls while I focused on selling insurance.

It was a win-win-win all around. Thankfully Eric saw the benefits as well, so we sealed the deal. We reached an agreement during the winter. Balloon Quest bought MBC, and I agreed to fly for Balloon Quest part-time for the next three years.

I flew for Balloon Quest/Capt. Phogg Balloon Rides in Fenton, Michigan, for the next 16 years, until 2019. Most of the time, I piloted large 10- to 12-passenger balloons flying paid passenger rides and averaged about 45 flights a year. It was nice to just show up and fly!

Michelle loved being a stay-at-home mom for our girls, and I could work full-time elsewhere. Another great outcome of this new arrangement was rekindling my friendship with Capt. Phogg. We had a blast flying together a few times and reminiscing about the good old days at BCA.

Starting around 2018, I began having the same premonition about flying balloons as I had some 30 years before when I gave up riding motorcycles. So, at the end of the 2019 flying season, I listened to my gut again and retired from flying balloons.

~ ~ ~

I will never forget my last flight. It was November 23, 2019. I remember the last 20 minutes of that flight like it was yesterday! It was a chilly morning flight with the temperature in the low 40s, and Eric and I took off shortly after sunrise. Eric was flying the big 12-passenger, 250,000-cubic-foot balloon. I was in the six-passenger 140,000-cubic-foot balloon.

There was patchy fog everywhere, which makes for an absolutely beautiful world to float through. All the many lakes and wetlands had thick fog rising off the water. We drifted in an east-southeast direction at about 400 feet above the ground, which took us toward my house and Holly High School.

Since the fields were saturated after a wet fall, we decided to aim for Holly High School's spacious parking lots for a dry hassle-free retrieval. I found there was a ton of "steering," almost 180 degrees between 500 feet and above, where the breeze was moving fast and heading southeast, and 200 feet and below, where it was slow and heading northwest.

Between those two altitudes, the direction gradually shifted from northwest to southeast. After ascending to about 1,000 feet at the beginning of the flight, I had to concentrate to stay low and slow to continue heading toward the high school.

We floated past our house, heading for Holly High School. I would go up to about 500 feet and quickly head southeast, then come back

The Balloonatics

down low again and go slowly northwest, thereby spiraling along the road that heads east toward the high school. I needed to line up perfectly southeast of the main parking lot on the opposite side of the road from the high school. Then I could ride the low breeze northwest into the main parking lot where Eric was going to land.

We watched Eric make his approach ahead of me. Eric landed in the middle of the big asphalt parking lot. He had been north of where I was and made it in easily. We ended up over the big farm field across from the high school and descended into the slow breeze, heading northwest. I immediately realized I had to be farther east to reach the same parking lot as Eric.

By rapidly heating the balloon, I ascended 200 feet into the easterly air current. Then I increased my elevation by adding more heat to the envelope to veer southeast before releasing hot air to descend. I did this twice before deciding that I was set up correctly. Then, leveling off at about 100 feet, we magically sat there not moving at all!

As usual, I chatted with the passengers during the flight, explaining my actions and pointing out interesting sights. Now here we just sat suspended, motionless. It was fantastic, and I made sure my passengers realized that.

I told them about how the winds are constantly changing as the day goes on and how we must use them and adapt as the winds change, even during the course of our short, one-hour flights. I whooped and cheered about how wonderful this flight had been with all the steering winds, and now we just sat there, suspended 100 feet above that field! I didn't want to end this fantastic flight, so I kept us suspended by periodically using the burner to maintain our altitude in that perfectly still band of air for about a minute.

Eric's crew had been there waiting for him when he landed, and they were all just watching us across the road. Eric had not deflated his balloon yet. They wanted to see how we fared first.

We sat there suspended, enjoying the moment, until I decided I had better make the best of it before the winds changed. I figured I was in the perfect spot to descend lower and ride that wind down low right to the parking lot next to Eric's balloon, so that is what I did. We descended to about 50 feet off the ground and drifted ever so slowly to the northwest, crossing the road. Then I ascended to clear the low power lines by a comfortable margin and descended again to float into the parking lot 100 feet away from Eric's balloon, with my ground crew there to greet us as well.

I have not been up in a balloon since that last magical flight on November 23, 2019, and to my amazement, I do not miss it. Guess I have been there and done that and have had enough of it. But man, was it ever a fantastic adventure!

Afterword

First, I want to thank you so much for reading my book! I hope you enjoyed it as much as I enjoyed writing it. Although it was a long and tedious process, it was also a ton of fun reliving all those crazy old memories. Also going through all the hundreds of old photos and VHS tapes and having them digitized to put on the website was an extremely long, expensive, but very enjoyable experience as well.

I have wanted to write a book about my ballooning adventures for a long time. In fact, I started many times in the past and got nowhere. I started seriously drafting this book on January 3, 2023. The breakthrough for me came when I quit drinking alcohol thanks to a book and online course I found called *Alcohol Lied to Me* by Craig Beck. If you enjoyed my book, please consider writing a positive review on Amazon. This will help others find my book and hopefully enjoy it as well. Thank you!

Career Statistics

- Flew 68 different balloons in 11 different sizes and classes from 56,000 cu. ft. AX-6 to 216,000 cu. ft. AX-11.
- Flew 2,693 flights, safely flying 14,401 human passengers, one dog named Lucky, and one Big Boy statue, thus averaging 5.35 humans and 0.00037 dogs/statues per flight.
- Over 6,000 bottles of champagne opened post flight!

Join Us on Our Adventures!

Please subscribe to my free private email list and join "The Balloonatics Club" where you will receive discounts on all the related MERCH available on my website and on all the books as well as be kept abreast of the publishing dates of all upcoming books.

Since writing *The Balloonatics*, I have been working on several new books that will be coming out soon. The first is called *California Trippin'* which is an account of the epic trip I took with two high school friends in 1976 to California the day after we graduated from Okemos High School in Okemos, Michigan. We drove straight through to Lake Tahoe, then on to San Francisco and down the coast to LA, San Diego, and Tiajuna, Mexico. A short but funny and exciting tale of teenage adventure.

The next one I am working on will be called *Tokemos High*, all about my friends and my crazy pot smoking, beer drinking, sex, drugs, and rock 'n' roll days at our alma mater Okemos High School from 1972–1976.

To stay connected and to check out all of the great *Balloonatics* merchandise, go to: www.theballoonatics.com or scan this QR code.

Made in the USA
Monee, IL
01 July 2025